T0313881

Framed by the Indiana highway 37 bridge, new Monon black-and-gold F-3As drum northward near Harrodsburg, Ind., in the late 1940s. The Barriger years had arrived, signaling a new era for the Chicago, Indianapolis & Louisville. *(J. F. BENNETT, JIM BENNETT COLLECTION)*

MONON
SECOND, REVISED EDITION

THE HOOSIER LINE

BY GARY W. DOLZALL
AND
STEPHEN F. DOLZALL

WITH AN AFTERWORD BY FRANK VAN BREE, PRESIDENT
MONON RAILROAD HISTORICAL-TECHNICAL SOCIETY, INC.

INDIANA UNIVERSITY PRESS • **BLOOMINGTON AND INDIANAPOLIS**

3

This book is a publication of

Indiana University Press
Office of Scholarly Publishing
1320 East 10th Street
Bloomington, Indiana 47405 USA

iupress.indiana.edu

first edition published by Interurban Press

The paper used in this publication meets the minimum require-
ments of American National Standard for Information Sciences—
Permanence of Paper for Printed Library Materials, ANSI
Z39.48-1984.

Cataloging-in-Publication data is available from the Library of
Congress.

ISBN 0-253-34083-7

2 3 4 5 6 21 20 19 18 16

DEDICATION
To our parents,
Paul and Betty Dolzall,
who had the good sense to raise us
in the company of
"The Hoosier Line"

Classic F-3 A-B-A locomotive set led by the 62 tow tonnage over the White River at Gosport, Ind., in the late 1940s at the start of Monon's "Barriger Years." (*J. F. BENNETT, MIKE SCHAFER COLLECTION*)

HOOSIER LINE

TABLE OF CONTENTS

In one of the most time-honored of Monon photographs, boys witness the embodiment of John. W. Barriger's Monon—the postwar, streamlined *Hoosier*, as it crosses Clear Creek in southern Indiana during the train's 1947 exhibition tour of the Hoosier Line. (J. F. BENNETT, JIM BENNETT COLLECTION)

PREFACE

THIS BOOK was created for a twofold purpose: one for the mind, and one for the heart.

For the mind, here is a chronicle of the Monon Railroad, with heavy emphasis on the extraordinary years 1946-1971. In the quarter century following World War II, the Chicago, Indianapolis & Louisville (the railroad's title until its nickname—Monon—became official in 1956) underwent an uncommon evolution, a myriad of changes. Consider: Immediately before World War II, the CI&L, ravaged by the Great Depression, was bankrupt (since 1933), in decline, old school. Its newest steam locomotive dated to 1929, its all-steel passenger coaches could be counted on the fingers of one hand, its traditional tonnage staples of Indiana coal and limestone were becoming uncertain, its passenger traffic was all but gone.

The early 1940s—*i.e.,* the war years—were mixed times for the Monon. The road's first diesel locomotives (four Electro-Motive yard switchers) were purchased, but attempts by its trustee to dieselize mainline freight operations were ruined by lack of funds. Passenger service was cut near the end of World War II to single round trips over Monon's primary routes: Chicago–Indianapolis, and Chicago–Louisville. And yet, in the troubled years of 1942-1946 was born the financial reorganization plan that would propel Indiana's home railroad into a postwar prosperity—and national fame.

On May 1, 1946, John Walker Barriger III was named president of the reorganized Monon. This bespectacled, diminutive man would leave his mark forever on the Hoosier Line, by standing over seven years of total change. Barriger, only 46 years old when he became Monon's president, but already with a score of years of railroad industry experience, orchestrated Monon's dieselization, rebuilt its passenger services, made massive purchases of freight equipment, and improved the road's physical plant. And whatever

level of skill Barriger held as a railroad manager, it was surely equaled by his penchant for creating publicity. Barriger proclaimed the Monon "America's guinea pig railroad" and pronounced an intention to turn this heretofore troubled property into a "superrailroad."

It is probable, if not certain, that John Barriger knew well that his stated goals were impossible, but nonetheless they gave the Monon a stature in the minds of bankers, press, freight customers, and fare-paying passengers that surely benefited the company.

When, on December 31, 1952, John Barriger resigned from the Monon and moved on to the New Haven Railroad, his successor was handpicked—Warren W. Brown, a man who had served as Barriger's vice president–traffic, and right arm. Warren Brown's tenure as president of the Monon never quite approached the flamboyance of the Barriger years, but nonetheless Brown proved an active railroad industry spokesman. His term on the Hoosier Line was one primarily of refinement. Dieselization was already complete, but freight equipment purchases and property improvements continued (albeit on a reduced level), passenger service was rationalized, and piggyback service introduced. Unfortunately, during Brown's tenure, increases in operating revenue were outpaced by rising operating costs, and the Monon's postwar prosperity began to erode.

Warren Brown departed the Monon at the end of 1958, and his successor—Carl A. Bick—proved to be the last of the men from the Barriger era. Bick had joined the Monon (from the Burlington) in 1950. While Bick remained as the Hoosier Line's president until December 31, 1961, true management of the Monon came under new hands in August 1960—when investors headed by midwest transit baron William C. Coleman gained working control of the Hoosier Line.

William Coleman, first as chairman, then (beginning in 1962) as president and chairman, envisioned a sec-

9

Slapping over the uneven rail joints of the lead track into McDoel Yard, Bloomington, RS-2 No. 24 has all but ended its journey with a local from the south. With the main line cleared, three Alco Century 628s start to pull, beginning their journey to Louisville on this hazy November 3, 1965. (KENNETH M. ARDINGER)

ond postwar transformation of the Monon—a "New Monon" as the company's annual reports soon proclaimed. His was an era marked by cost controls, by attempts (some successful, some less so) to expand Monon's freight traffic, by an ill-fated takeover attempt of the Chicago South Shore & South Bend, and by revitalization of Monon's diesel fleet. Coleman's greatest hope for the Monon—one he thought might secure the Monon as an independent road—never materialized. His dream was to make the Monon a major coal-carrying link between the Ohio River and Lake Michigan by constructing a barge unloading facility on the Ohio at Louisville and a Great Lakes port at Michigan City. But with the plan's demise (at the hand of the Interstate Commerce Commission), Coleman soon bid farewell to the Monon.

The final man to lead the Monon was Samuel T. Brown (no relation to Warren Brown), who succeeded Coleman as president and chairman in February 1967. Brown immediately moved the Monon toward merger, maintained the railroad in good physical condition, killed off the last Monon passenger train (in 1967), and kept freight revenues strong. On July 31, 1971, Brown saw the fulfillment of his merger quest—when Monon was merged into its 5,800-mile neighbor to the south, the Louisville & Nashville Railroad.

It is this remarkable quarter century that Chapters 4 through 6 of this book study, but not merely from the confines of a corporate board room. We explore the locomotives, the equipment, the events, the operations and the people that formed the Hoosier Line. The book concludes with a roster of Monon postwar steam and diesel motive power, and of postwar passenger equipment.

To provide a historical background, we provide Chapters 2 and 3 to account for the long, fascinating history of the Monon and its predecessors. We travel back more than a century, to 1847, and a time when a New Albany man named James Brooks founded a new railroad—the New Albany & Salem. Although Chapters 2 and 3 are meant primarily as a prelude, we think the reader will find in them an understanding of Monon history, and, perhaps, the most complete published record of the history of segments of the Hoosier Line, such as the Indianapolis & Louisville coal branch and French Lick branch.

And finally, for the heart: We hope that in the pages of this book the reader will discover something of the remarkable spirit of the Hoosier Line. We hope that for those who knew the Monon, this book will rekindle recollections of the *Tippecanoe* or *Thoroughbred* or *Hoosier,* of red and gray F-3s and black and gold C-628s and BL-2s, of depots at Lafayette or Delphi or Salem.

And for those who, by reasons of age or geography, never knew the Hoosier Line, we hope that this book will prove a worthy introduction. Chapter 1 keynotes our effort at recalling the spirit of the Monon, of being trackside on the Hoosier Line, but we trust something of the flavor of the Monon will be found in every chapter. Chapter 7 is a tribute to Lafayette Shops, the place where Monon's shopmen performed expert repairs and uncommon transformations to Hoosier Line locomotives, freight and passenger cars, and cabooses. Chapters 8 and 9 explore—primarily through photographs—the intriguing freight and passenger operations of the Monon during the years 1946-1971. A color album of Monon scenes is also presented to recall the sights of the Hoosier Line. And in Chapter 10, a brief summary of the fate of the Hoosier Line since its merger with the Louisville & Nashville is offered.

We hope that all our readers will enjoy this journey along the Hoosier Line.

Gary W. Dolzall
Stephen F. Dolzall

June 2001

Monon's *Thoroughbred* in its glory—paired red-and-gray F-3A's up front, observation-dining-parlor car on the rear—bends to a curve amid the scenic limestone-laden hills of southern Indiana. (*J. F. BENNETT, JIM BENNETT COLLECTION*)

1
MEMORIES OF THE MONON

A Personal Accounting of the Hoosier Line

EVERY TRAIN-WATCHER has a railroad he calls his own, a favorite property to haunt, a railroad taken to heart and thus unequaled by any other, regardless of its route map or the strength of its stock dividends. For two young Hoosier brothers, the Monon in its final quarter century became that special railroad.

The Monon was a comprehensible, comfortable, personable railroad. It did not overwhelm with 2-10-0s counted in the hundreds (like the Pennsylvania) or route miles counted in the thousands (like the Santa Fe). Nor did the Monon disguise its diminutive size, as did Florida East Coast with Miami-bound streamliners, or Central of New Jersey with countless commuters, or Clinchfield with 2-8-8-2s and Challengers. Monon was strictly uncomplicated and invariably friendly, i.e., perfect company for curious young train-watchers.

Consider the Hoosier Line's stature: At the end of World War II, the Chicago, Indianapolis & Louisville operated on 541 miles of track of which it owned 512. Very comprehensible numbers. Its system map? The Hoosier Line simply dropped an "X" down upon the state of Indiana, with its crossroads at a small (population 1,262 in 1946), quiet town named—what else?—Monon. From its namesake town, the legs of the railroad's "X" extended northwest toward Chicago, north to Michigan City, Ind., south toward Louisville, Ky., and southeast to Indianapolis. In effect, these lines formed two mainline routes: Chicago-Louisville, and Chicago–Indianapolis. The line from Monon to Michigan City could only be considered a secondary one, this

despite a historical significance that we'll explore later.

Branch lines off the Monon's "X" by this era numbered only two—both were fingers off the line to Louisville. From Wallace Junction, Ind., 105 miles south of Monon, the "I&L branch" wended its way 47 miles into the remote, coal-blackened hills of southwestern Indiana. And at Orleans, 62 miles north of Louisville, the French Lick branch left the main line and cast the Hoosier Line's tracks 17.7 miles, to the very front steps of the grand old French Lick Springs Hotel, a traditional, genteel resort hotel that was, in its halcyon, home to clandestine, but nonetheless infamous, gambling.

The Monon was, in spirit, a small-town railroad, at home in the likes of Rensselaer, Delphi, Cloverdale, or Mitchell. South Hammond, Ind., home of Monon's Chicago-area freight yard; Lafayette, location of Monon's main shops (and Purdue University); and Bloomington, home of a major south-end yard (and Indiana University) were the Hoosier Line's primary intermediate points. But aside from Hammond, no intermediate town counted more than 30,000 citizens in 1946.

When the Hoosier Line did venture into its large, end-point cities, it did so rather bashfully, and on borrowed rails—hence the difference in miles of track owned and operated. At Hammond's State Line Tower, Monon trains traipsed onto the Chicago & Western Indiana for the final 20 miles to Chicago's Dearborn Station. At New Albany, Ind., the Monon linked itself to the Kentucky & Indiana Terminal and used the K&IT bridge over the Ohio River to attain Louisville

Above: Bedford, milepost 245.8—Train 6, the northbound *Thoroughbred*, swings alongside the limestone depot. For the authors, the concrete platform at Bedford was the most important point on the Hoosier Line. (©1986, ROBERT'S STUDIO) Left: Red-and-gray, flat-ended observation-dining-parlor car born from an ex-U.S. Army hospital car at Lafayette Shops in 1948 wore a drumhead proclaiming "The THOROUGH-BRED" and an oscillating warning light. (DAVE FERGUSON'S PHOTO ART)

(K&IT's Youngtown Yard for freights, Louisville & Nashville's Louisville Union Station for varnish).

The Hoosier Line did enter Indianapolis on its own, snuggling a small freight yard and suburban Boulevard passenger station on the city's north side, but to send its passenger trains to Indianapolis Union Station required traveling the tracks of Big Four/Nickel Plate and Indianapolis Union Railway.

So much for the Monon's physical plant—unlike the New Haven's serpentine lines in New England, or Atlantic Coast Line in Florida, or the Chicago & North Western's granger branch lines of Iowa, it did not take a crystal ball to understand where the Hoosier Line went and how it got there.

Discoveries at Bedford

For us, through the 1950s at least, the Monon's most important point was Bedford, Ind., our hometown. For

it was there—on the concrete station platform, in the limestone depot, in Bedford's town square, and in the surrounding countryside—that we made our acquaintance with the Chicago, Indianapolis & Louisville. Naturally, if *you* knew the Monon, you'll probably disagree about the importance of Bedford. You'll argue that the tower at Lafayette Junction or the Wabash River Bridge at Delphi or the depot at Monticello was the finest train-watching spot on the Hoosier Line. And perhaps you're right. But given that this chapter is a personal accounting of the Hoosier Line, allow us our prejudice.

Bedford, milepost 245.8 (from Chicago), stood atop the limestone-laden hills of southern Indiana, with deep, rolling valleys to both north and south. Which meant Monon trains had to struggle with grades of 1.25% (southbound) and 1.40% (northbound) to attain the town of 12,000 citizens. And as was Monon's custom in New Albany, Lafayette, Monticello, and Frankfort, the company's trains trod right down the city streets of Bedford, in this case under the very shadow of the Lawrence County court house.

It was during the early and mid-1950s that we first came to know the Monon—*i.e.*, the post-World War II Monon, the post-receivership Monon, the Monon of Presidents John W. Barriger III and Warren W. Brown. It was a time when Monon's Chicago-Louisville *Thoroughbred*, brushed in red and gray, powered by Electro-Motive F-3As, called morning (northbound) and evening (southbound) at the depot. A time when train numbers 70 through 75 implied long strings of tonnage, headed by smoking, snarling quartets of black and gold Fs, bound for Louisville or Lafayette or South Hammond. A time when local freights might march down Bedford's J St. at eight miles per hour to the uneven rhythms of Alco RS-2 or Fairbanks-Morse H-15-44 road-switchers. A good time to be a train-watcher.

Consider the *Thoroughbred:* It was our firsthand evidence of the Barriger-era transformation of Monon's passenger service from moribund to notable. In the wake of the Hoosier Line's 1933-1946 receivership and World War II, the CI&L's varnish had withered to single day trains between Chicago-Louisville

(Nos. 3/4) and Chicago-Indianapolis (Nos. 31/30, the *Hoosier*). And north of Monon, to and from Chicago, even these trains were combined into one.

In September 1946, Barriger restored CI&L's passenger conveyances to the traditions of an earlier era—morning and evening trains between Chicago-Indianapolis, and day and night trains Chicago-Louisville, and even a connecting sleeper service to French Lick. At first, the trains carried on with the Hoosier Line's aged steam locomotives and heavyweights, but in 1946 Barriger's Monon purchased surplus U.S. Army hospital cars constructed by American Car & Foundry. Monon's Lafayette Shops and the skilled workers who punched time clocks there were enlisted to rebuild the cars, Raymond Loewy to style them, and in 1947-1948, 28 red and gray cars rejuvenated the Hoosier Line's passenger trains.

By our time trackside in Bedford, the overnight Chicago-Louisville *Bluegrass* had perished for lack of nocturnal patrons (and with it the French Lick train), and while Monon's Chicago-Indianapolis *Tippecanoe*

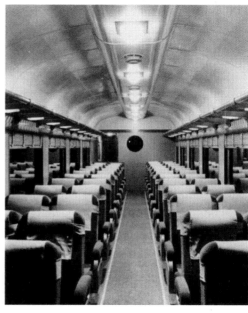

Left: At dowdy Dearborn Station, Chicago, Monon's Louisville-bound *Thoroughbred* makes its morning departure behind F-3A No. 84B, July 24, 1961. In the background, a Santa Fe Fairbanks-Morse H-12-44TS tends the passenger cars of its owner. *(ROBERT P. OLMSTED)* **Above:** Interior of Monon streamlined coach—comfortable seats with plain cloth headrests, huge windows with venetian blinds and a smooth ride atop six-wheel trucks. *(MONON, DOLZALL COLLECTION)*

and *Hoosier* carried on, they were beyond our sight in northern Indiana. But we were not to be pitied for the company of the *Thoroughbred.* We admit Monon Nos. 5/6 were not the *20th Century Limited* or *Super Chief* (all right, or even the *James Whitcomb Riley* or *Dixie Flagler* for that matter), but they were good company. In its heyday (read, through mid-1951), the *Thoroughbred* meant the arrival at Bedford of paired F units, head-end cars, shining, deluxe coaches, and a flat-ended, Mars-lighted observation-dining-parlor car.

For a youngster to stand on Bedford's platform and peer up at travelers in that dimly lit, mysterious observation car, or to follow No. 5's red observation beacon through the streets of Bedford and into the winter darkness, *was* a worthy endeavor. Or consider an encounter with, say, No. 6 north of Bedford—at Thornton or Harrodsburg or Diamond—her F-3s bending into a curve, the chant of EMD V-16s echoing from the limestone hills, flanges squealing, 400 feet of red-and gray-liveried steel stretched out behind. That was the experience of the *Thoroughbred* of our youth.

Another matter of intrigue to us in Bedford was far

removed from the drama of the *Thoroughbred.* It was the simple familiarity of our hometown yard goats. In 1953, Bedford merited its own switcher assignments, and it was stone—southern Indiana limestone—that gave reason for the CI&L to assign diminutive diesels there. Moving limestone, rough cut in blocks, from the quarries to the mills, then finished stone from the mills, was a Hoosier Line tradition.

And building sturdy, handsome, for-the-ages limestone depots—at the likes of Bedford and French Lick, Bloomington and Lafayette, Frankfort and Monon—had been Hoosier Line tradition, too. Monon's "Stone District" extended from Bedford north to Stinesville, 48 miles distant, but it was in the 25 miles from Bedford to Clear Creek to Bloomington that stone was without equal.

In the 1950s, the stone trade was enjoying something of a renaissance compared to its depths in World War II, which gave us opportunity to witness an Electro-Motive SW-1 or NW-2 bounding off into the valleys around Bedford, to call at Dark Hollow and Murdock and Walsh Mill, and do determined battle with strings

Peering from the darkened halls of red brick Lafayette Shops, Monon red-and-gray F-3A's 82A and 82B and black-and-gold 63B await their next call. Inside "Shops," Monon's workmen tended the Hoosier Line's equipment for more than three quarters of a century. (DAVE FERGUSON'S PHOTO ART)

of gondolas sagging under the weight of leviathan, cream-colored blocks of stone.

The quarries and mills of southern Indiana are now largely silent, the Monon's stone spurs abandoned, but for anyone who witnessed the toil of the EMD switchers, or the sights of Fairbanks-Morse and Alco roadswitchers' midnight prowlings to pick up gondolas and return them to Bloomington, or the thunder of stone blocks being loaded into battered mill gons, the memory will not be willingly forgotten.

Milepost 0—Dearborn Station

Allow us to move forward, to April 1959. That month, that year, our acquaintance with the Hoosier Line increased tenfold. No longer would we know the Monon only in the confines of Bedford. The event was a family trip to Chicago, by auto northbound—but by *Thoroughbred* back home. Which meant 245.8 miles of discovery, beginning at milepost 0, Dearborn Station, Chicago.

Dearborn! Ancient and brick, pillared waiting room, ground-level wooden platforms, and a maze of hand-thrown switches. At shortly before the stroke of 10 a.m., we walked past Dearborn's ample bumper posts, past the steel lattice supporting its dowdy, darkened trainshed, down the splintered wooden planks to find a red and gray coach with stepbox waiting. Monon's No. 5 shared the platforms that morning with better company—i.e., the trains of the Santa Fe—but never mind that, the *Thoroughbred* was adventure enough for us. On board, snuggled into our coach seats, perched nose to window, we awaited 10:05 and the gentle tug from the F-3A that would lead us home.

The tug came, our coach's six-wheeled trucks slogged through switch points, and No. 5 followed C&WI's path toward famed 21st Street Tower, past dozing, warbonnet-clad Santa Fe Fs, over the Pennsy diamonds, accelerating south toward 63rd St., Englewood, six miles distant. This Monon—the Monon of Chicago, Englewood and Pullman Junction—was uncommon to us, an urban Monon, a Monon surrounded by the likes of AT&SF, PRR, C&EI, RI and IC. But,

technically at least, it wasn't really the Hoosier Line—not until State Line Tower and Hammond, 19.8 miles from Dearborn.

After a brief pause at Hammond station, a depot shared with the Erie, No. 5 cast off through Maynard, Dyer and St. John, hustling into open country and soon attaining the 75 miles per hour that Monon employee timetable No. 11 would allow its engineer. This, the main line of the Northern Division of the Hoosier Line (Hammond–Lafayette), was flat (0.61 ruling grade southbound), and straight (89 miles of tangent), a hearty ride through rolling fields of corn, through small towns named Lowell and Shelby, Rose Lawn and Parr, over rivers named Iroquois and Kankakee.

Little less than two hours from the platforms of Dearborn Station, with a stop at Rensselaer history, No. 5 shuddered to the grip of clasp brakes on steel wheels, slowed and stopped at her sponsor's namesake —Monon, Ind. Baggage carts and a handful of passengers greeted our *Thoroughbred* as she stepped around the nine-degree curve at Monon, a curve that pointed our F-3A due south—toward Lafayette.

Barely two minutes were spent at Monon, precious little time to survey the sleepy town of brick buildings that gave the railroad its name, then with all the potency of an F-3's 567-series V-16, we were off, barreling at a mile a minute down 17-plus miles of tangent to Brookston (this, combined with 47 miles of straight track north from Monon to Westville on the Michigan City branch, formed a tangent of 64.58 miles—fourth longest in the country). But then, suddenly, the sprint was ending, the brakes reapplied, as the *Thoroughbred* nosed downgrade through Ash Grove and Battle Ground, descending on 0.85%, winding through one-degree curves, to clatter onto the 600-foot Wabash River truss bridge and swagger into the yards at Lafayette. From Hammond to Lafayette on Hoosier Line rails, 97 miles in one hour, 49 minutes with two stops. Average speed: 55.2 mph.

"Shops"

It was as the *Thoroughbred* stood in the yards for a crew change that we first witnessed, through our

Typical of Monon's flat Northern Division is this scene of BL-2 No. 36, trailed by head-end caboose 81223, bounding south toward Lafayette with a local in 1960. (J. PARKER LAMB)

Typical of Monon's flat Northern Division is this scene of BL-2 No. 36, trailed by head-end caboose 81223, bounding south toward Lafayette with a local in 1960. (J. PARKER LAMB)

coach's grand five-foot windows, the true heart and soul of the Hoosier Line—the mammoth, red brick edifice atop a hill—Lafayette Shops. To the men of the Monon, it was simply "Shops," nothing more need be said. Between the Wide Water branch of the Wabash River and Lafayette's Monon St., Shops in the 1950s snuggled a multistoried locomotive shop, transfer table, two car shop buildings, paint shop, and attending structures into some 45 remarkable acres.

And there, since it was opened in 1895, Lafayette Shops had tended the Hoosier Line's equipment, from coaches to gondolas, from boxcars to BL-2s. For us, its accomplishments were little short of legend: In the 1920s, Shops and its workmen rebuilt turn-of-the-century 4-4-0s and Ten-Wheelers and 4-8-0s with such skill that the company considered the locomotives new.

On March 23, 1948, Lafayette left the steam era behind, opening a diesel facility; in 1956-1957, Shops created from scratch eight notable "bay-window cupola" cabooses that would serve the railroad's conductors and rear brakemen well. And, of course, it had been Lafayette Shops, little more than a decade earlier, that had refashioned from surplus Army equipment the comfortable coach we rode home to Bedford that day.

Which brings us back to the story at hand: train No. 5. After four minutes in Shops Yard, the *Thoroughbred* clumped the short distance to Lafayette's snug depot, paused a few more minutes, then accelerated—to all of 10 mph—as it warily walked down Lafayette's 5th St. The citizens of Lafayette, like those of our hometown, were, of course, accustomed to having 115-ton, 50-foot-long F-3As and their trains march down the main street, and paid No. 5 little mind.

With Lafayette behind, the *Thoroughbred* ventured onto Monon's Southern Division, a curvy, up-one-hill, down-another property. Of the Southern Division's 199 mainline miles (Lafayette–New Albany), only 24.5 miles were level; grades reached 2.16%; there were 319 curves, and 80 bridges and trestles to cross. In short, it was a rugged, tough, unforgiving railroad—and an unforgettably scenic one.

Linden . . . Crawfordsville . . . Roachdale, each punctuated our journey with a brief station stop, then at little past 2 p.m., No. 5 paused at Greencastle—for 15 minutes. Why? Time to eat. By 1959, the *Thoroughbred* offered no diner, no lounge, no food. So at Greencastle a gentleman from a local eatery was enlisted to step aboard and sell sandwiches and the like. We don't recall the menu—but by 2 p.m., whatever it was probably tasted good.

In route miles, our journey was coming to a close—after Greencastle only 68 miles remained to Bedford. But between mileposts 177.8 and 254.8 we witnessed places that would, in future years, become cherished havens—Wallace Junction, the backwoods, tranquil yard where Monon's I&L branch cast off into coal fields; Gosport, where Monon shoehorned an ancient,

Top: On April 4, 1959, the southbound *Thoroughbred* calls at the namesake town of its owner—Monon, Ind. Hoosier Line F-3A 83B is easing around the 9-degree curve which will point No. 5 toward Lafayette. The track behind the station leads to Indianapolis; track at right is Monon's Michigan City line. (*J. PARKER LAMB JR.*) **Above:** McDoel Yard—Sixty cars in tow, including gondolas loaded with limestone blocks from the quarries of southern Indiana, Monon RS-2's 27. and 28 lope into Bloomington from the south end on June 14, 1963. (*KENNETH W. ARDINGER*) **Facing page:** A classic scene by the master of Monon photographers, J. F. Bennett, reveals the scenic beauty of the Southern Division. Three F-3's are heading a northbound freight at Gosport. Caboose of train has just cleared the bridge over the White River. (*J. F. BENNETT, JIM BENNETT COLLECTION*)

run-through depot between the Pennsylvania Railroad's Indianapolis-Vincennes branch and White River; Bloomington's McDoel Yard, populated by RS-2s and H-15-44s, F-3s and NW-2s; sweeping Harrodsburg Curve. And at 3:57 p.m., No. 5 arrived Bedford. We were back to our familiar concrete platform.

A Place Called McDoel

In January 1960, our family moved away from Bedford, to Bloomington, 25 miles north on the Hoosier Line. Which meant we exchanged Bedford's depot for Bloomington's similar, but larger, limestone station, and traded Bedford's small yard for a larger one—McDoel Yard. McDoel—the name recalled W.H. McDoel, a man who as general manager and then president (1899-1909) of the Monon brought change to the Hoosier Line just as certainly as John Barriger did nearly half a century later.

A few words on McDoel, the yard: Tucked on the south side of Bloomington, it counted among its assets long ladder tracks capable of holding 581 cars, rip tracks, a passing siding off the main line, a scale track, fueling racks and sand tower for servicing diesels, an aged yard office—and a 105-foot turntable that served what once had been an 18-stall roundhouse (although the old brick and wooden roundhouse had been trimmed by the time we arrived).

For mainline freights, McDoel meant pickups, setouts, and a crew change. Often it meant a trip to the fuel rack for the diesels. Locals worked the main line north and south, jobs were dispatched to venture down the stone district's spur tracks, and turns worked to both of Monon's branches—north to Wallace Junction and the I&L branch, south to Orleans and the French Lick branch. In short, there was much for young trainwatchers to experience—and Monon's yard crews never seemed to mind that we appeared with regularity on weekends to watch and ask questions, and, occasionally at least, beg rides in the cab of the yard switcher.

Our change of location to Bloomington, as it happened, coincided with change on the Hoosier Line. In April 1959—the same month as our journey on No. 5—Monon had discontinued the Chicago-Indianapolis *Tippecanoe* and *Hoosier*, leaving our familiar *Thoroughbred* as the lone surviving Hoosier Line passenger train. These were, in truth, relatively lean times for the Monon (in the years 1960 and 1961, the Hoosier Line turned its only net operating deficits after 1946).

With but one remaining passenger train, and red ink in the corporate books, Monon dispensed with the luxury of different passenger and freight paint schemes. The Barriger-era, Loewy-designed, red-and gray-passenger livery (inspired by Indiana University's cream and crimson school colors) was replaced, albeit slowly, on coaches and baggage cars and passenger-service F-3s with the Hoosier Line's freight colors —the black and gold of Purdue University. Unneeded passenger cars gathered in silent storage at McDoel, and among them was a pair of Monon's flat-ended observations, the cars that had so intrigued us a decade before in Bedford. Thanks to a kind-hearted Monon man who ushered us aboard one afternoon, we

discovered—belatedly—what it was like to snuggle into a parlor seat on one of Monon's uncommon observation cars.

Aged Veterans in Twilight

If the imprint of John Walker Barriger and his ilk was disappearing at the dawn of the 1960s, as control of the Monon passed to William C. Coleman and a "New Monon" was cast, surely Barriger's legacy remained in one form. And that was in the aged, veteran diesels that had stilled the exhaust of Monon steam more than a decade before, and which, through 1963, still toted every ton of Monon freight and forwarded every Monon coach. Their designations read F-3 and BL-2 and NW-2 (from Electro-Motive), RS-2 (from Alco), and H-10-44 and H-15-44 (from Fairbanks-Morse). Aside from the F-Ms, which in 1960-1961 had their original opposed-piston engines replaced by EMD 567s (more handiwork of the men of Lafayette Shops), the Hoosier Line's diesels were little changed from a decade before—except for the claims of time.

McDoel Yard was a wonderful place to make one's acquaintance with Monon's first-generation warriors, to peer into the oily, barely lit engine room of an F-3, to listen to the uncertain cadence of Alco's RS-2, to watch an NW-2 swim around on the uneven ladder tracks.

Of course, the show was even better when the old gladiators got down to serious business—take for example a quintet of black-and-gold F-3s challenging 130-odd cars and the twisting path of a railroad that

Above: Monon's diesel goliath: Alco C-628 No. 403 stands new at its builder's Schenectady (N.Y.) plant early in 1964. One of nine such titans purchased by Monon, the 403 was displayed at various Hoosier Line towns. *(ALCO, FRANK VAN BREE COLLECTION)* **Below:** Drama of Alco diesel's departure is evident as C-628's 404 and 403 blacken the sky over Bloomington, urging train 73 out of McDoel Yard bound for Louisville on November 13, 1965. *(KENNETH M. ARDINGER)*

climbed north out of Bloomington to Hunters, four miles away. On a grade that reached 2.16%, steepest on the Hoosier Line, with the rage of 80 pistons and 20 traction motors transferring 7,500 horses to the railroad, the Fs would claw their way through limestone cuts, digging, spitting sand, rocketing exhaust skyward, all to attain the tree-lined curve at Hunters which meant the hill had been conquered.

And even at that, there was more to this show—for heavy northbound freights received an assist from McDoel's yard switcher, which meant an NW-2 or RS-2 would snuggle into the rear coupler of a Monon caboose and push with fury through town and up the grade, then come waltzing back through Bloomington in victory. The same verve of the F-3s could be equally ascribed to Monon's RS-2s, which also added a wreath of charcoal smoke to any departure or engineer's opening of the throttle.

Goliath Comes to Bloomington

Train-watchers have a special grapevine, whether it be *Trains* magazine or the latest gossip from the yard clerk, and it is from such familiar sources that we expect to discover our railroad news. But one spring afternoon in 1964 we received big news, and it was the ordinary town newspaper that brought the message: The Monon would be displaying at Bloomington depot one of nine new diesels purchased from Alco. And not run-of-the-mill diesels, mind you, but "the nation's most powerful single-engine diesel electric."

It was a Saturday morn that our father accompanied us downtown, and our discovery was this: a goliath of a diesel, 69 feet long, 399,950 pounds, six axles, 2,750 hp, 4,000-gallon fuel tank, dual controls—all wrapped in Monon black and gold (with silver trucks) and numbered 403. The Alco C-628s had arrived, and the Hoosier Line entered the big leagues of dieseldom.

The C-628s, which cost the Monon $2,393,000, were evidence of William Coleman's "New Monon," purchased in anticipation of powering unit trains of coal from Coleman's proposed barge facility on the Ohio River to a dock on Lake Michigan. But in 1964, the plan was far from completion (and eventually was killed altogether by the ICC), so the big Alcos went to work on mainline freights. That translated into a remarkable experience anytime Monon freights 70-73 appeared at McDoel. It was the southbounds—No. 71 in the morning and No. 73 in the afternoon—that we most often encountered, to behold the burly C-628s slowly ease forward to take the slack out of their trains, then burst to life, pounding with sound, funneling black smoke over the south end of McDoel Yard, urging their tonnage toward Bedford and beyond.

The mid- and late-1960s proved, if anything, to be times of more rapid change on the Hoosier Line than even the early 1960s. For the Monon train-watcher, some changes were favorable, some less so. In 1965-1966, the men of Lafayette Shops again proved their skills, taking Monon's aging RS-2s into the brick erecting hall and rebuilding the road-switchers with new,

In a portrait of veterans in twilight, five black-and-gold Hoosier Line F-3's drag 132 cars north out of Bloomington, conquering a grade that reached 2.6 percent. Lead F-3 103 had just recently been renumbered from 64A in this June 14, 1963, scene. (*KENNETH M. ARDINGER*)

23

Left: With a Chicago & Western Indiana RS-1 standing aside, Monon train 5, the *Thoroughbred*, clatters out of Dearborn Station, Chicago, behind high-nose Alco C-420 501. The *Thoroughbred* had only months to live in this July 7, 1967, scene. *(JIM SCRIBBINS, WILLIAM A. RAIA COLLECTION)* **Below:** A quartet of Alco C-420's— stalwarts of the Monon in its final years— race train 70 over the Hoosier Line's flat, fast Northern Division near Roselawn, Ind. Date of the photo is July 30, 1971, one day before Monon was merged into Louisville & Nashville. *(ROBERT P. OLMSTED)*

1,600-hp Alco powerplants, and other refinements, re-numbering them from the 20 to 50 series. The result was that Monon began regularly splicing two C-628s with a single RS-2 on road freights. It was a peculiar trio to be sure, but one that served the railroad (and us train-watchers) well.

And then, in August 1966, more new motive power arrived—Alco C-420s—diminutive, 2,000-hp, four-axled kindred of the big C-628s. There were six—Nos. 501-506—and a pair (501-502) proved uncommon creatures, wearing hi-noses with steam generators tucked inside. It was this pair's duty to replace the aged Fs on the *Thoroughbred*, and they did so ably, if not with the style of the old EMDs. Considering that Alco road-switchers were not exactly synonymous with passenger carriage in the late 1960s, we were suspect that the C-420s felt most at home at old Dearborn Station, where they could count on the company of an elder sister—a Chicago & Western Indiana RS-1—casting about among the terminal tracks shuffling cars.

As for the experience of the passenger C-420s around Bloomington, by this time the *Thoroughbred's* schedule had been altered, the train passing southbound through Bloomington at 10:24 p.m., and northbound at 8:36 a.m.—which gave us the chance to witness No. 5 slice through darkened southern Indiana guided by its searing, yellow headlight, and to watch in daylight the gallop of the C-420s as they bobbed over rail joints departing Bloomington with No. 6. But the experience proved a short one, for on September 30, 1967, the *Thoroughbred* made its last run—and the Monon became a freight-only property.

As if the final departure of the *Thoroughbred* was not serious enough, there was more unsettling news in the summer of 1967. We heard it from a Monon switch-man one Saturday at McDoel: The burly C-628s that

we had so befriended were bound back to Alco—as trade-ins. With his hope of turning Monon into a heavy-duty coal carrier dashed, William Coleman had made his departure from the Hoosier Line in February 1967, and the road's new management—headed by Samuel T. Brown—saw little need for the ponderous (and often cantankerous) C-628s. A dozen more C-420s would serve the Hoosier Line better, and by the fall of 1967 the C-628s were gone and new C-420s were in their place on the head end of Monon trains 71, 73, *et al.*

Now, don't get us wrong—for the train-watcher there was little fault to find with the Alco C-420s. For mainline freights, Monon lashed them together in strings of three or four or five, tied 8,000 or so tons of freight behind, and dispatched them out of South Hammond and Lafayette and Louisville to battle grades from Borden to Gosport to Battle Ground.

During the closing days of the Monon in July 1971, the elderly round-house at McDoel is showing its age as RS-2 56 takes a spin on the turntable before being tucked away for the night. The appearance of

McDoel's roundhouse notwithstanding, the Monon was maintained in generally excellent condition to the end. (*GARY W. DOLZALL*)

Invariably, with throaty exhaust and undulating, whining traction motors, they succeeded at their tasks. The C-420s could pull—taking a trackside seat at Gosport to watch them tug 100 cars out of the White River valley proved that to us. And they could run— consider the sight of a quartet of C-420s rolling at 50 mph across the flatlands of the Northern Division.

And, unlike their departed bigger Alco kindred, the C-420s seemed right at home wandering in tandem down the tree-lined, less-than-certain right-of-way of the I&L branch, or stepping over the fragile timbers of the Kankakee River trestle on the Michigan City line, or strolling between the streets of Delphi headed to Indianapolis.

Farewell

April 1968: The directors of Monon and the 10 times larger Louisville & Nashville Railroad agreed in principle to the merger of the Hoosier Line into the L&N. It was merely the first formal step—stockholder approval came that August and ICC permission was sought in September 1968. It would take nearly three years for the ICC to grant its approval, and not until July 31, 1971, would the merger be consummated. But from late 1968 onward, we had little doubt that we were trackside for the final years of the Hoosier Line.

Given our attachment to the Monon, it might have seemed that these final years would be melancholy, or bittersweet at best. But, in truth, they were good years. The Hoosier Line was stable, in the black, and busy with tonnage. The Monon was going out with style. The Alco C-420s ruled the time freights and the maid-of-all-work RS-2s powered the locals and stone trains and even spelled the EMD switchers at yard work.

A handful of rusting but faithful 20-year-old F-3s and BL-2s lingered until near the end, and although the old EMDs were by this time primarily creatures of the Northern Division, they ventured through Bloomington often enough to remind us of what the chant of EMD V-16s and single-note air horns sounded like amid the echo-filled valleys of southern Indiana.

In spring 1970 came a final motive power addition to the Monon—eight new diesels built by General Electric, designated U23B. Alco was by then out of the locomotive business, so in a sense the 2,250-hp U23Bs were as close to more C-420s as Monon could come, but whatever management's reasoning, we soon applauded their decision. We first encountered U23Bs on an afternoon in early May 1970, four units affixed to the point of train No. 73. We watched them depart McDoel in a rampage of swirling sand and exhaust, then by car

Below: A trio of Alco C-420's, an aged RS-2 and one General Electric U23B are urged to life by the engineer of train 73 as Monon tonnage makes a gallant departure from Bedford in the Monon's final summer. (GARY W. DOLZALL) **Right:** GE U23B 602—one of eight purchased by Monon in 1970—leads a pair of Alcos and train 73 southbound at National, Ind., in July 1971. (GARY W. DOLZALL)

followed their rapid progress to Clear Creek and Diamond and Harrodsburg. Afterward, we had little doubt about the qualifications of Monon's newcomers.

Soon, the GEs and C-420s (and occasionally, the RS-2s) appeared together in lashups, and at times seemed to be in a contest as to which type could best blacken the Hoosier sky with diesel exhaust (the Alcos invariably won). At night, the Alcos and GEs shared an awesome trait of occasionally belching a visible sheet of orange flame from their turbo stacks, which made watching their passing in the darkened country-side at National or Gosport or Wallace Junction full of intrigue.

This chapter, and indeed this entire book, must eventually acknowledge the day of July 31, 1971, the time when "Monon" became but a division name on the Louisville & Nashville rather than the Hoosier com-

pany whose roots could be traced 124 years into history. In truth, the merger day came and went with limited fanfare, with few misting eyes, with no remarkable event. And thus we prefer to close our personal reflection on the Hoosier Line in another manner—with a Monon recall perhaps as dear as any we hold.

So journey with us back to a March afternoon in 1971, to the Monon's last winter, to a snow-covered hill overlooking Clear Creek and the Monon main line at Diamond, 5.4 miles south of McDoel. It was a cold, snowy Saturday, with roads nearly impassable. A day when prudence suggested staying at home. But we knew our time with the Monon was short and so we struggled by car and foot to that snow-dressed hill, to wait and hope for the arrival of train 73. We waited, and we chatted, to try to forget fingers and toes growing cold, until, from amid the sounds of winter's winds,

Monon memories: In March 1971, a mix of Alco C-420's and GE U23B's lead train 73 across the timber bridge at Diamond, Ind., passing like a specter vailed in nature's snowy white. (*GARY W. DOLZALL*)

we became aware of a distant but certain call, growing louder, louder.

We poured our attention toward the curve before us, waiting and silent, until a piercing headlight and a swirling dance of snow appeared, out-of-sync exhausts of Alco and General Electric V-12s cracking, as C-420 505 and Monon kindred led Louisville-bound train 73 across the timber bridge and into the stone cut below us, trailing boxcars and gondolas, piggyback flats and hoppers.

A deep red Monon caboose, ice clinging to its sides, snow pasted to its roof, slashed by, and then—so suddenly—train 73 was gone, disappearing like a specter in nature's veil of ghostly white. As we returned home, we knew our snowy journey had been worthwhile, for, just as so many times before, the Monon had given us a lifelong memory. We could ask nothing more.

MONON

THE HOOSIER LINE

Around the turn of the century—when the name Chicago, Indianapolis & Louisville was but a few years old—4-8-0 No. 203 challenges "the knobs" between Borden and Pekin, deep in southern Indiana. (*LLOYD J. KIMBLE COLLECTION*)

2
INDIANA'S OWN RAILROAD

Origins of the Hoosier Line
1847-1909

JAMES BROOKS was a remarkable man. Merchant, family man, civic leader—and railroad builder. Born in Orington, Maine, in 1810 and raised in Cincinnati, Ohio, Brooks settled on the north bank of the Ohio River at New Albany, Ind., in 1828. By the mid-1840s, Brooks was a noted New Albany businessman—and a man with a dream. James Brooks' vision: to connect the waterways of the Ohio River and Great Lakes by railroad. And it would take only seven years for young James Brooks to turn his dream into 288 miles of timber and rail.

In 1847, New Albany was the largest city in Indiana (population 7,000) and, in addition to standing on the bank of the Ohio, it rested at the southern end of an uncompleted McAdamized road, started in 1836 with Indiana state funds, but never finished. The road was to have run 170 miles through Indiana, from Crawfordsville to Greencastle, Bloomington, Bedford, Salem and New Albany. In Salem—35 miles north of New Albany—townsmen sparked talk of using this uncompleted road to connect Salem and New Albany via a new railroad. The time for James Brooks' idea had come.

The New Albany & Salem Rail Road

On May 20, 1847, in the tiny Hoosier hamlet of Providence (now Borden), midway between New Albany and Salem, James Brooks and six other men met to organize a company—the New Albany & Salem Rail Road. Action followed: On July 2, the new firm held its first shareholders meeting and Brooks was elected president; on July 8 its first board meeting was

held and the name "New Albany & Salem Rail Road" was established; and on July 31, 1847, Indiana Governor James Whitcomb proclaimed "the New Albany & Salem is duly organized."

The infant railroad was able to use the uncompleted McAdamized road's right-of-way because of an act passed in 1842 allowing private entrepreneurs to take over this and other defunct state road projects, and through an 1847 amendment allowing the Salem–New Albany road to be built instead as a railroad. In its charter and subsequent acts passed by a supportive Indiana legislature, the New Albany & Salem Rail Road gained valuable freedoms to raise funds and lengthen its route with little restriction.

On May 3, 1848, less than a year after James Brooks and his associates met for the first time, ground was broken at New Albany. Under the direction of Chief Engineer L.B. Wilson, grading began toward Salem, and the first tons of "flat bar" rails were ordered. Two passenger cars and freight equipment were ordered from Keck & Davenport and construction of a shop in New Albany began in 1849. In August 1848, the NA&S had ordered its first three locomotives—the *New Albany*, the *Providence*, and the *Salem*—from Philadelphia builder Norris & Co. Cost: $7,500 each. The *New Albany* arrived in its namesake city, carried on an Ohio River steamer, in spring 1849 (the other two locomotives arrived in 1850-1851).

On July 4, 1849, the NA&S operated an excursion run—three miles. A year later, another excursion ventured 22 miles, and on January 14, 1851, the first train reached Salem, fulfilling the promise of the railroad's

The New Albany & Salem extended into Lafayette in 1853, laying its tracks down Mississippi Street (later 5th Street). Could James Brooks have ever envisioned his railroad nearly a century later, when 4500 horsepower worth of black-and-gold EMD F-3's would draw tonnage down the same street? Monon 61 was photographed at 5th and Ferry, May 22, 1948. (C. R. ADAMS)

name. But James Brooks' ambitions for his railroad were far from complete. Indeed, as early as 1849 the NA&S had been letting construction contracts toward Bedford, and by 1850 on toward Gosport.

Crawfordsville, Ind., 56 miles north of Gosport and 170 miles north of New Albany, was the immediate construction goal of Brooks' railroad. There, a link could be made with the Crawfordsville & Wabash Railroad, a line chartered in 1846 to build from Crawfordsville to the Wabash & Erie Canal. Connecting with (and buying) the Crawfordsville & Wabash could take the NA&S 27 miles farther north, to near Lafayette. From there it would be less than 100 miles to Lake Michigan's shore.

James Brooks chose Michigan City, Ind., a Lake Michigan port city of 2,000 inhabitants, as northern

terminus for the NA&S. Michigan City offered a promising port, convenient connections with Great Lakes steamboats, and was—at the time—expected to grow into a large city. Contracts for the line from Michigan City to Lafayette, Ind., were signed in August 1851. Financing of the Michigan City–Lafayette line was certainly the most creative taken during construction of the NA&S. As did most railroads abuilding, the NA&S relied upon stock purchases from on-line communities for much of its funds. But the route from Michigan City to Lafayette was barely populated. Money had to come from another source—and that source was the Michigan Central.

The Michigan Central Railroad was deadlocked in a duel with competitor Michigan Southern to cross Indiana and enter Chicago. But the MC could not obtain a

The NA&S reached Gosport in 1854 and built its famed "run-through" brick depot along the bank of the White River. The depot would endure through the Hoosier Line's entire independent existence. Linn Westcott photographed the remarkable structure from the rear platform of a 1946 Monon inspection train. The historic structure was torn down by successor Louisville & Nashville in the late 1970's. (LINN WESTCOTT, COLLECTION OF KALMBACH PUBLISHING CO.)

charter from the state legislature. The NA&S, however, had its charter—with authority to build with little restriction. The Michigan Central and NA&S arrived at a mutually advantageous agreement in April 1851: the MC would use the NA&S's charter to build across northern Indiana, via Michigan City (and a connection with the NA&S) to Chicago.

In return, the MC would purchase $500,000 of New Albany & Salem stock. Brooks also saw the potential of this route to Chicago, and fostered plans of the NA&S to eventually control the Michigan Central's route from Michigan City to Chicago, but this never occurred. Of the stock income obtained from the Michigan Central, the NA&S earmarked $400,000 for its Michigan City-Lafayette construction and $100,000 to bolster south-end construction.

In southern Indiana, the NA&S was completed and opened to Orleans, 56 miles northwest of New Albany, on January 1, 1852, and rails were extended to nine miles north of Orleans by June 1852. That same month, the NA&S purchased control of the just-completed Crawfordsville & Wabash. Because of its original purpose of linking Crawfordsville with the Wabash & Erie Canal, the C&W had terminated south of Lafayette and quite distant from the town.

Crawfordsville, then competing with Lafayette as a business and farming center, saw the C&W link to the canal as a competitive advantage over its neighbor. Lafayette retaliated by building a plank road from its downtown to near—but not into—Crawfordsville. The NA&S, now that it controlled the Crawfordsville & Wabash, held entirely different plans for the C&W, and quickly went about plans to enter Lafayette, bridge the Wabash River, and eventually connect with its budding line from Michigan City.

By the spring of 1853, work on the NA&S was progressing up and down the line. The extension of the ex-Crawfordsville & Wabash line into Lafayette was built, and on March 11, the first NA&S train rolled into that city. In April, trains from New Albany reached Bedford, with six miles of rugged terrain and the east branch of White River conquered south of there. In

both Bedford and Lafayette, the NA&S strolled right through the heart of town on streets. Grading was under way on the Michigan City-Lafayette line and tracklaying, south from Michigan City, had begun in July 1852. Because of delays in the winter of 1852-53, it took 16 months to complete the job of joining Michigan City and Lafayette. By April 1853, the line from Michigan City had reached within 40 miles of Lafayette and joint rail/stage coach service was established, and in early October 1853 the Michigan City-Lafayette line of the New Albany & Salem was opened.

In that same month—October 1853—the NA&S extended its line through the rolling, sometimes rugged hills of southern Indiana as far north as Bloomington—home of Indiana University. By the following January, the ribbons of rail had reached Gosport, on the north branch of the White River, and an engine house had been built there.

From New Albany, 133 miles of railroad had been completed northward. From Michigan City via Lafayette to Crawfordsville, 119 miles of track was in place. Only 56 miles between Gosport and Crawfordsville remained to be completed. Actually, James Brooks had envisioned two lines radiating north from Gosport—the main line via Crawfordsville, and a 43-mile branch line to Indianapolis. Grading had begun on both projects in 1852, but while 1854 would mark the completion of the main line, it also marked abandonment of NA&S's plans for the branch.

Although the Indianapolis branch was graded to within 16 miles of its destination, the NA&S did not have the finances to complete both it and the main line. (The branch was, nonetheless, destined to be completed—as part of the Pennsylvania Railroad's Indianapolis & Vincennes Railroad.) As for NA&S's main line, tracklaying south from Crawfordsville began on

Ancient (Civil War era) photograph of an ancient locomotive: Although already re-lettered as LNA&C No. 2, this 4-4-0 was purchased by the New Albany & Salem, and, in fact, is likely NA&S's second loco-motive—originally the *Providence*—built by Norris in 1850. (*CSX TRANSPORTATION ARCHIVES*)

Standing beside the stock pens at Lafayette in 1870 is Louisville, New Albany & Chica-go 4-4-0 No. 9—the *Admiral*. Built (prob-ably using components from an old NA&S locomotive) in the LNA&C's New Albany shop immediately after the Civil War, the handsome 4-4-0 cost LNA&C $4985.93. (*DAVE FERGUSON'S PHOTO ART*)

June 20, 1853, Bainbridge was reached in November, and Greencastle early in 1854. Tracklaying then began north from Gosport as well, and on June 24, 1854, seven miles south of Greencastle, the track gangs met. The New Albany & Salem's last spike was driven at 4 p.m., June 24, 1854. At a cost of more than $6 million, James Brooks had fulfilled the promise he penned to stockholders in 1853, to extend the NA&S from the Ohio River to Great Lakes "as fast as means could be got to do the work."

The New Albany & Salem was opened for through traffic on July 3, 1854. Under the supervision of con-ductor S.B. Boroff, the first through train departed Michigan City at 5 a.m., averaged 16 miles per hour over the 288 miles, and pulled into New Albany at a few minutes past 10 p.m.

The next day—the 4th of July 1854—a celebration, bringing together dignitaries including the governors of Indiana and Kentucky, was held in New Albany. Together, the congregation rejoiced in what James Brooks, his associates, the muscle of Irish laborers, the power of blasting powder, and the steam potency of diminutive 4-4-0s had wrought.

The Louisville, New Albany & Chicago

Typical of so many formative 19th-century railroads, the New Albany & Salem dearly paid the price of its rapid birth. Overextended during its construction (witness its failed branch to Indianapolis), the road immediately suffered financial difficulty, and the economic panic of 1857 worsened its problems. The railroad was further weakened by the costs of relaying rail on 45 miles of line north of New Albany. On this portion, the NA&S had used "bar iron" rail, which proved troublesome and dangerous, and it was re-placed with "T" rails.

By October 1858, the New Albany & Salem was forced into receivership under D.D. Williamson of New York's Farmers and Traders Bank, and on February 4, 1859, James Brooks resigned his presidency. Under the trusteeship of Williamson, and with David Noble serving as president, the name of James Brooks' rail-road was, on October 24, 1859, changed to better de-scribe the aspirations of the railroad. The new name: The Louisville, New Albany & Chicago Railroad.

When the uncertain bond of North and South was broken by cannon fire at Fort Sumpter and the Civil War, the fledgling Louisville, New Albany & Chicago was pushed into a position of importance, being a north-south line that could feed Union troops and goods to the Mason-Dixon line. The LNA&C was heavily trafficked with both tonnage and troops during the war years, and the LNA&C felt the sting of war—from that redoubtable Confederate cavalry raider, General John Hunt Morgan.

"Morgan's Raiders," who caused heavy damage to

Road number of tall-stacked Louisville, New Albany & Chicago 4-4-0 is unknown, but other facts about this historic photograph are. Depicted is a LNA&C milk/passenger train standing at Lowell, Ind., 45 miles south of Chicago, amid the snows of winter 1886. (*FRANK VAN BREE COLLECTION*)

Historic 19th century scene at Monon reveals LNA&C 4-4-0 in background, wooden plank station platforms, and single-story Monon frame depot. (*DAVE FERGUSON'S PHOTO ART*)

Terminus for the Hoosier Line's passenger trains in Indiana's capital city was the red brick Victorian Indianapolis Union Station. The still-extant station, now completely rehabilitated into a shopping mall and train/bus station, was built in the mid-1880's; tracks, owned by Indianapolis Union Railway, were elevated in the 1920's. (*DOLZALL COLLECTION*)

dawn's light, headed by a pilot engine, and arrived in Michigan City at 8:25 a.m. There, after a stop, the train clattered onto the Michigan Central, bound for Chicago and on to Springfield, Ill., where Abraham Lincoln was buried.

More Troubled Times

At the end of the Civil War, traffic on the LNA&C plummeted. From 1865 to 1866, tonnage declined 36%; passenger traffic dropped by nearly half. Military traffic, of course, had all but disappeared, but the LNA&C's real problem was the Jeffersonville Railroad (eventually part of the Pennsylvania). With an extension opened into New Albany, the Jeffersonville Railroad began operating three daily passenger trains to Indianapolis, taking a substantial number of passengers away from the LNA&C. Because the Jeffersonville Railroad had tracks to the banks of the Ohio River (while the LNA&C terminated in downtown New Albany), it also had an advantage in plucking freight straight off the river steamers.

Rather than challenge the Jeffersonville Railroad, trustee Williamson threw in the towel. He noted that the Jeffersonville Railroad was "taking freights out of the river at a ruinous rate, so much so that we abandoned that traffic at once, and we did not even attempt to lay a track to the river, as it would not have benefited us at all."

For the frail LNA&C, there were still more problems: Bad weather resulted in poor crops, which left the LNA&C with less to haul. And Mother Nature brought destruction down on the LNA&C far more effectively than Morgan's Raiders had. In February and March 1866, fed by heavy rains and melting snow, Sugar Creek ripped away 200 feet of the LNA&C's bridge near Crawfordsville. At the same time, the railroad

the Louisville & Nashville Railroad's main line south of Louisville during the war, slipped into the Hoosier state in July 1863. At 10 a.m., on July 10, 1863, Morgan's Raiders rode upon Salem, and turned their fury on the LNA&C, burning the Salem depot and water tank, tearing up rails and ties, and burning nearby bridges.

The saddest, and yet most historic, duty ever performed by the Hoosier Line occurred at the conclusion of the Civil War, when the funeral train of slain President Abraham Lincoln rolled over the northern part of the LNA&C. After a stop in Indianapolis, Lincoln's funeral train departed the Hoosier capital at midnight, April 30, 1865. It traveled north to Lafayette via the Lafayette & Indianapolis Railroad (later part of New York Central's Big Four).

At 3:20 a.m., on the morn of April 30, 1865, somberly lighted by bonfires set at trackside by mourning crowds, the funeral train crept onto LNA&C rails at Lafayette Junction. It moved north through the

Most infamous feature of the Bedford & Bloomfield—the Owensboro Tunnel—is visible in the background as tunnel workers pose in this remarkable 19th century photograph. Locomotive in foreground is a B&B narrow-gauge 2-4-0. *(LLOYD J. KIMBLE COLLECTION)*

Rhode Island Locomotive Works built LNA&C's first 2-8-0's—low-boilered Nos. 64-67—in 1887. Eventually, the Hoosier Line would purchase 40 2-8-0's. *(LLOYD J. KIMBLE COLLECTION)*

Pin-striping adorns 63-inch drivers of Rogers-built LNA&C 4-6-0 No. 90 when new in 1890. *(ALCO HISTORIC PHOTOS)*

lost its bridges over Monon Creek at Bradford (later to become Monon, Ind.), and smaller bridges near Greencastle. Other bridges, including the Wabash River crossing, were seriously damaged. Then that August, LNA&C lost more bridges—near Ellettsville and Gosport—to flood waters. LNA&C's superintendent, B.F. Master, estimated repair costs at $45,000. And there was more trouble: South of Bedford, between Juliett and Hitchcock, LNA&C's track, laid on log stringers, became so unstable that it was necessary to install new ties and sand ballast on nine miles of line.

Despite its troubled economics and battle to merely keep its main line open, the LNA&C did, nonetheless, make attempts at improvement after the Civil War. In 1866, the road purchased 50 box and stock cars from the Ohio Falls Car Co., and at its New Albany shops built 44 coal cars and 26 flatcars. A new station was built at Quincy, and a new blacksmith shop at New Albany. Considered, but not built, was a branch leaving the main line at either Bainbridge or Putnamville bound for the coal fields of Clay County. At the north end of the railroad, LNA&C looked to the completion of Michigan City's harbor, and expected increased tonnage of lumber, salt, plaster and farm produce from that port.

But the LNA&C's attempts at stability failed. By October 1868, the railroad was again facing foreclosure and James F. Joy of Detroit, Mich., was named receiver. The railroad was sold, and on June 24, 1869, was reorganized as the Louisville, New Albany & Chicago Railway. In control was a New York group with John Jacob Astor at its head.

Over the next three years, the LNA&C endured total financial and legal turmoil. Following a suit by junior bondholder John S. Shaw, who held the 1869 sale of the LNA&C to be illegal, the railroad was again placed in receivership (under George H. Chapman) in 1871. The road again underwent foreclosure sale in December 1872, and control was again gained by the Astor interests. For the next eight years, the LNA&C would lead a quiet existence with few improvements and no expansion.

A Crossing at Bradford

While the LNA&C of the 1870s slumbered, there was railroad activity elsewhere in Indiana that would

This two-story frame depot at Monon was an 1893 expansion of the single-story depot depicted on page 33. The K-2-class 4-6-2 eased up to the platform was built by Brooks in 1906. In 1916, this station would be replaced by a limestone structure. (*DAVE FERGUSON'S PHOTO ART*)

change the face of the Hoosier Line. On September 3, 1872, a railroad—the Indianapolis, Delphi & Chicago—was organized to build between its namesake cities. Reorganized was, in truth, a better term, because the ID&C had been first incorporated by Delphi business-men in 1865, but construction had never been started. But in 1872, there was strong reason to renew the ID&C. A projected railroad giant, the Chicago & South Atlantic—envisioned to reach from Lake Michigan to the Atlantic Ocean (Chicago to Charleston, S.C.)—searched for a path across northern Indiana toward Chicago. And the ID&C's charter provided just such a route.

By 1874, with the financial backing of the Chicago & South Atlantic, grading began on the ID&C. Within a year, the majority of the line north of Delphi—pro-jected to run northwest to Monticello, Bradford (where it would cross the LNA&C), Rensselaer and Dyer (where connections into Chicago could be made on existing railroads)—was graded. Then suddenly, the ID&C lost its parent. In late 1875, the Chicago & South Atlantic fell into economic disarray—and finally total collapse. For a second time, the Indianapolis, Delphi & Chicago had been stillborn.

Enter John Lee. In 1877, Lee (of Crawfordsville) and Delphi businessmen again renewed plans for the ID&C. This time the railroad was cast not as part of a dreamed-of Titan such as the ill-fated C&SA, but as a three-foot, narrow-gauge line intended to provide low-cost competition to standard-gauge roads. Because the

Louisville, New Albany & Chicago provided a means to transport rail and equipment, construction of the ID&C began at Bradford. Under the guidance of builder S.N. Yeomen, the ID&C laid its narrow-gauge railroad from Bradford northwest to Rensselaer, 15 miles, by February 1878. By the end of 1878, the ID&C had extended southeast from Bradford to Monticello, and in September 1879 the road reached one of its namesake towns—Delphi. Conquered were crossings of the Tippecanoe River (at Monticello) and the Wabash River (north of Delphi).

But in 1880, the luckless ID&C again—for a final time—faltered. Control of the Indianapolis, Delphi & Chicago passed to its builder, S.N. Yeomen, largely because the ID&C was unable to pay for his construc-tion work. Yeomen reorganized and renamed the road the Indianapolis & Chicago Air Line, planned entry into Chicago via rights on the budding Chicago & Western Indiana, and made the decision to recast the railroad—in standard gauge. In September 1880, tracklaying began south from Dyer, and by the end of the month had reached Lowell, 15 miles. By May 1881, the line was nearly complete from Dyer to Delphi. And the Indianapolis & Chicago Air Line had a larger suitor—the Louisville, New Albany & Chicago.

Years of Expansion

Following its nearly decade-long sleep, the LNA&C of the 1880s made a rapid expansion. At the start of

Hoosier Line Ten-Wheelers 28 (right) and 32—built in 1880 and 1881 respectively—stand surrounded by crew members at Perry, Matthews & Buskirk quarry in the stone district at Bedford in a scene from early in the Twentieth Century. (*LLOYD J. KIMBLE COLLECTION*)

Power from the Baldwin Locomotive Works was relatively rare on the Hoosier Line, but one such example was lanky 2-8-0 No. 82, built in Philadelphia in 1892. (*H. L. BROAD-BELT COLLECTION*)

History at Mitchell: U.S. presidential candidate William Jennings Bryan addresses a throng at Mitchell during his 1896 campaign. Mitchell depot was built in 1892; the locomotive—standing with a southbound freight—is LNA&C 2-8-0 No. 72, built by Rogers in 1887. (*LLOYD J. KIMBLE COLLECTION*)

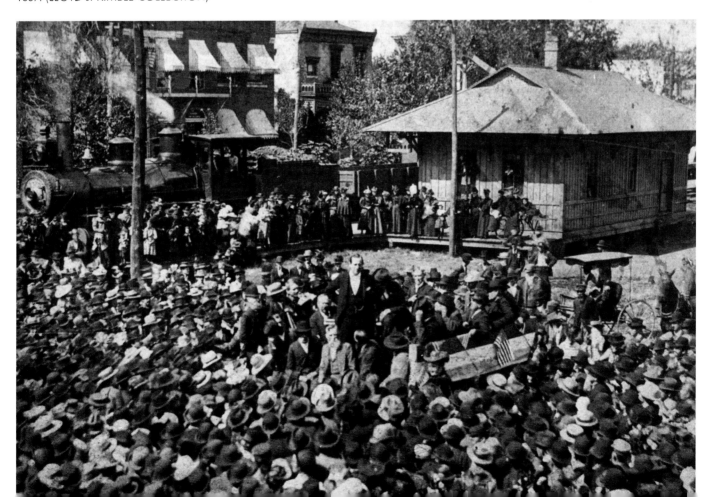

Classic turn-of-the-century southern Indiana scene includes Pekin station, windmill, local folk gathered on station platform, and Hoosier Line 4-4-0 104. (*LLOYD J. KIMBLE COLLECTION*)

MONON ROUTE
CHICAGO, INDIANAPOLIS & LOUISVILLE RAILWAY

BETWEEN

Chicago

Indianapolis
Cincinnati
Louisville
AND THE
Famous
French Lick
AND
West Baden
Springs

W. H. McDOEL,
President

B. E. TAYLOR,
General Manager

CHAS. H. ROCKWELL,
Traffic Manager

FRANK J. REED,
General Passenger Agent

STROMBERG, ALLEN & CO., CHICAGO.

JANUARY, 1906

the decade, the LNA&C was a branchless railroad of 288 miles—a railroad described by its own president, R.S. Veech, as a company with "a line starting at no place and ending nowhere, without a place or habitation in any of the great cities." But by the end of the decade, the LNA&C would count its trackage at 509 miles and send its trains into Chicago, Louisville and Indianapolis.

The first move came on May 20, 1881—when the LNA&C and Indianapolis & Chicago Air Line agreed to consolidate. The consolidation, with the LNA&C as surviving partner, was ratified by stockholders on June 7, and soon the Indianapolis & Chicago Air Line became simply the "C&I Division" of the LNA&C. The line from Dyer to Delphi was opened in August 1881 and it had also been fully converted to standard gauge.

By this time, the tiny hamlet of Bradford, site of the crossing of the LNA&C main line and C&I Division (and location of an enginehouse which New Albany & Salem built there in 1853), was renamed after the creek which flowed nearby. Bradford became Monon, Ind., and the "Monon Route" name was born.

There was more expansion to come: On the north end, the Indianapolis & Chicago Air Line's intention had been to sweep its rails northwest from Dyer to meet the Chicago & Western Indiana at Dolton, Ill.

The LNA&C management had other plans—the LNA&C would instead build north to Hammond, Ind., where it could connect with the C&WI at the Indiana/Illinois border. (This would prove a two-step process. On January 9, 1882, the road opened four miles of line from Dyer to Maynard Junction and used the Chicago & Atlantic—later the Erie Railroad—to attain the state line and C&WI. Then, in June 1884, the LNA&C built its own line from Maynard, through Hammond, to a direct connection with the Chicago & Western Indiana.) The LNA&C signed a 999-year lease with the C&WI with rental at $84,000 per year. The C&WI would take LNA&C's passenger trains into the heart of downtown Chicago, at its 12th Street depot (Dearborn Station was built in 1885). And while Monon also gained downtown Chicago freight facilities, it built a facility of its own at South Hammond.

As the LNA&C secured its permanent entry into Chicago, progress at the south end of the C&I Division toward Indianapolis also progressed—slowly. At the end of 1881, grading was completed south from Delphi to Frankfort and Sheridan, and in February 1882 grading was completed south to Broad Ripple, less than 10 miles from Indianapolis. Track gangs were laying rail both north and south from Frankfort. Finally, in October 1882, the LNA&C pushed its rails to Howlands (between the present sites of Broad Ripple and the

A remarkable photograph of the Perry, Matthews & Buskirk quarry at Bedford, May 23, 1900, includes CI&L 4-6-0 31 ready to couple onto Hoosier Line flatcars loaded with massive limestone blocks. (CSX AR-CHIVES)

Indiana State Fairgrounds), linking itself to the Lake Erie & Western's (later Nickel Plate) existing line for entry into downtown Indianapolis.

Local passenger service out of Indianapolis began on March 24, 1883, and later in the year, when the LNA&C reached agreement to use Indianapolis Union Station, the railroad inaugurated through Chicago-Indianapolis service. (LNA&C saved one final adjustment in its Indianapolis trackage until 1888, when it built two miles of track from Howlands to Massachusetts Ave., where it connected with both the LE&W and Cleveland, Columbus, Cincinnati & Indianapolis [later Big Four, NYC] for trackage rights into Indianapolis Union Station.)

With entry of the LNA&C into Indianapolis, speculation abounded that the road would push on—to Cincinnati. But the rumors were false, and the Monon Route in future years would instead settle for joint service with the Cincinnati, Hamilton & Dayton (later the Cincinnati, Indianapolis & Western) to reach Cincinnati.

The LNA&C had one other major move in hand at the start of the 1880s—to cross the Ohio River and reach Louisville. In 1881, the LNA&C purchased land at 14th Street in Louisville and built two 30-foot by 195-foot freight houses there. Then, in 1882, the road contracted with the Pennsylvania for trackage rights

In providing a low-gradient alternative to the old NA&S main line between Harrodsburg and Clear Creek, the Indiana Stone Railroad criss-crossed Clear Creek and rambled through some of the Hoosier Line's finest scenery. A half century after the ISRR was built, passengers aboard train 5, the *Thoroughbred*, could rejoice in the works of W. H. McDoel as the southbound train neared Harrodsburg. (*J. F. BENNETT, JIM BENNETT COLLECTION*)

Ornate MONON ROUTE number plate adorns the smokebox of CI&L 4-4-0 No.100 as it unloads passengers in the snow at an unknown location during the winter of 1900. Note the snowplow affixed to No. 100's pilot. (*LLOYD J. KIMBLE COLLECTION*)

from New Albany to the Louisville Bridge, and with the Louisville Bridge & Depot Co., to cross the waters of the Ohio and enter Louisville. The "great cities"—Louisville, Indianapolis and Chicago—that Monon president Veech had wished for were now the LNA&C's terminal cities.

To "The Springs"

Given the complexity of modern corporate structure, it is perhaps incongruous that a simple, handwritten, two-page document signed by 15 men could give life to a railroad—but on July 13, 1885, it happened. The railroad was the Orleans, Paoli & Jasper Railway, born—according to its articles of incorporation—to build from Orleans to the town of Jasper, 50 miles. The LNA&C's main line, of course, passed through Orleans, and on the new OP&J's board were three LNA&C officials: Vice President and General Manager John Carson; General Superintendent W.R. Woodard; and Traffic Manager W.H. McDoel. A branch line for the LNA&C was in the making.

The existence of the Orleans, Paoli & Jasper as a company proved very brief. Within a year, the paper company was purchased by the LNA&C and was renamed the Orleans, West Baden & French Lick Springs Railway. There were four reasons for the OWB&FLS to be built: passengers, lumber, stone and coal. French Lick and adjoining West Baden, some 17 miles from Orleans, was already forming into a resort hotel mecca, popular for its "Pluto water" with visitors from as far as St. Louis. The LNA&C looked to the hills southwest of Orleans to provide stone tonnage from quarries and timber from forests. And beyond French Lick, toward Jasper, bituminous coal rested under the Indiana soil.

By July 1886, work on the OWB&FLS had begun, with General J.S. Casement its contractor. In October 1886, rail reached from Orleans to Paoli (10 miles) and by February 1887 grading was under way to French Lick. Rail for the OWB&FLS was coming off the

LNA&C's C&I Division, as the parent railroad had purchased 4,599 tons of new 60-lb. rail to improve its Chicago–Indianapolis line. The OWB&FLS was marked by a number of small trestles, grades of up to 1.76%, and one dominating structure—a curving, 1,600-foot-long pine trestle over Lost River just north of Paoli.

Contracts were expected to be let in March 1887 for construction to Jasper (at a cost of $430,000), but the move was delayed by other activities of the LNA&C. In truth, the OWB&FLS proved aptly named, because it would never be extended beyond "the Springs." (Instead, the Southern Railway would complete a line from Jasper to French Lick and a connection with the Monon in 1908.)

The OWB&FLS was completed to French Lick early in the summer of 1887 and service began in August. The Monon Route's French Lick branch was in place.

The Remarkable, Rustic "B&B"

One month to the day after the LNA&C had acquired the Orleans, Paoli & Jasper in 1886, the expanding Monon Route purchased itself another branch line—this one largely complete. It was the three-foot, narrow-gauge Bedford & Bloomfield, which despite its name ran 41 miles west from Bedford through Bloomfield to Switz City, Ind. At a cost of $200,000, the LNA&C acquired the railroad, five locomotives, 93 freight cars (including 23 flatcars), one coach, one baggage car, and two combines. Although the "B&B" was a poorly built narrow-gauge line, the LNA&C saw in it potential to haul tons of southern Indiana limestone.

The heritage of the B&B could be traced to the late 1860s, and a plan to link Effingham, Ill., with Bedford. To accomplish this, four narrow-gauge properties had been formed. From west to east, the first was the Springfield, Effingham & South Eastern, incorporated on March 10, 1869, which completed 57 miles of railroad from Effingham to the Illinois/Indiana border by

1880. In 1880, 31 more miles of narrow-gauge was opened from the state line to Switz City by the Bloomfield Railroad (which had been formed in 1874).

Moving east, the next link was the Bloomfield Rail Road (the word "railroad" in its title being two words), incorporated in October 1874, which built six miles of trackage from Switz City to Bloomfield, including a 600-foot wooden bridge over the West Fork of White River near Bloomfield (it collapsed under a stone train in July 1884 and was rebuilt). And the fourth property was the Bedford, Springville, Owensburg & Bloomfield, formed on November 9, 1874. During the years 1874-1877, the BSO&B was built, laid with 35-lb. rail on untreated wooden ties and earth ballast, venturing through hill and valley on grades that reached 2.25%. A 1,362-foot tunnel was bored west of Owensburg.

In 1883, the BSO&B was reorganized as the Bedford & Bloomfield and a year later it acquired the Bloomfield Rail Road, bringing the Bedford–Switz City line under one ownership. The LNA&C purchased the B&B from the Bedford Rolling Mill Co. (The Effingham–Switz City portion of narrow gauge would eventually be standard gauged and evolved through the Indiana & Illinois Southern, then the Indianapolis Southern, to become part of Illinois Central's Effingham–Indianapolis line.)

For the LNA&C, the B&B of 1886 offered a lesson in the frailty of rustic narrow-gauge lines. Almost immediately upon LNA&C's takeover of the B&B, 100 feet of the Owensburg tunnel collapsed and had to be rebuilt in the summer of 1886 at a cost of $4,986. Bridges on the line, including the White River bridge, were in poor condition and had to be repaired and braced.

Despite its weaknesses, the B&B was a welcome addition to the LNA&C, which at the end of 1886 proclaimed that B&B stone tonnage had increased 50%. To handle the extra tonnage, LNA&C purchased 15 flatcars and five boxcars for service on the B&B.

The most serious problem on the B&B, of course, was that it was a narrow-gauge branch of a standard-gauge railroad. Transferring stone from narrow-gauge flats to standard-gauge flats at Bedford was costly. The LNA&C's short-term solution, undertaken in 1887, was to standard gauge 6.1 miles of main track from Bedford to Avoca, along with 3.5 miles of sidings and spurs, enabling LNA&C's own locomotives to serve the largest stone quarries, which were located around Bedford and Dark Hollow. Use of dual-gauge track allowed the B&B's trains to still enter Bedford.

Improvements in Indiana

The closing years of the 1880s and the early 1890s were undoubtedly among the most uncommon of the Monon Route's history. In the railroad trade press of the period, the LNA&C was regularly associated with expansion: In 1886, rumors of extension of the C&I Division toward Cincinnati persisted; in 1887, LNA&C was credited with plans to build a branch from the main line at Bainbridge to Brazil, Ind., and nearby coal fields.

Also in 1887 (and again in 1890), the LNA&C was reported ready to build a branch from Bennettsville (north of New Albany) to Cementville and/or Jeffersonville. In 1889, the Monon Route was reported to be planning a line from Salem north to Indianapolis. And in the early 1890s there was thought of casting the French Lick branch on to Evansville. None of these routes was ever turned to roadbed and rail, but other moves of the LNA&C were very real.

Between 1888 and 1896, the LNA&C made massive

Left: The I&L branch was young, and ballasted only with dirt, on the day an unknown photographer turned his camera on CI&L 4-6-0 92, standing at Patricksburg, Ind., 19 miles from Wallace Junction. (STEPHEN J. DAVIDSON COLLECTION) **Below:** With the construction of the Indianapolis & Louisville in the years 1906-1907, the Hoosier Line at long last attained via its own rails the coal deposits near Victoria and Midland, in southwestern Indiana. (DAVE FERGUSON'S PHOTO ART)

improvements to its often uncertain physical plant. On the Chicago-Indianapolis line, timber Howe truss bridges were replaced with iron and masonry bridges in 1892 and 1893. Depots at Rensselaer, Monon, Monticello and Delphi were enlarged and a depot was built at Cedar Lake in 1893. A depot was constructed at Broad Ripple in 1894, and the following year a new station was built at Kirklin. In 1896, the LNA&C built a new yard, enginehouse and turntable at Belt Junction in Indianapolis. The LNA&C also built a new freight house in Indianapolis in 1896 (LNA&C had previously used the LE&W's freight house), and replaced its 49th Street, Chicago, enginehouse that had burned.

On the ancient New Albany-Michigan City line, wooden bridges over White River in southern Indiana were replaced with iron between 1888 and 1892. Also in 1892, a depot was built at Mitchell, a freight house at Bedford, and a 10-stall roundhouse at Bloomington. In 1893, all iron rail on the Michigan City line was replaced with steel rail and depots were built at Salem, Clear Creek and Bedford. Ladoga, Romney and Greencastle Junction received new depots in 1894 and Chalmers the next year. And in 1895, the LNA&C opened a massive new shop facility at Lafayette (see Chapter 7). In 1896, seven new steel bridges were built on the main line, and a new passenger and freight depot built at Crawfordsville.

On the French Lick branch, new stations were built at West Baden and French Lick in 1889 and eight miles of 56-lb. rail was installed in 1892. And on the B&B, the Owensburg tunnel was remade (at a cost of $27,000) in 1894, and the following year the entire length of the B&B was widened to standard gauge. The renewed B&B was laid with 52-lb. steel rail taken off LNA&C's Monon-Indianapolis line, and with replacement of the B&B's last iron rail, the Monon Route was equipped entirely with steel rails.

Catastrophe in Kentucky

As the LNA&C undertook its line improvements in Indiana, it also moved to extend out of the Hoosier state. On October 2, 1888, the LNA&C signed a lease with the Kentucky & Indiana Bridge Co. The agreement, effective for 99 years as of July 19, 1889 (at an

annual rate of $65,000), would send LNA&C's trains across the Ohio on the K&I's bridge rather than that of the Louisville Bridge Co. The new agreement ignored the LNA&C's 1882 contract with the Louisville Bridge & Depot Co., and incensed the Pennsylvania (owner of the LB&D Co.) and the Louisville & Nashville. The L&N soon refused to interchange traffic with the LNA&C.

If the uncommon move by the LNA&C needed explanation, the road's plans became clear on March 1, 1889, when the Monon Route signed a 30-year lease of the Louisville Southern, a railroad that terminated on the K&I in Louisville and wended its way 83 miles southeast to Burgin, Ky., and a connection with the Cincinnati Southern (later the Cincinnati, New Orleans & Texas Pacific, part of the Southern Railway).

On October 18, 1889, LNA&C signed another agreement with the Louisville Southern—this for a 30-year lease of its "Lexington Extension," which left the LS main line at Lawrenceburg, Ky., and headed east to Lexington and Georgetown, Ky. In that same month, LNA&C concluded an agreement with the Ohio Valley Improvement & Contract Co., the firm which held construction rights to build the Richmond, Nicholasville, Irvine & Beattyville Railroad. The LNA&C agreed to guarantee principal and interest on $2.3 million in bonds in exchange for two-thirds of the RNI&B's capital stock. The RNI&B would link with the "Lexington Extension" at Versailles, Ky., and extend another 94 miles east to Beattyville, Ky. The Monon was bound for the coal fields of Kentucky.

The LNA&C's grand plans to reach Appalachia began to destruct on February 22, 1890, the day John Jacob Astor died. Suddenly, control of the LNA&C by its directors became fragile, and less than a month later the worst was realized. At the Monon's March 1890 annual meeting, it was revealed that a maverick, Dr. William L. Breyfogle of New Albany, had gained control of the LNA&C, holding nearly three-quarters of its voting shares. Breyfogle ousted most of the LNA&C's leadership, seated himself as president, and repudiated the agreements on the K&I bridge, on the "Lexington Extension," and on the RNI&B.

The LNA&C was thrown into legal confusion. On March 27, 1890, the Louisville Southern took posses-

sion of both its main line and the "Lexington Extension" and gained protection against the LNA&C from Kentucky courts. Litigation over the LNA&C's financial responsibility for the RNI&B's bonds dragged on for half a decade, but in 1896 was decided against the LNA&C. In the interim, Breyfogle was himself ousted from the Monon's presidency in March 1891 (replaced by Samuel Thomas), following an ill-planned, questionably financed scheme to build a railroad (the Fort Wayne, Terre Haute & Southwestern) from LNA&C's main line toward western Indiana coal.

In August 1896, with its financial burden increased by responsibility for the RNI&B bonds and with its traditional investors alienated, the LNA&C fell into receivership. President Thomas announced the news to shareholders: "On the 24th of August, a receiver was appointed for your company. The credit of the corporation, which had been excellent, was destroyed by the judicial decision from suits arising out of an alleged guarantee by your company of the bonds of the RNI&B." (Of the Kentucky lines Monon briefly held, the RNI&B and "Lexington Extension" eventually became part of L&N; the Louisville Southern part of the Southern.)

The Chicago, Indianapolis & Louisville

Fortunately for the Monon Route, its new receiver was longtime LNA&C employee W.H. McDoel (who had served the railroad as a freight agent, traffic manager and general manager). In the ensuing reorganization, Samuel Thomas remained president and gained considerable control over the railroad, and McDoel served as vice president and general manager. On July 1, 1897, the Monon Route entered a new era with a new corporate name—the Chicago, Indianapolis & Louisville Railway Co.

As the new Monon Route moved toward the 1900s with its new corporate name, it continued the physical improvements that had been interrupted only by the Breyfogle disaster and its brief receivership. McDoel, as general manager since 1891, had been responsible for orchestrating the improvements of the final years of the LNA&C, and he—along with Chief Engineer F. Hall—continued on with the CI&L.

In the summer of 1897, even as the reorganization was being completed, work on improving the grades and curvature of the Monon–State Line portion of the CI&L was beginning. Major work was undertaken at Cedar Lake, Lowell and Rensselaer. At Cedar Lake, the old line, which included eight curves of up to six degrees, was replaced with a new line with only three curves of a three-degree maximum, and the grades were reduced to less than a half percent (from 1%). The relocation did, however, require construction of a wooden trestle over a bottomless bog south of Cedar Lake—the structure to become known as Paisley trestle.

At Lowell, similar grade and curvature reductions were undertaken, and at Rensselaer, a curve of six degrees was reduced to three degrees and grades were evened out (from a maximum of 1.2% to .4%). Rail replacement, ongoing on the line since the mid-1890s, continued, with 70- and 75-lb. rail being installed. Along the entire CI&L, construction of new stations also continued through the end of the century: In 1897 a passenger station was opened at Brookston; and in 1898 new depots were built at Greencastle, Harrodsburg, Campbellsburg and Cedar Lake, and freight houses were constructed at New Albany and Hammond. In 1899, a new station went up at Wanatah, a freight house at Cedar Lake, and an enginehouse at Bedford.

Since its construction, one of the most rugged, difficult portions of the old NA&S main line rested between Harrodsburg and the town of Clear Creek. Running via Smithville, the line was hampered by grades in excess of 2% and was prone to washouts. The CI&L's largest motive power could handle but 15 loaded freight cars over this section. To solve this operating problem—and to tap the limestone-rich valley of Clear Creek—the CI&L chartered a new railroad on January 3, 1898. The company was the Indiana Stone Railroad, formed to build 9.2 miles of new main line between Clear Creek and Harrodsburg, plus three miles of quarry spurs. Work on the ISRR was completed and the line leased to the CI&L in September 1899. On the ISRR, the maximum grade was .57% and the CI&L could increase tonnage on Bedford-Bloomington trains by 110%. Immediately, the Indiana Stone Railroad became the CI&L's main line, while the old line through Smithville was reduced to a double-ended branch.

Into the 20th Century—and the Coal Fields

As the CI&L neared the 20th century, changes in its leadership and control occurred that would forever influence the CI&L. On April 25, 1899, President Samuel Thomas stepped down, selling his interests in the CI&L to famed financier J.P. Morgan of New York. The masterful W.H. McDoel became CI&L's president.

In 1900, along with the Southern Railway and the Baltimore & Ohio Southwestern, the CI&L acquired one-third ownership of the reorganized Kentucky & Indiana Bridge Co. (and with the K&I's 1910 construction of a new bridge from New Albany to Louisville, CI&L would permanently switch its operations to the Kentucky & Indiana Terminal). Most importantly, in 1902 the Louisville & Nashville and Southern Railway, through J.P. Morgan & Co., jointly gained control of

Evidence of the rapid growth in motive-power size at the turn of the century is Monon 4-8-0 No. 203. Built by Brooks in 1898, the Mastodon would survive—as No. 223—into the Barriger era. (*ALCO HISTORIC PHOTOS*)

the CI&L with over 75% of its stock. L&N/Southern influence would endure for nearly half a century.

And at long last, with the birth of the 20th century, the Monon made its often-dreamed-of entry into the coal fields of southwestern Indiana. When it did, the CI&L entered via three different routes.

The Monon's first entry into the coal fields came through a trackage lease agreement. On September 30, 1902, the CI&L signed a lease with the Indianapolis Southern (a successor to ex-narrow-gauge Bloomfield Railroad and a predecessor of the Illinois Central) for trackage rights on 10 miles of line from Switz City through Linton to the mining district of Victoria, Ind. In combination with the Monon's B&B branch, these trackage rights—valid for 25 years—gave the Hoosier Line access to mines in Sullivan and Greene counties. Another result of the trackage rights was that CI&L's passenger service on the B&B was extended on from Switz City to Linton. Many passengers were coal mine workers.

On May 1, 1903, the Hoosier Line gained its second entry into coal country—again via trackage rights—when it contracted with the Pennsylvania for use of the "I&V" (Indianapolis & Vincennes) from Gosport to Switz City for the transport of coal only. This arrangement still required use of the Indianapolis Southern's Switz City–Victoria tracks to reach the coal fields, but offered Monon the advantage of bypassing the B&B with coal trains. Despite ballasting and rail replacement programs during the McDoel era, the B&B remained a difficult to operate line prone to washouts—and derailments.

Although Monon trains had finally attained coal country through trackage rights, the arrangement was far from ideal. Monon was reliant upon competitors for its entry into the region—and the coal fields were quickly being laced with other roads' rails. By 1900, the Indianapolis Southern (IC), Chicago & Eastern Illinois, Pennsylvania, Southern Indiana Railway (eventually the Milwaukee Road), and Big Four (later the New York Central) all had entered the area.

In truth, the seeds had been planted for the Monon's third and best route into western Indiana in 1899. On March 20 of that year, officers of the CI&L participated in the creation of the Indianapolis & Louisville

Railway Co. The I&L's charter provided for construction of a 100-mile railroad from Indianapolis through Marion, Hendricks, Morgan, Putnam, Owen, Clay, Sullivan and Greene counties to Switz City. Among the nine-man I&L board were five with CI&L links, including ex-President Samuel Thomas (still a CI&L director) and President McDoel (who owned the majority of I&L shares).

Despite the I&L's charter, and even at this late date, the CI&L struggled with its reach toward coal. No construction was started on the I&L, and in April 1902 the CI&L board discussed—and approved—an alternative. It was the "Coal Field Division," which was projected to build from the CI&L main line at or near Quincy either to Switz City (and a link with the B&B and Indianapolis Southern) or to a point on the Indianapolis Southern where Monon held trackage rights. But on May 16, 1902, the CI&L board quickly rescinded its plans for the Coal Field Division and instead decided that the CI&L would guarantee the bonds of the still-unbuilt I&L.

With attention turned back to the I&L, the road's original charter was amended on March 7, 1903—to allow construction all the way to Evansville, Ind. The proposed extension southwest from Victoria would pass through Knox, Pike, Gibson, Warrick and Vanderburg counties.

Finally, early in the summer of 1903, real progress on the I&L began. On June 9, 1903, President McDoel reported to his board that a route for the I&L had been surveyed from the Monon main line south of Cloverdale to Victoria. Construction costs were estimated at $19,000 per mile. But at the same time, McDoel recommended that construction on the I&L main stem be delayed in favor of building spur tracks from Victoria to coal properties of the Chicago & Indiana Coal Co. In 1904, a line from Victoria to Andromeda was built to reach Shirley Hill Mine, and another spur off this line was built to reach Little Giant Mine (total trackage, 11 miles). Until the I&L main stem could be built, these spurs would be reached via the B&B and Indianapolis Southern.

In March 1905, at McDoel's recommendation, the final form of the I&L was agreed upon by Monon's board. The I&L would begin not at Indianapolis, but on the Monon main line between Cloverdale and Quincy, at a place to be named Wallace Junction (after CI&L Engineer W.A. Wallace). It would extend not to Evansville, but to Victoria. (In fact, the final I&L took on very much the route of the unbuilt "Coal Field Division.") To assure CI&L control of the Indianapolis & Louisville, the Monon took a 99-year lease on the I&L effective January 1, 1906.

The construction route of the I&L ran from Wallace Junction roughly southwest to Patricksburg, Clay City, Howesville, Midland and Victoria. There the new line connected with the spur tracks built in 1904. Primary contractor for the I&L was Dickason Construction Co., and once grading began in early 1906 it took but a year and a half to complete the line. Rail for the I&L was mostly 67- and 75-lb. relay rail from CI&L's main line. During construction of the main stem of the I&L, the decision was made to build yet another spur—a 4.7-mile line from Vicksburg to the Cloverleaf Mine at Cass, Ind.

The I&L was turned over by its contractor for CI&L

Standing tall and elegant atop 73-inch spoked drivers, CI&L 301 was one of only a pair of 4-4-2's owned by the Hoosier Line. The Atlantics, built in 1901, ran the fast Northern Division early in life; they ended their careers—as Nos. 390 and 391—in the 1930's working the French Lick branch. (HAROLD K. VOLLRATH COLLECTION)

The first Pacifics—4-6-2's—owned by the Monon were built by Brooks in November 1905. CI&L 351 was second among the group of five (Nos. 350-354). Driving wheels stood 69 inches tall. (ALCO HISTORIC PHOTOS)

operation on October 1, 1907, with the Vicksburg spur opening that December. In complete form, the I&L counted 59.7 route miles, with another 10.2 miles of sidings and mine trackage. With the opening of the I&L, the trackage rights agreement with the Pennsy's I&V became redundant and the last Monon coal train ventured over the I&V in 1907.

The Indianapolis Southern trackage rights agreement was left intact, since it provided backup mine access via the B&B (although little coal was moved via the B&B after the opening of the I&L). A second advantage of retaining the IS trackage rights was that, together with the I&L, it provided Monon access to the west end of the B&B branch when the Owensburg tunnel suffered one of its frequent collapses (Monon would use the I&L and IS trackage rights as a back-door entry into the Switz City area into the 1920s).

For the Ages

With completion of the I&L, the breadth of the Hoosier Line was, for all intents and purposes, settled for the remainder of its life. A look at Monon's final route map in 1971 would reveal few changes from the year 1908. As the presidency of W.H. McDoel closed on November 1, 1909, he could look with pride at the accomplishments of his CI&L (and those of the LNA&C he served). For even during the years of building the Indiana Stone Railroad and Indianapolis & Louisville, McDoel's improvement program for the CI&L had flourished.

Between 1900 and 1909, there was extensive construction of new water and fuel stations, new turntables were built at the likes of Bainbridge and Switz City and Lafayette, and enginehouses built at Gosport and New Albany. New station construction could be found up and down the Monon. In 1901, the CI&L built a new stone station at Frankfort, and in 1902 the noted limestone depot at Lafayette was erected.

In 1903, the Bedford freight and passenger stations were built anew after fire destroyed both, and passenger depots also went up at Ketchums (on the Indiana Stone RR) and Kirklin. In 1904, a new station was built at Raub, the Borden station was enlarged, and a new brick freight house was built at Louisville. Also in 1904, a line relocation was undertaken on the French Lick branch at Lost River (north of Paoli), and the original 1,600-foot timber trestle there was replaced with an 870-foot steel trestle.

Putnamville and Shelby received new stations in 1905, LaCrosse, Medaryville and West Baden (the latter a stone station) in 1906. In 1908, the stone depot at French Lick was built, a new wooden depot was erected at Ellettsville, and a combination passenger/freight station took form at Linden. In 1909, a new station went up at Salem and improvements were made to Lafayette Shops.

And, in addition to Monon's physical plant improvements, the McDoel era on the CI&L brought rejuvenation to CI&L's rolling stock and locomotives. Nowhere was this more obvious than in the Hoosier Line's enginehouses. As late as 1896, the Monon Route had been a railroad of primarily small motive power—of 0-4-0s and 4-4-0s, of 0-6-0s, 2-6-0s and Ten-Wheelers. Only a score of 2-8-0s, purchased between 1887 and 1892, could be considered potent motive power.

But in the McDoel years of 1897-1909, the Monon Route took delivery of more than 60 steam locomotives. Among them were the last pairs of passenger-service 4-4-0s and 4-6-0s the Monon would buy, but also included were a dozen new 0-6-0s for switching, 22 potent 4-8-0s and nine more 2-8-0s for tonnage, and two 73-inch-drivered Atlantics and 13 K-class 4-6-2s for varnish. In CI&L's McDoel-era motive power stood many locomotives destined to serve until the very end of steam on the Hoosier Line . . . to a time when a man in many ways similar to W.H. McDoel would ascend to the presidency of the Monon.

Epitomizing Monon's Age of Steam years, J-class 2-8-2 No. 577 and crew pose on September 20, 1940, near Linden, Ind. Monon's first major freight-car purchases since the 1920's came in 1940, with 200 hoppers from Pullman-Standard making up the majority of the purchase. Extra 577 South is moving 100 of the new hoppers from Lafayette to the I&L branch to be distributed for coal loading. (*J. C. ALLEN & SONS INC.*)

3

FROM GLORY TO BANKRUPTCY TO REBIRTH

The Hoosier Line, 1910-1946

THE MONON in the years immediately following W.H. McDoel's term as president was a railroad of confidence and strength. In 1910, the CI&L carried 3.5 million tons of freight and 1.9 million passengers, and grossed $5 million doing so. Its tonnage came primarily from the earth of the Hoosier state—coal from the I&L and stone from the southern Indiana quarry districts accounted for nearly half of Monon's freight business; grains and produce from the fields of Indiana another 12%. The CI&L owned 122 locomotives, 107 passenger-service cars, 5,287 freight cars (plus 68 leased from the I&L), and 279 service cars. And the Hoosier Line was firmly in the black—at the end of 1910, profits for the year stood at $1.1 million.

The years 1910-1914 saw the final sizable growth to Monon's route map. First, in 1910 Monon built a spur from the main line at Horseshoe (later Murdock) 2.5 miles into the hills north of Bedford, terminating at the Furst-Kerber mill near Oolitic. This line allowed the CI&L to further tap the limestone deposits of southern Indiana. Next, in 1911-1912, the Hoosier Line (through the I&L) added to its coal field trackage. A new 4.4-mile spur was built from the I&L main line at Midland to Lattas Creek Mine.

Concurrently (in 1911), the Monon Coal Co., owned by the railroad, was formed to establish holdings in the coal region. The Lattas Creek spur also provided the Hoosier Line with a link to the Chicago, Terre Haute & Southeastern (later Milwaukee Road) at Lattas Junction. By using 1.3 miles of CTH&SE trackage rights, the Monon reached Gilmore Mine. By 1912, the Monon had gained access to six Monon Coal Co. mines capable of producing 6,000 tons of coal a day. Midland was fast becoming the hub of Monon coal field operations, being the site of a new assembly yard, engine terminal, and Monon Coal Co. coal washer.

On March 15, 1914, perhaps the most unusual (and destined to be a short-lived) addition to Monon's map occurred. The CI&L purchased the 40-mile Chicago & Wabash Valley Railway, which connected with the Monon main line at McCoysburg and ran in a north-westerly direction through the small town of Dinwiddie, Ind., then terminated approximately five miles east of Cedar Lake.

If ever there was a property that went from "nowhere to no place," the C&WV was it, but in this short line, which had been built by Benjamin J. Gifford between 1898 and 1912, the Monon saw potential for an inexpensive second main track. Gifford had died in 1913, and the Monon purchased the Chicago & Wabash Valley from his estate. Monon planned to build a link from Dinwiddie to the CI&L main line near Cedar Lake in 1915, thus, in effect, double-tracking some 45 miles of its Northern Division. But construction of the connecting track was delayed, and in truth it would never be built, leaving the C&WV a poor, unwanted branch of the Monon operated only as far north as Dinwiddie.

Following W.H. McDoel's retirement as president, the Hoosier Line witnessed a revolving door presidency for nearly half a decade. Ira Rawn, the man who succeeded McDoel as president, served the Hoosier Line for only a few months before tragically taking his own life in July 1910. Fairfax Harrison, who would later gain fame as president of the Southern Railway

The combination of steam locomotive and camera seemed a guarantee to draw a crowd in the early Twentieth Century—witness 1903-built Monon 4-8-0 218 standing at the new Salem depot of 1909. The 4-8-0's, giants in their day, were needed to battle the grades of Monon's south end. *(LLOYD J. KIMBLE COLLECTION)*

Remote was an ample description of the lone track and turntable at Switz City, Ind. CI&L 4-8-0 242, built as No. 214 in 1902, had been renumbered prior to World War I. *(HULCE MARTIN COLLECTION)*

(and who would give birth to Southern's green and gold steam locomotive livery), served as Monon president from August 1910 to December 1913.

Frederic A. Delano, uncle of U.S. President Franklin Roosevelt, was Monon president from December 1913 to August 1914 (rather amazingly, Franklin Roosevelt's father—James Roosevelt—had also served as a Hoosier Line president, in 1883-1884). Finally, with H.R. Kurrie, who became president in 1914, the Monon found another long-term leader. Kurrie would serve the CI&L as president and then a trustee until 1938.

Despite the frequent changes in the president's chair, the Monon made steady progress in the period before World War I. In addition to its trackage extensions, Monon made significant improvements to its physical plant. Beginning in 1911, the CI&L began installation of automatic block signals (semaphores). The first signaled section, between Fair Oaks and Monon, was completed in December 1911. During 1912, the route from the Illinois/Indiana border to

Massachusetts Ave. in Indianapolis was equipped with signals. And by the end of 1913, the main line was signaled south to Bloomington. By late 1916, the semaphore signals, destined to be a familiar, comforting sight to everyone who knew the Monon, were extended south to Orleans.

Passenger station construction, so widespread during the McDoel years, continued, albeit on a much reduced level. Construction began on new passenger depots at Bloomington, Rensselaer and Hammond in 1911; at Bainbridge in 1913; and at Pekin and Monon in 1916. These years immediately prior to World War I were the halcyon days of Hoosier Line varnish. If, for example, a traveler peered into the yellow, black and red CI&L timetable of January 1916, he would find frequent service on the Monon's main lines and some form of service on all its branches.

On the Indianapolis line, the Monon sponsored four trains in each direction over the length of the route, and in fact, three of these trains—the *Daylight Limit-*

Another early J. F. Bennett photograph recalls all the rural flavor of southern Indiana railroading. Harrodsburg depot (built in 1898) and water station stood on the bank of Clear Creek; beyond the distant semaphores, the original NA&S-built main line via Smithville swung right and the newer Indiana Stone Railroad main swung left. (*J. F. BENNETT, JIM BENNETT COLLECTION*)

World War I was in the wind when Monon Ten-Wheeler 107 journeyed into Smithville with four wooden Hoosier Line coaches. In 1916, five passenger trains a day still ran via the Smithville line, but the Depression would strangle passenger service on that route, and in 1935 all through service was discontinued. (*J. F. BENNETT, JIM BENNETT COLLECTION*)

One of noted photographer J. F. Bennett's first Hoosier Line works was this scene of a Monon 4-6-0 leading wood heavyweights on the French Lick branch circa 1916. The steel trestle over the Lost River north of Paoli replaced the original wood trestle (depicted in chapter 2) during Monon's 1904 line relocation on the branch. (*J. F. BENNETT, JIM BENNETT COLLECTION*)

ed, *Mid-day Special,* and *Night Express*—continued on to Cincinnati over the Cincinnati, Indianapolis & Western. The fourth train—the *Hoosier*—which had been inaugurated by Fairfax Harrison—was the CI&L's premier Chicago-Indianapolis service.

On the Chicago-Louisville route, the Monon offered day trains 5/6 and overnighters 3/4 over the distance (with through cars to and from French Lick), while a series of additional trains either ran on portions of the main line as locals (i.e., between Chicago-Lafayette and Bloomington-Louisville) or helped form an intricate connecting service funneling passengers toward French Lick Springs. French Lick was the trump card of Monon passenger services, and, together with the Pennsylvania Railroad, Monon offered two trains a day in each direction between Indianapolis and French Lick. These trains operated Indianapolis-Gosport Junction over the Pennsy's "I&V" line (the line originally started as an NA&S branch) and Gosport Junction-French Lick via the Monon. All told, six passenger trains a day in each direction trod over the 17.7-mile French Lick branch.

In addition, Monon offered two trains daily in each direction on its Michigan City line, daily except Sunday trains on the I&L to Victoria and on the B&B to Switz City, and even daily except Sunday mixed trains on the Chicago & Wabash Valley branch. The result of Monon's expansive passenger service was that from 1911 through 1917, the Hoosier Line carried more than two million passengers each year.

The years immediately before WWI also saw freight traffic growth—tremendous growth. In 1911, Monon toted 3.6 million tons of freight; in 1917, the figure stood at 6.2 million tons. To accommodate the ton-

nage, freight car ownership was pushed up (from 5,287 in 1910 to 6,675 in 1915, for example), and improvements to freight facilities were made.

In 1910, the yard at Bloomington—christened McDoel Yard in honor of Monon's extraordinary past president—was doubled in capacity, from 358 to 702 cars. A new roundhouse and turntable and new coal and water stations were built at McDoel. A new roundhouse was built at Michigan City in 1915, and the roundhouse at Indianapolis was expanded in length and six new stalls added. In 1918, Midland Yard, just six years old, had to be expanded. And on the main

Mikados—2-8-2's—first arrived on the Monon in 1912 in the form of 25 500-class J-1's such as 504 standing at Gosport shortly after its birth at American Locomotive Company's Brooks plant. (*RICHARD BOWEN COLLECTION*)

Left: Mammoth steam: In 1914 and 1916, CI&L purchased eight burly 2-10-2's from Alco. CI&L 606, from the Class of 1916, stood for its portrait with a crew at Bloomington's McDoel Yard in June 1937. *(DOLZALL COLLECTION)* **Below:** Ten potent J-4-class 2-8-2's—Nos. 570-579—built by Alco at Schenectady, N.Y., in October 1929 proved to be the Hoosier Line's final new steam locomotives. *(ALCO HISTORIC PHOTOS)*

line, Monon had begun laying 100-pound rail in 1914.

As for motive power, the McDoel-era philosophy of equipping the Monon with larger, more potent motive power continued. For freight service, the Monon purchased five H-3 class 2-8-0s in 1910, seven H-6 Consolidations in 1911, then—in 1912—turned to the 2-8-2 in a big way, accepting delivery of 25 J-1 Mikados. In 1914, the Hoosier Line added the 2-10-2 to its roster, taking a quintet of the beasts onto the roster for Southern Division service. Three more 2-10-2s followed in 1916, and 10 more 2-8-2s (five J-1s, five J-2s) came in 1918. For its passenger trains, Monon purchased 4-6-2s: three K-4 class Pacifics arrived in 1911; three K-5s in 1912; and three K-6s in 1916. All of Monon's new motive power—freight or passenger—was built by the American Locomotive Co. (Alco).

In 1916, the CI&L simplified its corporate structure by purchasing the properties of the Indianapolis & Louisville and the Indiana Stone Railroad. In colorful Hoosier Line fashion, the I&L stockholders meeting to confirm these events was convened in ancient, NA&S-built Gosport station on September 21, 1916.

World War I—First Signs of Trouble

On January 1, 1918, with World War I raging in Europe, the United States Railroad Administration took control of all American railroads—Monon included. USRA control would last through February 29, 1920. For the Hoosier Line, the event effectively

marked a change in eras—from a time of steady increases in freight traffic and strong passenger traffic, to a time of fluctuations in freight traffic and the near-total decline of the passenger train.

In 1918 and 1919, Monon's freight levels dropped (from 6.2 million tons in 1917 to 5.7 million tons in 1919), then rebounded (to 7.5 million tons) in 1920, then plunged again (to 5.6 million tons) in 1921. But

Bloomington's yard, christened McDoel Yard after Monon's famed president, underwent expansion in 1910 and again in the 1920's. Heart of the yard was the roundhouse, which in its brick and frame construction was typical of other CI&L roundhouses, including those at Indianapolis, New Albany and Hammond. *(LLOYD J. KIMBLE COLLECTION)*

Above: Monon K-2 Pacific 412 charges down tangent track at Shelby, Ind., with six-car train 38, the *Chicago Limited*, bound from Indianapolis to Chicago (with through cars from Cincinnati) in the summer of 1928. (*J. F. BENNETT, JIM BENNETT COLLECTION*) **Right:** Built in 1922 to cater to affluent Indianapolis north-siders, Monon's Boulevard Station stood adjacent to the Indiana State Fairgrounds. (*LINN H. WESTCOTT, COLLECTION OF KALMBACH PUBLISHING CO.*)

Handsome Monon Route K-4 Pacific 431 (originally No. 404), built by Brooks in 1911, draws then-nameless train 6 from Louisville through the south side of Chicago, bound for Dearborn Station, on October 12, 1934. (PAUL EILENBERGER, HAROLD J. STIRTON COLLECTION)

then, tonnage began a climb in the 1920s—to 6.5 million tons in 1922; to eight million tons in 1925; to a staggering 9.8 million tons in 1928.

Passenger service at first fluctuated in a pattern similar to freight traffic, but, in 1921, began a rapid decline. By the mid-1920s, the Monon was carrying around a million passengers a year—only half the level of half a decade before—and by 1928 the passenger count had dropped to 690,000 passengers carried. The proliferation of the automobile and improving highways had all but demolished Monon's extensive passenger service.

Despite the vagaries of the 1920s, the Hoosier Line proceeded on its steady improvements program. And while not great, the Monon's improvements of the 1920s proved significant in that, for all intents and purposes, they would represent the last major improvements to the Hoosier Line until after World War II.

A number of Monon's actions of the early 1920s related to passenger service, and thus, given the urgent decline of passenger traffic by the end of the decade, provided little return. In 1923, the CI&L contracted for a 12-mile test section of Automatic Train Control between Fair Oaks and Rensselaer. The test section, expanded to 20 miles, was opened in 1924, and it impressed Monon's management enough that by 1927 the CI&L's entire passenger-heavy South Hammond–Indianapolis line was equipped with ATC. Monon equipped 50 locomotives with ATC equipment. Between 1923 and 1925, Monon participated in the track elevation project for Indianapolis Union Station, which included building new fills, retaining walls, and a bridge at East Street. Related to this project, Monon built a new two-story freight house in Indianapolis late in 1924.

A freight-train derailment on April 9, 1924, resulted in the collapse of a portion of Monon's Wabash River bridge north of Lafayette. A new pier and two new spans were required in the repair. (J. F. BENNETT, JIM BENNETT COLLECTION)

To cater to passengers on Indianapolis' then-affluent north side, in 1922 Monon constructed Boulevard Station at 38th Street. San Pierre received a new depot in 1924, and the last in the long line of Bedford stations, a handsome limestone structure, was built in 1926. What proved to be Monon's last new passenger steam locomotives—three K-5A 4-6-2s—were built by Alco in January 1923.

Improvements for freight hauling included three locomotive orders—all for Mikados. At the same time Alco built Monon's last Pacifics, it also built three J-1A 2-8-2s; in 1926 Monon took delivery of six J-3

Above: The engineer of tall-stacked CI&L K-4 Pacific 432 surveys the loading of baggage, mail and passengers upon Monon varnish as his charge pauses at Hammond, Ind., August 1, 1936. (COLLECTION OF BOB LORENZ) **Right:** Two decades into its career—and far from its original Southern Division stomping grounds—Monon 2-10-2 600 lends its 66,700 pounds of tractive force to lugging a transfer freight on the Chicago & Western Indiana in Chicago, October 7, 1934. (HAROLD K. VOLLRATH COLLECTION)

2-8-2s from Alco; and in 1929 the Hoosier Line accepted 10 burly Alco-built J-4 2-8-2s which were destined to be the last new steam locomotives Monon would buy. During the mid-1920s, Monon's Lafayette Shops undertook a major locomotive rebuilding program, and the locomotive shop was expanded (see Chapter 7).

McDoel Yard at Bloomington was further expanded in 1923, and in 1928 a new turntable and water tank were built there. A telephone dispatch system was set up on the Lafayette–Louisville line in 1928-29, and additional block signaling was also completed on the south end of the railroad between Fogg and Borden. In the quarry district around Bedford, the Monon gained two spurs in the mid-1920s. The Baltimore & Ohio, which reached Bedford via a branch that left its Cincinnati–St. Louis main line at Rivervale, Ind., abandoned operations on the branch in January 1924. The following year, Monon purchased a portion of this trackage from Bedford a short distance to Blue Hole Mill. In

1927, the CI&L also took over the Bedford & Wallner Railroad, a 2.8-mile quarry line that connected with the ex-B&O trackage.

Not all of the changes were on the south end: Abandonment of the west end of the Central Indiana Railroad in 1929 allowed the Monon to pick up industrial trackage at Ladoga, and Michigan City's yard was expanded in 1928-29.

A remarkable number of improvements on the Monon during the 1920s were not planned, but rather were required by "acts of God." Fire destroyed the French Lick freight house in 1921 and Monon constructed a new brick structure there. On April 9, 1924, a freight train derailment on the Wabash River bridge dumped freight cars—and a portion of the bridge itself—into the river. A new pier and two new steel girder spans were required to rebuild the bridge. In 1926, the CI&L's enginehouse and machine shop at Monon burned (they were replaced in 1928). And in 1927 a

Brake shoe smoke curls up around heavyweights as a Monon 4-6-2 draws northbound varnish into backwoods Wallace Junction. The I&L branch existed to the right. (*J. F. BENNETT, JIM BENNETT COLLECTION*)

spectacular blaze took down the Lafayette Shops coal chute. It was replaced with a 500-ton concrete coal tipple that stands to this day.

The 1920s—January 1922 to be exact—also marked the beginning of a quaint Hoosier Line ritual that endured into the Barriger era. It was the "Cedar Lake Ice Harvest." Each January, Monon employees were dispatched to lineside Cedar Lake, where ice blocks were cut from the frozen lake and loaded onto a train to be transported to CI&L ice houses up and down the line. The original "harvest" in 1922 netted the Monon 33 freight carloads of ice; by the early 1940s Monon crews were loading more than 300 cars of ice during each remarkable harvest.

The Depression and Demise

During the 1920s the CI&L had been a profitable railroad, although those profits were tempered by the passenger train decline and by rapidly escalating operating costs. During the Monon's period of control by Louisville & Nashville and Southern, its long-term economic strength was also affected by issuing rather generous stock dividend payments to its parents. But no matter the case, it is certain that few railroads the Monon's size could have weathered the total collapse of its traffic that the railroad would soon endure.

It was on Black Tuesday—October 29, 1929—that the stock market crash came, the first step in America's plunge into total economic depression. The effect on the Hoosier Line was catastrophic: From the record 9.8 million tons of freight hauled in 1928, Monon's tonnage plunged to 4.1 million tons—less than half—in 1933. Passenger traffic reached seemingly absolute depths: In 1932, Monon carried only 173,362 passengers—less than 1/20th the number it had carried 15 years before!

By mid-1933, Monon's passenger service was reduced to three trains—the *Tippecanoe, Hoosier* and *Mid-Night Special*—between Chicago and Indianapolis (the service to Cincinnati ceased in 1927 when Baltimore & Ohio purchased the Cincinnati, Indianapolis & Western). Trains 3/4 and 5/6 still rolled Chicago-Louisville, but the French Lick service was but a shadow of early days. Only trains 3/4 had connecting through cars; the joint PRR-Monon service via Gosport Junction was gone. Also gone was all CI&L passenger service on the Michigan City line, the I&L, and the Bedford & Bloomfield. The C&WV branch still had its mixed train service—as far as Kersey, Ind.

The inevitable occurred in 1933. Running out of cash, Monon applied to the federal Reconstruction Finance Corporation's Railroad Division for a $500,000 loan. The head of the RFC's Railroad Division was a man named John Walker Barriger III, who concluded that $500,000 alone could hardly save the CI&L. He

A white plume of smoke hovers over the southbound *Hoosier*, train 31, as it sweeps out of Chicago, bound for Indianapolis, on May 1, 1939. The power is K-4 Pacific 430; note the baggage-mail car lettered THE HOOSIER. (*PAUL EILENBERGER, HAROLD J. STIRTON COLLECTION*)

felt only total reorganization could revitalize the Hoosier Line.

Without the loan, Monon fell bankrupt, and on December 30, 1933, the Monon filed for reorganization under Section 77 of the National Bankruptcy Act. Monon president Kurrie and Holman D. Pettibone were named co-trustees. The Monon, of course, was not the only company in the railroad industry to suffer bankruptcy as a result of the Depression. The list of the fallen was counted in the dozens and included the likes of the Seaboard Air Line, Milwaukee Road, and Missouri Pacific, and the great railroad locomotive builder, Baldwin Locomotive Works.

The Monon would not return an annual profit again

until 1939, and given that fact, improvements to the railroad in the 1930s were virtually nonexistent. Only a new ice house at Indianapolis and 200-ton coal chute at Wallace Junction (both built in 1937) brought change to the CI&L's property. In 1937, bridge work, which had been deferred, was resumed, and in 1939 two spans of the White River bridge at Indianapolis were replaced. But for the most part, even standard maintenance fell by the wayside, and the condition of the railroad and its equipment slowly disintegrated.

As the Depression wore on, lines of stored locomotives grew behind Lafayette Shops. Nicknamed "Klondike," these weed-grown storage tracks became burdened with derelict locomotives missing cabs, side

rods, drivers and tenders. Many of the locomotives would never again serve the railroad whose name they carried. Wholesale disposal of the pitiful lot began in 1936 when 28 steam locomotives were retired. Of the 173 locomotives carried on the CI&L roster in 1930, only 113 would survive to the next decade.

Freight and passenger cars suffered the same fate as did Monon's locomotives—only worse. Between 1930 and 1940, freight car ownership dropped from 6,620 to 3,610 (and many of the remaining cars were in poor condition); passenger car ownership declined from 99 to 55. The Monon was cannibalizing itself to survive at all, and the pairing off was not restricted to locomotives and rolling stock.

Above: At 11:30 a.m. on August 13, 1945, Monon train 31, the southbound *Hoosier*, begins to roll out of Frankfort, Ind., behind K-4 Pacific 432. This was the late World War II period when the Monon operated only one Chicago-Indianapolis train. (*RICHARD J. COOK*) **Left:** The markers of train 33, the southbound *Tippecanoe*, are carried by an open-platform observation as the C&IL train stands at Indianapolis Boulevard Station, ready for its five-mile jaunt on to Union Station. Scene is from the 1930's. (*DR. KENNETH ADKINSON COL-LECTION*)

Facing page: In the late steam era Monon's 1911-built H-6 2-8-0's ruled CI&L's Indianapolis line freights, a CI&L 286 does here, working ove grass-covered tracks at Sheridan, Ind on August 18, 1942. (*MALCOLM D. M(CARTER*)

Since the 1920s, the Bedford & Bloomfield branch had produced little traffic, except for the portion serving Bedford's quarry district. In March 1935, a cave-in of the Owensburg tunnel closed the west end of the B&B. The Chicago & Wabash Valley, likewise, produced little tonnage, and with Monon's original dreams of using it for a double track long dead, the C&WV served no real purpose. On April 10, 1935, the CI&L requested permission to abandon 33.7 miles of the B&B from Avoca (near Bedford) to Bloomfield (Monon's trackage rights on the Illinois Central to Switz City had expired in 1923). Permission was also requested to abandon the entire C&WV branch. The abandonment petitions were granted, and final Monon operations on the majority of the B&B and the entire C&WV occurred on December 31, 1935. (Some spur trackage on the B&B around Bloomfield was taken over by the Illinois Central.) Already that year, the Monon had removed the Bedford & Wallner spur, and ceased through operation on the original NA&S main line between Harrodsburg and Clear Creek (any chance for further operation via Smithville died in the winter of 1939/40 when a major washout occurred on the line).

World War II

By the end of the 1930s the American economy was rebounding, and with the early 1940s came the industrial buildup associated with war in Europe and impending war for the United States. As the Monon entered this historic decade, it was under the stewardship of L.F. DeRamus.

Longtime president and trustee H.R. Kurrie had died on Christmas day of 1938 at the age of 63. He had served the Monon as president for 24 years, the longest tenure of any Hoosier Line president in history. DeRamus was familiar with the Monon because he came to the CI&L from parent Southern Railway, where he had served as general manager–western lines. In August 1939, DeRamus became chief executive officer of the CI&L and in April 1941 he was appointed a co-trustee.

Although America's entry into World War II following the Japanese attack on Pearl Harbor on December 7, 1941, spawned perhaps the greatest U.S. railroad effort in history, the Monon was little affected. The majority of war movements were east-west and the CI&L was a north-south railroad. The Monon was not the primary artery from any great industrial centers, and, in fact, World War II actually depressed portions of Monon's traditional traffic—stone being the most important example.

Because of limitations on construction and manpower, demand for limestone fell well below even the levels of the Depression. And it was at the start of the 1940s that the coal mines Monon's I&L branch served first began to expire. In total, Monon totaled 5.6 million tons of freight in 1940; its peak wartime tonnage—in 1944—was only 6.7 million tons.

The situation was different with regard to passenger service: World War II nearly tripled the number of passengers Monon carried, from 149,000 in 1940 to a peak of 424,000 in 1944. But when one recalled the two million passengers carried annually by the CI&L during the years 1911-1917, it showed that Monon passenger service was still far from its glory years. In fact, despite its increases in passengers carried, Monon saw its passenger service slashed in early 1945 by the Office of Defense Transportation to single daytime Chicago-Indianapolis trains (the *Hoosier)* and Chicago-Louisville trains (Nos. 3/4). French Lick rail passenger service was discontinued.

At lineside, the Hoosier Line of the 1940s was one of contrasts, of continued decline braced with the piecemeal improvements that slowly improving economics

In a scene typical of the old-school, pre-dieselization Monon, J-1 2-8-2 No. 524 draws tonnage across Clear Creek on the scenic portion of the Hoosier Line built as the Indiana Stone Railroad. Photograph is undated, but is circa World War II. (*J. F. BENNETT, FRANK VAN BREE COLLECTION*)

could provide (CI&L operated in the black from 1939 throughout the war).

The CI&L's mileage contracted from 549 miles in 1939 to 541 miles in 1945. In 1939, 1942 and 1945, portions of the I&L's Andromeda spur were cut off as mines expired. In 1942, the I&L's Lattas Creek spur was trimmed back to Lattas Junction and in 1945 it was shortened further. The closing of mines all along the I&L branch was already becoming serious—during 1945 the closings of Peabody Coal mine No. 48 and Maumee Collieries mine No. 25 resulted in a loss of 30% of the I&L's coal carloadings.

During 1943, the remnant of the B&B branch was shortened further, trackage to Avoca being abandoned so that the line was little more than a four-mile spur to the Dark Hollow stone quarries. And, in 1945, five miles of trackage on the silent old main line via Smithville was torn up. During its years of disuse, the Smithville "main line" had been employed to store strings of Monon's decrepit freight cars, and before the tracks could be ripped up, crews first had to cut down trees that had grown up between the long-stored cars.

In 1940, Monon made its first large freight car purchase since the 1920s. CI&L received 10 steel 70-ton covered hoppers and 200 steel 50-ton coal hoppers (but that same year Monon had to retire 684 freight cars).

In 1941, Monon took delivery of 150 steel boxcars, 10 more covered hoppers, and 60 flatcars. All told, in the years 1940-1944, Monon would add more than 750 new freight cars to its fleet.

Alas, the severity of the rolling stock problem was hardly cured. In April 1942, the ICC inspected the Monon's equipment and concluded that—new steel cars aside—the CI&L's freight equipment had an average of only five years of service remaining. About a group of 1,500 Monon gondolas, the ICC reported: "They fall in the class of deferred retirement rather than deferred maintenance. ... In normal times, cars in this condition would be ordered scrapped as they arrive on the bad order track." Only 15% of Monon's freight cars at this time were of all-steel construction.

Physical improvements to the property remained few. In 1940, work was restarted to complete the automatic block signal system on the southern end of the railroad. When, on October 2, 1941, semaphores were placed in service between Orleans and Fogg and Borden and New Albany, the automatic block system started 30 years before was finally complete on the entire main line. The signals to equip the last portions of the Southern Division main line were available only because signal blocks were being lengthened on the Indianapolis line. In 1940, a track elevation in Louis-

Left: The birth of dieselization: Monon's first diesel—Electro Motive SW-1 DS-50—was built in February 1942, then was placed in service at Monon, Ind. Two months later, three more diesels—EMD NW-2's DS-1 (**below**), DS-2 and DS-3—arrived on the Monon for service at South Hammond and McDoel Yard, Bloomington. DS-50 and DS-1 display the black-and-white livery Monon's first diesel switchers wore. (*BOTH PHOTOS, ELECTRO-MOTIVE DIVISION, GENERAL MOTORS*)

ville required Monon to relocate its freight house. The new location, ironically, was across an alley from the site of the LNA&C freight house of 1881. In 1941, a new roundhouse was built at South Hammond, replacing one destroyed by fire.

What was, perhaps, the Monon's major event of the early 1940s—a start toward dieselization of the railroad—occurred on July 22, 1941, when the CI&L ordered a modest fleet of Electro-Motive FT road diesels and yard switchers. The diesel switchers—black-clad SW-1 DS-50 and three NW-2s (DS-1, DS-2, DS-3)—were delivered in 1942. The SW-1 went to work at Monon, the NW-2s at South Hammond (two units) and McDoel Yard. But the FTs were canceled, and despite the best attempts of trustee DeRamus (see Chapter 4), full dieselization of the Hoosier Line would need to wait until after World War II.

Reorganization at Last

It had been in 1937, as the U.S. climbed out of the Depression, that reorganization of the Monon was first considered, but that attempt was stillborn, and the next attempt did not begin until the war period. In September 1943, the ICC granted its blessing to a reorganization plan brought by a group of Monon bondholders, and on June 28, 1945, the plan, slightly revised, was approved by Federal Judge M.L. Igoe in Chicago. On January 11, 1946, the plan was accepted by Monon's creditors and on April 24, 1946, Judge Igoe signed an order turning over the railroad to a reorganized CI&L effective May 1, 1946.

Control of the reorganized CI&L was placed in the hands of three "stock trustees" who would oversee the railroad for 10 years. The three men appointed were Arthur T. Leonard, then vice president of the City National Bank & Trust Co. of Chicago; Homer J. Livingston, vice president of the First National Bank of Chicago; and John E. Dwyer, Chicago manager of Otis & Co. The Hoosier Line's reorganized capitalization stood at $30,014,791, compared to a previous capitalization of $46,060,000. Debt was set at $16,528,296, none of which bore fixed interest. Although the L&N and Southern could have regained a large share of lost Monon control through stock purchases in return for traffic agreements, neither southern neighbor came to terms with the new CI&L.

At long last, after 12 years, four months in bankruptcy and the better part of a half century under L&N/Southern domination, the Monon was reorganized—and independent. The Hoosier Line was at the eve of a new era.

John Walker Barriger III, president of the Chicago, Indianapolis & Louisville, May 1, 1946, to December 31, 1952. *(LINN H. WESTCOTT, COLLECTION OF KALMBACH PUBLISHING CO.)*

4
THE BARRIGER YEARS

Seven Years of Change, 1946-1952

JOHN WALKER BARRIGER III was a man of 46 years when he was elected president of the Chicago, Indianapolis & Louisville on May 1, 1946. He was a Texan by birth, born in Dallas on December 3, 1899, but it had been in the northeast, with the great Pennsylvania Railroad, that he'd begun his railroad career—as a 17-year-old shop hand at Pennsy's Altoona (Pa.) Shops.

After taking leave to attend the Massachusetts Institute of Technology (MIT), Barriger returned to the Pennsylvania, where his jobs ranged from accident investigation to assistant yardmaster at Altoona. In 1927, Barriger left railroading to enter into an investment firm, but his bond to railroading remained strong. In 1933, Barriger became chief of the Reconstruction Finance Corp.'s Railroad Division—the position he held when he turned down Monon's 1933 loan request—and he servd as reorganization manager of Monon's neighbor to the west, the Chicago & Eastern Illinois.

During World War II, John Barriger served his nation, and still, its railroads. He became associate director of the War Department's Division of Railway Transport, and in May 1942 was dispatched as federal manager to another of the Monon's troubled midwestern neighbors, the Toledo, Peoria & Western. Barriger was soon elected vice president of Chicago's Union Stock Yard & Transit Co. (a position he would continue to hold while Monon's president), and in April 1946 was named to a short tenure as manager of the Diesel Locomotive and Railroad Division of Fairbanks-Morse at Beloit, Wis. Then, at the behest of the Monon's three stock trustees, John Walker Barriger came to the Hoosier Line.

In the past one hundred years, Monon has not always met the highest ideals of railroad service. It has had shortcomings, of course. But this same, friendly road has served the people of Indiana for one hundred years, which is, in itself, deserving of recognition. For, be it human, animal, or mechanical, nothing can live for one hundred years without having something basically sound within it.
John Barriger

It was with this knowledge of the Hoosier Line's weaknesses and admiration for its spirit that John Barriger arrived on the Monon. During his tenure on the CI&L, Barriger attempted to overcome the weaknesses and retain, even enhance, the Hoosier Line's friendly nature.

John Barriger dreamed large. And his dream for the CI&L, publicly at least, took the form of a "superrailroad." Writing in *Trains* magazine's July 1947 issue, Barriger noted, "It is our ambition to make a little 'superrailroad' out of the Monon. To me, the term 'superrailroad' means integrating the best engineering methods and standards of operation in a railway's entire property." With his penchant for public relations, Barriger was prone to overstatement. He well knew the Monon, with its curving, rugged main line, street running, et al., could never fully become the embodiment of a "superrailroad."

But "superrailroad" or no, John Barriger did have extraordinary plans for the Hoosier Line. He would modernize and expand passenger service (and expect

Symbolic of the Monon that John Barriger and company inherited in May 1946, aged 2-8-2 No. 554 draws a short French Lick local north-ward under the highway 37 bridge at Harrodsburg. (J. F. BENNETT, JIM BENNETT COLLECTION)

passenger service to be profitable); he would renew Monon's right-of-way; he would make massive purchases of new freight equipment and improve freight operations. And, more often than not, John Walker Barriger would succeed.

The Starting Point

The Hoosier Line at the end of World War II—the CI&L Barriger inherited—was a railroad undergoing financial reorganization and rebirth—but still a railroad of aged equipment and uncertain service. In 1945, Monon had hauled 5.5 million tons of freight (of which it originated only 37%), with its steam locomotives producing 899,842 freight train miles. Coal, although threatened, remained CI&L's number-one commodity (1.6 million tons), with stone and lumber and grains each providing over 200,000 tons of freight. As for varnish, Monon passenger trains had rolled 460,188 miles (versus 781,935 in 1944), and carried 261,082 passengers. Total operating revenue in 1945 was $11.5 million. Net operating revenue: $1.7 million.

At 12:01 a.m., May 1, 1946—the moment the Barriger era began—CI&L rostered 74 steam locomotives (of six different wheel arrangements) with an average age of 27.4 years, and only the four diesel switchers purchased in 1942. Tending this aged group of Hoosier Line veterans was costing the Monon 64 cents per mile

At the time John Barriger became president of the CI&L, the road sponsored only one Chicago passenger train departure. At Monon, the train split into sections for Indianapolis and Louisville. On June 22, 1946, burly K-6 Pacific 451 leads this combined consist—10 cars strong—away from 63rd Street station—"Little Englewood"—on Chicago's south side. (HAROLD J. STIRTON)

for freight locomotives, 41 cents per mile for passenger locomotives. Freight car ownership stood at 3,002 cars, fully 1,200 of which were overdue for immediate retirement. The passenger car fleet counted slightly over 50; only four of 18 coaches were all steel, the oldest coach was 44 years of age, the oldest baggage car was no less than 57 years into its career.

Monon's passenger service consisted of single daytime Chicago–Indianapolis trains (Nos. 30/31, the *Hoosier*) and unnamed Nos. 3/4 between Chicago–Louisville. The *Hoosier* was equipped with coaches, parlor car and diner; Nos. 3/4 with coaches and a restaurant-lounge. Between Monon and Chicago, the trains were combined into a single consist (an operating arrangement begun at the start of 1946 when trains 3/4 became daytime runs).

Monon carded three second-class freights in each direction (Nos. 71, 73 and 75 southbound; Nos. 70, 72 and 76 northbound) between South Hammond and Louisville, one between South Hammond and Indianapolis (Nos. 175/176), one between Lafayette and Michigan City (Nos. 56/57), plus locals. But Monon's sched-

ules meant little. Often, freight cars were left to accumulate at yards until a full-tonnage train could be put together and dispatched.

The Seeds of Dieselization

When John Barriger and Monon's new directors (headed by stock trustee Arthur T. Leonard as chairman) first met in May 1946, motive power was their immediate concern. It is well recognized that John Barriger orchestrated the Monon's dieselization; but the instrumental role that CI&L's previous trustee, L.R. DeRamus, played in the Hoosier Line's dieselization is less remarked. In fact, when the Monon directors met on May 10, 1946, and discussed dieselization, the question was not whether to place diesel orders, but how to treat new diesel orders already placed with Electro-Motive by trustee DeRamus.

The vision of dieselizing the Monon was half a decade old when John Barriger arrived. The first spark of dieselization on the Hoosier Line had occurred in 1940, when Electro-Motive's famed FT demonstrator

65

Top: Prelude to dieselization: Grandfather of Electro-Motive's F-unit line—EMC FT demonstrator 103—worked on the Hoosier Line for seven days during its 83,000-mile exhibition tour of 1939-40. The olive green-and-yellow diesel easily outperformed CI&L's best steam, the J-4 Mikados, and set the stage for Monon's postwar dieselization. The Electro-Motive F-3, **above,** became the backbone of that dieselization under Barriger. Among the first of Monon's F-3's built was black-and-gold F-3A 62, standing in the snow at its maker's plant in La Grange, Ill., December 1946. *(BOTH PHOTOS, ELECTRO-MOTIVE DIVISION, GENERAL MOTORS CORP.)*

No. 103 worked on the CI&L. The four-unit (A-B-B-A) 5,400-hp, olive-and-yellow prototype FT spent seven days on the CI&L, covering the entire Chicago–Louisville main line, but working primarily between McDoel Yard, Bloomington, and K&IT's Youngtown Yard in Louisville. Electro-Motive 103 spent 141 hours in active service on the CI&L, and rolled up 1,896 miles.

For testing, it was operated in three different configurations. In a test of a two-unit A-B set (2,700-hp), the diesel lugged 2,050 tons from Louisville to McDoel in three hours, 44 minutes. In three-unit (4,050-hp) form, the FT hauled 3,000 tons from Louisville to McDoel in three hours, 51 minutes. And with its full, A-B-B-A, 5,400-hp lashup, FT 103 forwarded 3,750 tons of freight from Louisville to McDoel in three hours, 18 minutes. In comparison, Monon's most potent steam locomotive—the J-4A 2-8-2 (with booster)—could handle 2,150 tons from Louisville to McDoel (ruling grade was the 1.5% climb up the "Knobs" north of Borden) on a schedule of roughly four hours.

Following Electro-Motive 103's remarkable demonstration on the CI&L, Monon's DeRamus had taken his first step toward an early dieselization of the CI&L —the July 22, 1941, diesel order to Electro-Motive. The Monon ordered the four diesel switchers which were delivered in 1942—and two 4,050-hp A-B-A FT diesel sets. The FTs were earmarked to dieselize Monon's mainline freight operations, but the dire financial condition of the CI&L eventually precluded consummation of such a purchase. The FT order was canceled on December 4, 1941, three days before Japan's attack on Pearl Harbor and America's entry into the war.

World War II and the War Production Board's restrictions on diesel production left the CI&L little hope of dieselizing for the next four years. But as the war concluded, the Monon—still under trustee DeRamus— again prepared for diesels. In May 1945, Monon ordered four additional EMD NW-2s, then in September increased this order to five units. In December

Right: Celebration of the first diesel arrival during the Barriger era took place at Lafayette on November 5, 1946. Delivery of black-and-yellow Fairbanks-Morse H-10-44 switcher No. 18 was cause for the event. After celebration, 18 went to work in Lafayette yards. (*J. C. ALLEN & SONS, INC.*) **Below:** Monon's *Day Express* stands at Rensselaer with two thirds of GM's A-B-A F-3 demonstrator set No. 754 on the point. Monon borrowed, then purchased, the ex-demonstrators after the Ash Grove wreck (see pages 72-73). The demonstrator cab units became Monon 85A&B; the booster became 65C. (*GEORGE W. HOCKADAY*)

1945, the CI&L placed another order—with Electro-Motive for 18 freight-service F-3s. A dozen F-3As were to be paired in 3,000-hp, A-A sets, and were to be assigned road numbers 3000A/B–3005A/B. Four F-3As and two F-3Bs were to be linked in A-B-A, 4,500-hp sets and given road numbers 4500A/B/C–4501A/B/C.

In January 1946, Monon changed its order for NW-2s again—not in quantity, but in model. The order was changed from NW-2 switchers to EMD's NW-5 light road switcher. The NW-5 was actually little more than an NW-2 with road trucks and short hood and could have served as a yard switcher or in light road service. Finally, in March 1946, the pre-Barriger CI&L dealt its final order to Electro-Motive—this time for passenger diesels. On March 29, 1946, Monon ordered a trio of EMD E-7A passenger units, to be road numbers 2000-2002.

During this same period, the Hoosier Line reached agreement with the Baldwin Locomotive Works to do a study of dieselizing the Monon. Baldwin responded with a proposal to fully dieselize the railroad—with BLW diesels, of course. At the time, Baldwin was introducing its postwar line of diesels which included 660- and 1,000-hp diesel switchers, 1,500-hp road switchers, 1,500-hp freight cab units, and 2,000- and 3,000-hp passenger cab diesels.

When Barriger took the presidency of the Monon, he and his board inherited the EMD orders placed by DeRamus—and Baldwin's proposal. In July 1946, Barriger acted, appointing Colonel F.E. Cheshire as his chief mechanical officer and announcing—on July 29—his intention of dieselizing the Monon. The existing EMD orders by the trustee were agreeable to the new management, with changes. The NW-5 order was re-cast to its original form—for four NW-2s. As for the Fs: Instead of six A-A freight sets, the order was revised to two sets (road numbers assigned: 3000A/B–3001A/B). The A-B-A sets, meanwhile, were increased in number, to four A-B-A sets (4500A/B/C–4503A/B/C). The E-7s were canceled altogether on July 8, 1946.

In September 1946, more refinements to the Monon's dieselization order were made: The F-3 order was increased to include four freight-service A-A sets which were to be numbered 51A/B–54A/B. The order for four A-B-A sets remained the same, except road numbers assigned were changed to 61A/B/C–64A/B/C. Two new orders, each for one unit, were placed: From Fairbanks-Morse, Monon ordered a 1,000-hp H-10-44 switcher for use at Lafayette. And from Alco-GE, Monon ordered a single 1,500-hp RS-2 road switcher, to be used for passenger service between Bloomington and French Lick Springs.

Text continued on page 70

67

Barriger-era transition: Diesel meets steam at Gosport as new F-3 61 brings train 72 north on the main line and J-2 Mikado 551 stands on the siding with a southbound extra freight bound for Bloomington. (*J. F. BENNETT, FRANK VAN BREE COLLECTION*)

Of the nine Alco-GE RS-2's Monon received in 1947, Nos. 21-23 were delivered in a short-lived black-and-yellow livery; Nos. 24-29 wore the black-and-gold design which would become synonymous with Hoosier Line tonnage. Monon 23 was photographed at Lafayette on September 23, 1947. *(LOUIS A. MARRE COLLECTION)*

In addition to switcher No. 18, Fairbanks-Morse contributed two road-switchers to the Monon diesel roster, H-15-44's 36 and 37 (later renumbered 45-46). Month-old No. 37 switched at Franklin Street in Michigan City on January 7, 1948. *(PERRY F. JOHNSON)*

The thinking—and rethinking—of Monon's diesel requirements continued through the fall of 1946. On November 4, 1946, the CI&L directors authorized Barriger to place yet another F-3 order—for eight passenger-service F-3As, to be used in A-A lashups, equipped with steam generators, and numbered 81A/B–84A/B. This would be Monon's postwar passenger power. And finally, Monon made its last adjustment to its freight-service F-3 order: The order for A-A sets was again reduced back to two A-A sets (to be numbered 51A/B–52A/B). With this order, the count of F-3s ordered stood at 24 units (16 for freight service, eight for passenger)—and that is the number that would actually be delivered.

As for Baldwin Locomotive Works and its dieselization proposal, Barriger was uninterested. In fact, the Baldwin proposal caused some embarrassment to the Monon, because Baldwin had undertaken the study and proposal with the understanding that no diesel orders had been placed, when, in fact, the trustee's EMD orders were on the books. At any rate, aside from its switcher line, Baldwin was a relatively unknown commodity in the diesel marketplace in 1946 and early teething problems with its postwar 608SC

power plant did Baldwin's reputation little good. The sight of burly Baldwin diesels—perhaps "Babyface" freight cabs or AS-16 road switchers—in Hoosier Line colors was left only to train-watchers' imaginations.

The Diesels Arrive

The first evidence in steel of Monon's diesel orders arrived on November 5, 1946. At Lafayette, a crowd of 500 guests gathered to witness the Hoosier Line's acceptance of Fairbanks-Morse H-10-44 No. 18. Chief mechanical officer Cheshire termed the black-and-yellow switcher "the first material evidence of the beginning of Monon's modernization program." Then, with its brief moment in the spotlight complete, the F-M switcher took up duties at Shops Yard, a toil it would fulfill virtually all its life on the Hoosier Line.

A bigger event awaited early in 1947: On January 6, standing in front of a gold-and-black Hoosier Line F-3A at Indianapolis Union Station, John Barriger accepted a gold-plated reverser lever from Electro-Motive General Manager C.R. Osborn—and with it CI&L's 16 freight-service F-3s. Monon's four new NW-2s (Nos. 14-17) also arrived in January 1947, and

Above: Uncommon among diesels was the Electro-Motive BL-2 (BL standing for "branch line"). The unit was a transitional design from the fully streamlined F-units that dominated in the 1940's toward the multi-purpose, bidirectional road-switchers of the 1950's. Monon 30, delivered in April 1948, was the first BL-2 built. *(DAVE FERGUSON'S PHOTO ART)* **Right:** Monon's steam era concluded June 29, 1949, when B-8 No. 95 (ex-35, nee 23) served its last day as New Albany switcher. The 0-6-0 was officially retired on September 14, 1949; here, the 42-year-old switcher was photographed resting forlorn, minus rods, at McDoel Yard after its retirement. *(J. F. BENNETT, JIM BENNETT COLLECTION)*

delivery of its eight passenger-service F-3As would follow in May. Alco-GE made its first diesel contribution to the Monon's diesel roster on February 15, 1947, when RS-2 21 was placed into service—and at a ceremony at French Lick was christened and lettered the *Hoosier Belle.*

With delivery of Barriger's first round of diesels, the Hoosier Line had increased its ownership from the four diesel switchers of 1942 to 34 units. It was the beginning of the end for steam. From May to November 1946, the Monon retired and sold 11 of its 74 steam locomotives. By year-end of 1946, Monon's active steam counted less than 45; by the end of 1947 Monon would roster only 18 steam locomotives.

In February 1947, Colonel Cheshire reported to Barriger and the board on his requirements to complete the Monon's dieselization. Cheshire felt the Monon required 19 more units—28,500 horsepower. He requested—and was authorized to negotiate for—16 1,500-hp road switchers, one more F-3B (to transform one A-A set into a 4,500-hp A-B-A set), and one more A-A set of passenger-service F-3s. The immediate re-

sult was that in March 1947 the CI&L ordered eight additional Alco-GE RS-2s, six Electro-Motive 1,500-hp BL-2 road switchers, and two Fairbanks-Morse H-15-44 road switchers. The additional A-A set of passenger service F-3s and the lone freight-service F-3B were also reserved.

But early on the morning of June 3, 1947, Monon's budding dieselization program was thrown into turmoil. Monon trains 70 and 75 met head-on at Ash Grove, Ind. All six F-3s involved were badly damaged; three would have to be scrapped. Matters worsened when little more than a month later, at Fogg, Ind., on July 13, 1947, F-3 A-B-A set No. 63 derailed and was seriously damaged.

As an emergency measure to help replace the strick-

Text continued on page 74

AT THE STROKE of 3:00 a.m., on the clear, dark morn of June 3, 1947, Monon train No. 70 stood ready to depart Shops Yard in Lafayette, bound for South Hammond. F-3s 64A, 64C and 64B were coupled to 53 cars and a caboose. In the hands of the train's crew was train order 207, which read "No. 75 Eng 62 meet No. 70 Eng 64 at Ash Grove." Train 70 eased out of Shops at 3:10 a.m., crossing the Wabash River, climbing toward Ash Grove, 7.7 miles distant, bound for its meet with train 75—and history.

Twelve minutes after departing Lafayette, train 70 neared Ash Grove, rounding a one-degree curve, ascending a .76% grade, rolling at 40 mph, its crew confident that train 75 would be in the clear on Ash Grove siding, honoring the CI&L timetable instruction which read "All northward trains are superior to trains of the same class in opposite direction."

But instead, train 70 and its crew rounded the curve to witness the glare of a headlight, to plunge head-on into train 75, which had overrun Ash Grove siding and was sliding downgrade at 35 mph.

The tragedy of 3:22 a.m., June 3, 1947, left the engineer and fireman of northbound No. 70 dead. In the cab of F-3A 62B—power of train 75 (along with F-3s 62C, 62A)—the engineer was injured, the front brakeman killed (the fireman of train 75, in the second unit at the time, survived). Diesels were twisted and lay askew amid 15 derailed freight cars (most coal hoppers) that jackknifed and piled atop each other in the cut where the collision occurred. F-3 62B, the lead unit of train 75, rested upside down at a 90-degree angle south of the main line; F-3A 64A, the operating unit of train 70, was spun 180 degrees and sat, crushed, half under a coal hopper. Both lead units, along with F-3B 64C, were beyond repair and were later scrapped.

In the Interstate Commerce Commission investigation that followed, the engineer of train 75 recalled that he had grown "drowsy" and was unaware that his train had passed three red semaphores and Ash Grove siding. The ICC concluded, matter-of-factly, that the Ash Grove disaster, the worst accident of Monon's postwar era, was caused by "failure of the inferior train to obey a meet order and signal indications."

Top, both pages: With tragedy only days away, Monon F-3 sets 62 and 64 were photographed at Lafayette. The 62 set appears at Lafayette Junction on May 20, 1947, the 64 set is at Shops on May 27. Only seven days after the latter photo was recorded, the two sets met head on. (BOTH PHOTOS, MALCOLM D. McCARTER)
Above: Big hooks are in place to lift F-3A 62 upright; it was repaired, and in 1963 became Monon 105. (DAVE RANDOLPH COLLECTION)

June 3, 1947

Below: Monon F-3A 64B is littered with coal and squeezed between hoppers and F-3A 62B (upside down atop cut). CI&L lost three new F-units in the accident; the greater loss came with the deaths of three Hoosier Line trainmen. *(DAVE RANDOLPH COLLECTION)*

en F-3s, CI&L arranged use of Electro-Motive's three-unit (A-B-A) F-3 demonstrator set No. 754, which had completed its sales tours. The EMD demonstrators arrived on the Monon in late June and by the next month, EMD offered to sell the trio to the Monon for $412,991. Monon accepted. The ex-demo F-3A cab units (equipped with steam generators) became Monon 85A/B, and were used as dual-service (freight or passenger) units. The ex-demo F-3B became Monon 65C and was assigned to freight service.

These events gave Monon reason to further revise its EMD orders pending from March 1947. The ex-EMD demo F-3As erased the need for the set of passenger F-3s ordered in March 1947, and this order was canceled. But in their place, two BL-2 units were added to the existing BL-2 order, making a total of eight of the EMD road switchers on order. The two additional BL-2s would replace the two F-3As destroyed at Ash Grove. The F-3B from the demonstrator set likewise fulfilled the need for an additional F-3B, but since one F-3B had been destroyed at Ash Grove, this order was left intact.

Eventually (in early 1948), the Monon revised its orders one last time. It decided to replace the two wrecked F-3As in kind rather than with BL-2s, and changed the BL-2 order back to six units and added two freight-service F-3As.

The results of Monon's March 1947 orders—and revised orders—were built and placed in service on the Hoosier Line between the springs of 1947 and 1948. The Alco RS-2s were numbered 22-29. Monon Nos. 28-29

were ex-Alco RS-2 demonstrators 1501 and 1500 which the Monon requested be included in its order after Barriger learned they were available. For steam generator-equipped RS-2s, the ex-Alco demonstrators' price of $137,000 each was a relative bargain. Monon's new Fairbanks-Morse H-15-44s were numbered 37-38, and its six BL-2s were given road numbers 30-35. The three new F-3s took the numbers of their kindred destroyed at Ash Grove (F-3As 62B and 64C; F-3B 64C).

Delivery of Monon's March 1947 orders would have brought CI&L's diesel ownership to 53 units, but in January 1948 there had been a sale. Monon SW-1 DS-50 (since renumbered No. 1) was deemed too light and of too little horsepower to be of use to the Monon, and was sold to United Electric Coal Co. of Chicago.

A Suggestion from Electro-Motive

As 1948 neared its close, so did the steam era on the Monon. Only seven steam locomotives (comprising the 0-6-0, 4-8-0 and 2-8-2 wheel arrangements) would survive on the Hoosier Line roster in early 1949 (and of those only four were in daily service). In October 1948, Monon's board approved the final retirement of all steam—and the removal of all steam-servicing facilities on the Monon—as quickly as management deemed appropriate. That same month, Electro-Motive presented a report to the Monon detailing what it felt were the final steps to the CI&L's dieselization. The report recommended the purchase of a final five diesels —three 1,500-hp road switchers and two 600-hp switchers. On November 1, 1948, John Barriger recommended that the Monon accept EMD's proposal and the board approved. At a cost of $627,782, the CI&L ordered three additional EMD BL-2s, and two SW-1s. Given that the CI&L had, less than a year earlier, sold

Reborn: After disappearing at the start of World War II, the *Tippecanoe* was reborn on July 21, 1946. Little more than a month later—on August 25—the southbound *Tippecanoe* behind K-5A No. 443 strides over the Chicago & Western Indiana main line at 88th Street, Chicago. (*JOHN F. HUMISTON*)

In the fall of 1946, Monon's Chicago-Louisville day train, No. 5, brakes for its station stop at Bedford with K-6 Pacific on the point. Within a year, diesels would take over and the 4-6-2 would be retired. (LINN H. WEST-COTT, COLLECTION OF KALMBACH PUBLISHING CO.)

its original SW-1 because it was "unsuitable" to Monon service, the purchase of a new pair of SW-1s was a curious decision indeed.

Monon BL-2s 36-38 arrived in April and May 1949 (requiring the F-M H-15-44s to be renumbered 45-46); Monon No. 38 proved to be the last BL-2 built. The SW-1s (Monon 5-6) arrived in August 1949, and were stationed at New Albany and Bedford. With these units' arrival, the Hoosier Line's dieselization was complete. On July 13, 1949, Monon officially retired its last two Mikados—J-2s 560 and 565—and on September 14, 1949, the steam era died, when 4-8-0 No. 229 and 0-6-0 No. 95 were retired. Monon 95, stationed at New Albany, had actually been the final Hoosier Line steam locomotive in service. Its fires were dropped for the last time on June 29, 1949, and the sounds of Hoosier Line steam were quieted forever.

The Coming of Red and Gray

Along with dieselization, John Barriger was a true disciple of passenger service. He felt passenger service could be profitable on the CI&L, and that its high visibility kept a railroad in the public mind and thus helped produce freight revenue. But the passenger equipment and service that Barriger's Monon assumed in May 1946 were far from good assets.

Upon taking control of the CI&L, Barriger envisioned a resumption of Monon service in a traditional form—two trains a day in each direction Indianapolis–Chicago, day and night trains in each direction between Chicago and Louisville, and a sleeper connection to French Lick for the nighttime Chicago-Louisville trains. Service of this scope, if not of the quality Barriger envisioned, had existed on the CI&L as late

as 1944. But Barriger, of course, would add new qualities to the CI&L's passenger service—namely, red-and-gray diesels and streamlined passenger cars.

Barriger's first moves had to use CI&L's existing equipment—aged passenger cars and 4-6-2s. On July 21, 1946, Barriger made his first changes to Monon's passenger service. The *Hoosier* between Chicago and Indianapolis, which had become a morning train during the schedule reductions of 1945, was returned to its traditional evening departures (5 p.m. out of Indianapolis; 5:15 p.m. from Chicago) and its schedule improved from roughly 4½ hours to four hours flat. Taking its place in the morning was the *Tippecanoe*, running on a slightly slower schedule. Both trains carried heavyweight coaches, parlor car and diner. Under Barriger, the *Tippecanoe* carried train Nos. 11/12, while the *Hoosier* became train 14/15. The Hoosier Line's Chicago–Louisville service was again run independently of the morning Chicago-Indianapolis trains, and offered morning departures from Chicago and Louisville with early evening arrivals. The consist included coaches, parlor-lounge and diner.

The next move came in September 1946. Barriger planned the reinstatement of overnight Chicago-Louisville service, complete with a connection to French Lick, and brought it before Monon's board on September 16, 1946. He proposed a service start of September 29, and indicated that a pair of baggage-mail cars would need to be rented and a contract with

Pullman signed for the sleeping cars. On September 25, the board approved and the contract with Pullman was signed—the service was ready. The nocturnal Chicago-Louisville train made its first departures from Chicago and Louisville as proposed on September 29. The train was designated Nos. 3/4 and named the *Night Express*. It carried coaches and Pullman sleeping cars, Chicago-Louisville and Chicago-French Lick. The connecting train to operate over the French Lick Branch (train 23/24) ran between Bloomington and French Lick, making its connection with the *Night Express* at McDoel Yard. The daytime Chicago-Louisville varnish, meanwhile, was christened the *Day Express* and took train numbers 5/6.

With these changes, Barriger had—in less than five months—transformed the structure of the Hoosier Line's passenger service to match his vision. But his biggest challenge—equipment renewal—remained. Barriger had two factors to consider: cost and delivery. Despite Barriger's enthusiasm for passenger service, the Hoosier Line could ill afford to spend millions of dollars to revitalize its passenger conveyances, and the delivery schedules of the major passenger carbuilders —in the midst of the American railroads' great postwar race to streamline their trains—were well out into 1948. Barriger found his answer in the U.S. Army hospital cars that had been constructed by American Car & Foundry in 1944-45 and, with the war's end, were stored surplus.

On September 25, 1946, Barriger brought before Monon's board his proposal to purchase the Army hospital cars, asking to purchase 23 cars to be converted into coaches, dining-lounge-parlor cars, parlor cars, and one business car. The board approved purchase of 20 cars (instead of 23), and indicated that cost —including conversion at Lafayette Shops—should not exceed $550,000. Barriger projected the rebuilding process would run into summer of 1947. Financing was arranged for the cars by December, and in early January 1947 the purchase was made. At the same time, Barriger convinced Monon's board that eight more ex-hospital cars should be purchased, and that purchase was made in April 1947, bringing the total to 28 hospital cars acquired.

During late 1946 and early 1947, other passenger

A string of U.S. Army hospital cars stands outside Lafayette Shops in September 1947 awaiting their turn at rebuilding. Six-wheeled General Steel Castings trucks, retained in rebuilding, gave the cars a rather husky appearance. (C. R. ADAMS)

The Train of

WHEN, in the summer of 1947, Monon's new *Hoosier* made its debut, it was not the first diesel-powered, streamlined passenger train to ride Hoosier Line rails. That distinction fell to a blue-and-silver, four-car conveyance that rolled on to the CI&L in May 1947—General Motors' *Train of Tomorrow*.

At the conclusion of World War II, the lightweight, streamlined American passenger train was in its glory. Before the interruption of the war, in the years 1934-1942, the diesel streamliner had evolved from fixed-consist lightweights the likes of Burlington's original *Pioneer Zephyr* to flagships such as Santa Fe's 1937 lightweight *Super Chief* and Illinois Central's 1942 *Panama Limited*. In 1945, the Burlington built the first dome car, adding even more enthusiasm to the railroads' quest to reequip their postwar passenger trains.

In 1944, General Motors, together with Pullman-Standard, developed plans to construct the ultimate train for the postwar era—the *Train of Tomorrow*. An embodiment of the latest passenger train design, the *Train of Tomorrow* would tour the nation's railroads, generating public interest, and—presumably—diesel orders for Electro-Motive and passenger car sales for Pullman-Standard. Completed in the spring of 1947, the *Train of Tomorrow* was drawn by a 2,000-hp Electro-Motive E-7A (road No. 765). The four cars of its consist—a chair car, diner, sleeper and lounge-observation—were all equipped with domes ("Astra-Domes" in GM's terminology). And it fell to the Monon to be the rather unlikely host of the *Train of Tomorrow*'s official inaugural run.

After break-in test runs (including a Chicago-Wallace Junction turnaround on the Monon), the *Train of Tomorrow* made its official debut on May 26, 1947. With press, company officials, and invited guests on board, the

omorrow

Left: On May 26, 1947, General Motors' *Train of Tomorrow* rounds Harrodsburg curve bound for French Lick on its inaugural run. EMD E7A 765 leads chair car *Star Dust*, diner *Sky View*, sleeper *Dream Cloud* and lounge-observation *Moon Glow*. *(J. F. BENNETT, JIM BENNETT COLLECTION)* **Facing page:** Its maiden 279-mile journey all but complete, the *Train of Tomorrow* eases along the tree-lined platform at the French Lick Springs Hotel. *(GENERAL MOTORS)* **Below:** Stretching 411 feet from pilot to buffer plate, the *Train of Tomorrow* commands the attention of the residents of Lafayette as it ventures down 5th Street. *(JIM BENNETT)*

Train of Tomorrow departed Chicago's Dearborn Station and reeled off 278 miles on the CI&L's main line and French Lick branch to pull up before the ancient yellow brick edifice of the French Lick Springs Hotel. The passengers were guests at the "Springs" for the night, before the *Train of Tomorrow* returned north over the Monon to Chicago on May 27. The following day—May 28, 1947—the *Train of Tomorrow* was christened at a dedication ceremony near Chicago's Soldier Field.

On June 2, 1947, its display in Chicago over, the *Train of Tomorrow* began an exhibition tour that would take it through the eastern U.S. and bring a million visitors to trackside. The following year, the *Train of Tomorrow*, complete with its E-7A, was sold to the Union Pacific for Portland–Seattle service. It would never return to the CI&L, but with the events of May 26-27, 1947, the histories of GM's *Train of Tomorrow* and the Hoosier Line had forever been linked.

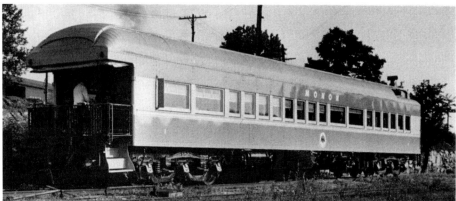

Above: Barriger was so enthusiastic about overnight sleeper service that he proposed buying 10 heavyweight sleepers from Pullman in 1947. In truth, only four would be purchased, in 1949. Among them was *Sir Henry W. Thornton*, a 10-section, 2-compartment, 1-drawing room sleeper, standing in red and gray at French Lick Springs. *(RICHARD BOWEN COLLECTION)* **Left:** Fresh from Shops, Monon business car No. 1 stands at Lafayette in June 1947. Previously Tennessee Central No. 100, the car was purchased for $42,000 at the end of 1946. Its two-tone gray livery was unique. *(DAVID W. CHAMBERS, RICHARD J. COOK COLLECTION)*

Steam-generator-equipped, red-and-gray passenger-service F-3A (No. 81) stands beside the first black-and-gold F-3A (No. 51) inside Lafayette roundhouse on September 10, 1947. Wide logo reading MONON ROUTE on freight F-3 was rare; roundhouse was soon demolished. *(C. R. ADAMS)*

Steam-generator-equipped, red-and-gray passenger-service F-3A's arrived on the Hoosier Line in May 1947. Handsome No. 84 receives a wash at Lafayette. (DAVE FERGUSON'S PHOTO ART)

equipment purchases were undertaken. The eight F-3As to power Monon's new passenger trains were ordered in November 1946, and that same month Barriger was authorized to purchase Tennessee Central Railway business car No. 100 at a cost of $42,200. This purchase made the ex-Army hospital car slated for conversion to a business car available for rebuilding into a revenue passenger car. In February 1947, Barriger proposed purchasing 10 sleeping cars from Pullman for use on the Chicago–Louisville and Chicago–French Lick services. Discussions on the sleeping car purchases continued into May 1947, when the board finally approved negotiations for purchase of five sleepers (four sleepers would eventually be purchased, but not until November 1948).

When Monon's new passenger-service F-3As (81A/B-84A/B) arrived on the Hoosier Line in May 1947, the diesels introduced the new livery that the Hoosier Line's postwar streamliners would wear—Monon red and gray. To give the postwar Monon a striking new appearance, John Barriger had retained noted industrial designer Raymond Loewy to style the new equipment, inside and out. The exterior result was the Hoosier Line's handsome Indiana University-inspired passenger colors of two shades of gray separated by a wide middle band of what was termed "Monon red."

White striping (itself bordered by gold pinstripes), white lettering, and a new Monon corporate logo completed the design.

Concurrently, Monon's black-and-gold freight scheme was created, first appearing on the F-3 freight diesels delivered in 1947 (Monon's diesel switchers of 1942 were delivered in a spartan black-and-white livery, while the H-10-44, the NW-2s, and the first three Alco RS-2s of 1946/47 wore a short-lived black-and-yellow scheme).

Although the 28 ex-Army hospital cars were yet to roll out of Lafayette Shops in May 1947, Monon immediately put its new red-and-gray F-3As to work. The diesels were first utilized on train 3 (the southbound *Night Express*) and train 6 (the northbound *Day Express*) and then other trains as the number of F-3s on the property increased. The F-3As were first employed on the Chicago–Louisville trains because they could substantially better the performance of Monon's 4-6-2s on the rugged Southern Division main line. On June 8, 1947, Monon revised its Chicago–Louisville schedules to take advantage of the diesels' ability to accelerate much faster than the 4-6-2s, cutting as much as 50 minutes off scheduled times (train No. 6). By this time, the French Lick connection (train 23/24) was also dieselized—with Alco RS-2s.

First streamlined coach outshopped at Lafayette was No. 21, rebuilt from ex-Army hospital car 89377. In red-and-gray form, the car weighed 150,600 pounds, measured 84 feet, 6 inches over buffers, and held coach seats for 46 passengers. *(FRANK VAN BREE COLLECTION)*

The Streamliners Arrive

The passenger F-3s were Monon's good news in the early summer of 1947; the bad news was that Lafayette Shops' conversion program for the ex-Army hospital cars was running behind schedule due to material and labor shortages, and the cost of conversion was proving higher than expected. While awaiting its own new passenger fleet, Monon had been forced to lease a number of passenger cars and the rental costs for these cars were also mounting.

But in late July 1947—just in time to participate in Monon's Centennial celebration—the first set of new equipment was ready. During the last week of July and into August, Monon's new *Hoosier*—F-3s 81A/81B, mail-baggage car No. 11, three deluxe coaches (Nos. 21-23), dining-bar-lounge No. 51, and parlor-observation No. 71—toured the breadth of the Monon, from New Albany to French Lick, from Lafayette to Michigan City. Although Monon rejoiced in calling this first set of equipment its new *Hoosier*, in truth the new car set would first serve on the northbound morning *Tippecanoe* and southbound evening *Hoosier*.

Text continued on page 84

Left: When the passenger F's first made their appearance on train 5 on May 18, 1947, J. F. Bennett photographed the train north of Harrodsburg. *(J. F. BENNETT, JIM BENNETT COLLECTION)*

Facing page: Barriger-era rebirth of passenger service on the French Lick branch took the form of Alco RS-2 power and heavyweights. RS-2 No. 24—an institution on the branch—stood with its consist in late 1947. *(DAVE FERGUSON'S PHOTO ART)*

Change in the streets of Lafayette: In two 1947 views on 5th Street, transformation of the *Day Express* is recorded as Mikado 510 and F-3A's 81A&B urge No. 5 southward only months apart. *(Steam—PAUL EILENBERGER, HAR-OLD J. STIRTON COLLECTION; diesel—ROBERT M. STACY)*

MONON
THE HOOSIER LINE

In late July and early August 1947, Monon's new *Hoosier* made its exhibition tour: **Above:** Rolling down 5th street, F-3A's 81A&B fly white flags (denoting an "Extra" train) and draw crowds in downtown Lafayette on July 27. *(DAVID W. CHAMBERS, RICHARD J. COOK COLLECTION)* **Facing page, bottom:** Crowds also gather as the two-unit, six-car train ventures over the Michigan City line on August 9, 1947. *(MALCOLM D. McCARTER)* **Left:** At French Lick, wooden steps are in place at the end of parlor-observation No. 71 for visitors to board the train, which also includes baggage-mail car 11, coaches 21-23 and dining-bar-lounge 51. *(JIM BENNETT)* **Facing page top:** Timetables (printed in red and gray of course) for Monon's new era of passenger service featured the F-units. *(MIKE SCHAFER COLLECTION)*

As John Barriger watches, Mrs. Emil Schramm christens the *Tippecanoe* at Indianapolis Union Station on the morning of August 17, 1947. That evening, at Chicago, the same train set would inaugurate streamlined *Hoosier* service. *(DAVE FERGUSON'S PHOTO ART)*

On August 17, 1947—christened at Indianapolis Union Station as the *Tippecanoe* by Mrs. Emil Schramm (wife of the president of the New York Stock Exchange)—the train set made its first revenue run to Chicago. That evening, in a more publicized ceremony at Dearborn Station, the same train set was christened *Hoosier* by noted cartoonist John T. McCutcheon and made its first southbound run. It was not until November 1947 that a second, nearly identical six-car set of rebuilt cars was placed in service, allowing both the *Hoosier* and *Tippecanoe* to employ new equipment in both directions every day.

With the Indianapolis trains properly equipped, Monon turned its attention to the Chicago–Louisville trains. By February 1948, five new coaches (Nos. 27-31) were ready to be put in service on the Chicago-Louisville route. On February 15, 1948, overnight trains 3/4 were renamed the *Bluegrass,* while day trains 5/6 took the name *Thoroughbred.* Along with new coaches and new name, train 5/6 also received a schedule change. The morning departures from Chicago and Louisville were changed to early afternoon (1:35 p.m. from Chicago; 12:01 p.m. from Louisville), which resulted in late evening arrivals. At the same time, Monon's board approved a request by John Barriger that two of the hospital cars still to be rebuilt be configured as dining-parlor-observation cars for use on the *Thoroughbred.* Until these cars entered service

in mid-1948, the *Thoroughbred* would carry a heavy-weight dining-lounge car with its new coaches.

During the lengthy hospital car rebuilding program, several different mixes of car configurations were discussed, and into 1948 the reconstruction of one ex-hospital car as a full diner was planned. However, it was realized that a full diner would be of little use on any of the Hoosier Line's trains, and when Monon made the decision to build the dining-parlor-observations for train 5/6, the full diner became moot. Finally, at the end of 1948, the conversion program for the 28 hospital cars at Lafayette Shops ended. When it did, the final mix among the 28 cars stood at two baggage/mail cars; six deluxe coaches; eight coaches; three dining-bar-lounges; two dining-parlor-observations; five grill-coaches; and two parlor observations. From the original $550,000 allocated for the first 20 hospital cars, the program had bulged another $200,000-plus for the eight extra cars purchased, and cost overruns had exceeded a quarter million dollars. In total, the Monon had invested roughly $1 million on its new passenger car fleet.

With the *Hoosier, Tippecanoe, Thoroughbred,* and *Bluegrass* (and connecting service to French Lick) in its red-and-gray public timetables, with eight new F-3As and 28 new passenger cars in service, the Hoosier Line's postwar passenger service was at its zenith.

A Budd at Bloomington

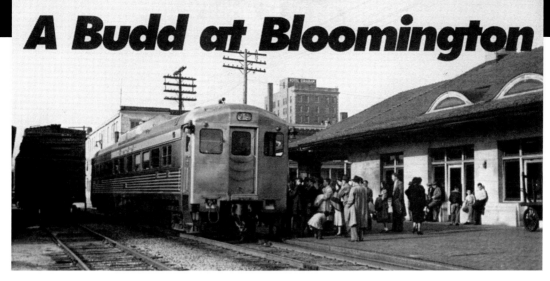

THE BUDD Rail Diesel Car (RDC) was an idea born of the late 1940s, an attempt by Budd Co. and General Motors to put the gas-electric rail motor cars of earlier decades into modern guise.

The prototype Budd RDC-1 was constructed at Budd's Red Lion (Pa.) shops in the summer of 1949, and was introduced at Chicago on September 19, 1949. It measured 85 feet long, was bidirectional with enginemen's compartments at both ends, was powered by two 275-hp Detroit Diesel (GM) two-cycle power plants, and used an Allison Division (GM) torque-converter transmission. Inside, the RDC-1 could accommodate 90 passengers.

With John Barriger's interest in passenger service, it came as little surprise that a proving tour of the RDC-1 that included the Pennsylvania, New York, Susquehanna & Western, Chicago & Eastern Illinois, Chicago & North Western, and Western Pacific also included the Hoosier Line. For two weeks—from April 1 through April 15, 1950 —Budd's RDC-1 worked in revenue service on the Monon.

The RDC-1 was based at Bloomington during its stay. Each morning at 6:40 a.m., it departed Bloomington and galloped 132 miles to Monon, arriving at 9:30 a.m., in time for passengers to connect with the northbound *Tippecanoe* to Chicago. The Budd car waited at Monon to meet the southbound *Tippecanoe*, then, at 11:05 a.m., headed south. On this journey, it ran beyond Bloomington to Bedford, arriving there at 2:40 p.m.

After a quick servicing, the RDC-1 began the second journey of its day by departing Bedford at 3:30 p.m. It arrived Monon again at 7:05 p.m., this time to connect with the northbound *Hoosier,* waited at Monon to meet the southbound *Hoosier,* then journeyed back to Bloomington, arriving at 11:00 p.m. The next day, the little RDC would begin its 578-mile cycle once again. In addition to Bloomington, Bedford and Monon, the RDC-1 made station stops at Greencastle, Crawfordsville and Lafayette.

Despite Monon's promotional flyers for the Budd RDC-1 proclaiming it "Another Step Toward Monon's Service Goal," and John Barriger's interest in a regularly scheduled Monon-Bloomington train following the demise of the *Bluegrass,* there is little evidence that the Hoosier Line seriously considered purchasing Budd Rail Diesel Cars. The RDC never was the subject of serious discussions by the CI&L's directors.

For train-watchers of the 1950s wanting to witness a small midwestern railroad operating a Budd RDC, a trip to the C&EI would have to suffice.

Above: Passengers wait to board Budd's RDC-1 at Bloomington as the bidirectional diesel rail car prepares to journey north toward Monon on April 8, 1950. **Bottom:** Northern endpoint of the experimental RDC service was Monon, where the car made connections in the morning with the Chicago-Indianapolis *Tippecanoe* and in the evening with the *Hoosier.* Date: April 8, 1950. **Below:** On the same day, the southbound demonstration run makes its station stop at Lafayette. *(THREE PHOTOS, MALCOLM D. McCARTER)*

Symbolizing the renewed urgency John Barriger placed on moving tonnage, Monon J-4 class 2-8-2 No. 571 blurs past Limedale tower, which guarded the intersection of CI&L's Chicago-Louisville line and Pennsylvania Railroad's Indianapolis-St. Louis main. Date: August 1946. *(HAROLD J. STIRTON)*

The Freight Future

Regardless of the zeal with which Barriger's Monon approached passenger service, it would be freight service—tonnage—that would decide the future of the CI&L. The armada of black-and-gold diesels purchased by the Monon were the most visible part of the Hoosier Line's freight-service rebirth, but there had to be more. The freight carpool was derelict, traffic promotion weak, freight movements slow, the railroad's physical plant in poor condition.

Even before the diesels' arrival, Barriger made his first improvements to freight scheduling. First, trains were run to the schedule, regardless of tonnage—or lack of it. And as much as four hours, 25 minutes was cut from the schedules of Monon's Chicago-Louisville freights (train numbers remained 71, 73, 75 southbound and became 70, 72 74 northbound). The old Michigan City-Lafayette trains (56/57) retained their numbers but were extended to Michigan City-Louisville runs. Trains 175/176 between Monon and Indianapolis were replaced by Nos. 90/91 operating between South Hammond and Indianapolis. The changes took effect July 21, 1946. Additional scheduled freights were added (see Chapter 9) and further cuts in running times were made as the diesels arrived and line improvements were made.

In 1946, the Monon ordered 500 all-steel, 50-ton, 40-foot boxcars and 100 70-ton covered hoppers for 1947 delivery. In 1947, 550 more freight cars were ordered—100 70-ton coal hoppers, 300 50-ton gondolas, 50 70-ton mill gondolas, and 100 additional 50-ton boxcars, all for 1948 delivery. By the end of Barriger's tenure on the CI&L, more than 1,500 freight car orders had been issued.

If any man could conjure national publicity from the purchase of a simple, 40-foot, Pullman-Standard boxcar, it was John Barriger. Monon's first 500 boxcars delivered in 1947 carried road numbers 1-500, and the "CIL 1" became a celebrity. Monon indicated the intent of its simplified numbers was to "reduce figure-writing and errors," but, of course, the publicity was welcome, too. Boxcar 1 was released from Pullman-Standard's Michigan City plant the first week of May 1947. It was moved to French Lick for display (May 7-9), then was shown at Bloomington and Lafayette before being loaded for the first time at Crawfordsville on June 13.

Car 1 ran in general service, roaming as far as Miami (on the Seaboard) and Los Angeles (on the Santa Fe) until June 1948, when it was displayed at Bedford for the Indiana Limestone Centennial and then—from June 20 through September 1948—was the centerpiece

Above: F3A No. 63 and mates provide proud leadership for CI&L tonnage at Harrodsburg. In all likelihood, this was a publicity set-up—the consist pulled by the spotless locomotive ends at the edge of the photo and has no caboose. *(J.F. BENNETT, COLLECTION OF MIKE SCHAFER VIA ELECTRO-MOTIVE)* **Left:** Barriger did not limit publicity to new locomotives. The most famous boxcar in the land, CI&L 1, toured the Monon in 1947 and was exhibited at the 1948 Chicago Railroad Fair. Number 1 was built in May 1947 by Pullman-Standard's Michigan City plant. *(FRANK VAN BREE COLLECTION)*

of Monon's exhibit at the 1948 Chicago Railroad Fair. For more than a decade, "CIL 1" would remain the land's most noted boxcar.

To fill its boxcars and hoppers and gons, *et al.,* Barriger himself led the Monon's traffic promotion, and, on October 1, 1947, hired Warren W. Brown off the Nickel Plate Road as his vice president-traffic. Together, Barriger and Brown oversaw a rebuilding of the CI&L's Traffic Department, increasing the number of off-line sales offices, seeking out new industrial development, and seemingly forever traveling to special events to promote the Monon in general—and freight traffic in particular.

In the Footsteps of McDoel

The parallels of the Monon under presidents W.H. McDoel and John Barriger were many, and in no way was this more true than in Barriger's rebuilding of the CI&L's physical plant. Little money had been spent on maintenance of the Hoosier Line's right-of-way during the receivership years. During 1934-1945, an average of $218,000 per year was spent on fixed property improvements and an average of $1.1 million spent annually on maintenance. In the Barriger years, those figures would nearly triple.

During 1946-1952, massive ballasting and tie renewal programs were undertaken, most bridges were repaired, and rail replaced. More than 125 route miles of 112-lb. and 115-lb. rail was installed on the Chicago-Louisville and Indianapolis lines, and by the end of 1950 the entire State Line–New Albany main line was equipped with 100-lb. or heavier rail. Rail of 90 lbs. taken off the main line was used to replace 75-lb. rail on

the Michigan City line. The arrival of the diesels required that new fueling facilities and fuel storage tanks be built at all the Monon's larger yards.

And there were two major projects undertaken during the Barriger years: the Cedar Lake Cutoff, and replacement of the Wabash River bridge at Delphi. (Barriger also advocated other major improvements, including relocating the Monon out of its street-running environments. In 1951, the railroad considered an extension from Bedford off the old B&B to tap business at the Crane Naval Ammunition Depot. Early in his term as Monon president, Barriger even went so far as to suggest rebuilding the Indianapolis line into a 100-mph railroad that would allow Chicago–Indianapolis passenger trains to run on a schedule of 2½ hours, but these ideas were dashed by the realities of available finances.)

Ironically, the Cedar Lake mainline relocation undid one of W.H. McDoel's improvements of some four decades earlier—Paisley trestle. The 962-foot-long wooden trestle carried trains over Paisley bog, a seemingly bottomless quicksand trap. When McDoel's Monon built the trestle, piles were driven 90 feet into the bog without finding solid footing. Because of the unstable nature of the trestle—not to mention the danger of having a train derail into the bog—trains were restricted to 25 mph on the trestle.

In 1947, work began on relocating Monon's main line from Armour to Creston, 3.67 miles. The new line would take higher ground, bypassing Paisley bog—and Cedar Lake—to the west. L.F. Racine, chief engineer of the Monon, supervised the relocation, which was subcontracted to three firms. In addition to ridding the Monon of Paisley trestle, the new line reduced the curvature and grades on the route and moved the Monon away from the shore of Cedar Lake, where people often used the tracks as a path to the little

resort town's beaches and piers. The Cedar Lake Cut-off was opened on the morning of November 30, 1948, with the southbound *Tippecanoe* standing behind John Barriger at the ribbon-cutting ceremony.

As work at Cedar Lake was ending, the renewal of the Wabash River bridge at Delphi was beginning. CI&L Chief Engineer Racine was again in charge. The old bridge, with spans dating from 1892 to 1909, consisted of seven through-truss spans, with a short I-beam span at the north end and two 75-foot girder spans at the south. During the steam era, the frail, 1,212-foot bridge limited Monon to using 2-8-0s on freights into Indianapolis, and speed over the bridge was restricted to 15 mph.

Work began in September 1948; the plan was to replace the mixture of truss and girder spans with 15 heavy deck-plate girder spans, which first required seven new piers to be constructed and eight piers to be repaired. Then, one by one, the old trusses were launched into the river below and replaced by two

Facing page: Cedar Lake: On June 20, 1948, Monon F-3 62 heads train 73 ushering freight south toward Lafayette. South of Cedar Lake stood Paisley trestle, which on October 10, 1948, felt the weight of train 5 (above), the *Thoroughbred*, advancing behind F-3 84. (BOTH PHOTOS, JOHN F. HUMISTON)
Right: Monon's 1947-48 relocation away from Cedar Lake and Paisley trestle removed two of the Northern Division's scenic highlights, but allowed for far safer operation. On November 30, 1948, the southbound *Tippecanoe* stands at the ribbon-cutting ceremony that opened the Cedar Lake cutoff. (FRANK VAN BREE COLLECTION)

The aged truss bridge (portions dated to 1892) over the Wabash River at Delphi limited Monon to using nothing larger than 2-8-0's such as H-6 No. 283 on its Indianapolis line freights. In 1948-49, Monon replaced the 1212-foot span with a girder bridge. *(W. A. AKIN JR., COLLECTION OF KALMBACH PUBLISHING CO.)*

girders. The Indianapolis line was taken out of service for six hours, 45 minutes a day, starting at 9:45 a.m., after the passing of the northbound *Tippecanoe*. The southbound *Tippecanoe* was detoured, and then, by the arrival time of the evening *Hoosiers,* the track was back in service. In December 1949, the new Wabash River bridge was complete. Cost: $300,000.

Mixed Returns

For the student of railroading, for the train-watcher, the Barriger-era transformation of the Monon—diesels, streamliners, physical improvements, and the like—was cause for fascination. But what of a stockholder's view—what of tonnage hauled and passengers carried? And the unforgiving bottom line? The results were mixed: Tonnage was a winner, carrying the road to relative prosperity, but Barriger's red-and-gray experiment—passenger service—was less fortunate.

In 1946, despite the Hoosier Line's expanded passenger service (CI&L passenger trains operated 39,000 miles more than they did the previous year), ridership decreased from 261,000 to 213,000 passengers. But 1945 had been an aberration, the last of the travel-heavy war years, and Monon's new service had only been in place a few months. In 1947, passenger traffic did rebound—to 259,000 passengers carried, almost the equal of 1945. And yet, to carry that number of passengers, CI&L's expanded passenger service had reeled off 806,000 miles—almost double that of 1945. Total passenger train revenue stood at $1.2 million. In 1948, there seemed to be real promise: With the streamliners in service, passenger count increased to 307,000 and total passenger train revenue hit $1.6 million, as the Hoosier Line's passenger trains rolled 805,000 miles. But then, in 1949, the decline began anew. At year's end, only 245,000 passengers had been carried,

revenue totaled only $1.3 million, and mail and express revenue (which had been improving) decreased 14%.

By August 1949, Barriger had met with his board to discuss passenger train deficits, which were running approximately $85,000 a month on an out-of-pocket basis. Barriger recommended that the two Chicago-Indianapolis trains be retained, but with equipment changes to the *Tippecanoe*. The parlor-observations (cars 71-72, shared with the *Hoosier)* should be dropped from the *Tippecanoe* for lack of patronage, and be replaced with "grill-parlor" cars. For this, two grill-coaches—Nos. 68-69—were soon reconfigured to grill-parlors (also later called dinette coaches) and renumbered 81-82.

Barriger also recommended changing the schedule of the northbound *Thoroughbred*, moving its Louisville departure up from 12:01 p.m. to 9:30 a.m. And he recommended discontinuance of the *Bluegrass* and its French Lick connection (which together were losing $40,000 per month). To utilize existing equipment and keep two-train frequency on the most patronized part of the Chicago-Louisville line, Barriger suggested a new Monon-Bloomington train, to connect at Monon with the southbound *Tippecanoe* and northbound *Hoosier.* Agreement was reached on all of Barriger's proposals except the last—the new, Monon-Bloomington train would never be born.

On September 24, 1949, the *Bluegrass* made its final run, and with it came an end to Monon's last scheduled service to French Lick Springs. Barriger himself explained the demise of trains 3/4 to the public: "For some time, the public's response [to the night trains], while not adequate in terms of revenue to meet the operating costs, was encouraging because a steady improvement in passenger traffic and revenues was registered. The trend reversed itself last October and has been downward ever since."

Although Barriger's Monon-Bloomington operation was never realized (save a short Budd Rail Diesel Car test in 1950), one final new train name was to appear in the Monon's timetables during the Barriger years—*Varsity*. On December 1, 1949, Barriger proposed to his board that a new Chicago-Bloomington weekend train be run to accommodate the heavy college student travel along the Monon. With the understanding that the train could be withdrawn if unprofitable, the proposal was approved. The *Varsity* made its debut on Friday, January 6, 1950. Carrying train Nos. 1/2, the *Varsity* ran northbound from Bloomington (departure 5:00 p.m.) to Chicago (arrival 9:35 p.m.) on Fridays, and southbound Chicago to Bloomington (on a similar schedule) on Sundays. The *Varsity* endured until college's summer vacation, making its last run on June 18, 1950, never to return during the Barriger era (rather surprisingly, during Warren Brown's presidency, the *Varsity* would make a brief return to Monon's schedules at the start of 1953, only to disappear forever on May 29, 1953).

From 1950 onward in the board room of the Hoosier Line, the "passenger deficit problem" required repeated discussion. But for the remainder of the Barriger years, no other major reductions would occur in the Monon's passenger services (although discontinuance of all service south of Bloomington was considered in February 1952). Meanwhile, passenger totals and revenues continued to falter. In 1950, only 201,000 passen-

Ex-EMD demonstrator F-3A's 85A&B, used as dual-service units and dressed in black-and-gold, lead the *Thoroughbred* north toward Bloomington. Location of this J. F. Bennett photograph is one of the photographer's favorites: bridge E-8 over Clear Creek north of Harrodsburg (also see pages 8, 39, 60 and 80). *(J. F. BENNETT, JIM BENNETT COLLECTION)*

gers rode the Monon's trains; in 1951 the total dipped to 196,000; and in the final year of Barriger's Monon presidency, only 172,000 passengers would step aboard the Hoosier Line's red-and-gray trains. Total passenger train revenue by 1952 had dipped to $813,000, passenger train miles to 534,000. The Monon's great passenger train experiment was a failure.

In defense of the Barriger-era passenger service, it can be said that Monon's passenger train decline was slower than the national railroad average. In the years 1946-1952, Monon's passenger count dropped 20%; the national average for all U.S. railroads was a drop of 46%. During the brief halcyon days of red and gray—the years 1947 and 1948—the Monon's increasing passenger trade flew in the face of a national decline of 9%. But across the country, despite the American railroads' great investment in new streamliners, the passenger business was again in rapid decline (in the decade 1946-1955, passengers handled by all U.S. rail-

roads dropped from 452 million to 185 million). Monon's investment in coaches and parlor cars, grill-coaches, and red-and-gray Fs would never pay off.

Tonnage and Profits

Just as Monon's postwar passenger experiment was a failure, its revitalization of freight service was a success. In 1946, Monon matched its 1945 traffic figures (5.5 million tons of freight hauled; $10 million in freight revenue)—then launched into a period of traffic growth. In 1947, freight traffic grew to 6.4 million tons and freight revenue climbed to $14.7 million. In 1948, the Hoosier Line's black-and-gold diesels lugged seven million tons of freight and produced $16.6 million in freight revenue.

With 1949 came a national decline in freight traffic, and Monon proved no exception to the trend—the

Text continued on page 94

100 Years After James Brooks

IT WAS by chance that the 100th anniversary of the birth of Monon's original predecessor—the New Albany & Salem —fell during John Barriger's presidency of the Hoosier Line. But, in fact, the timing could not have been more perfect. Barriger was a man who took advantage of any opportunity to promote the Monon, and with a year passed since the CI&L's reorganization, there was indeed reason to celebrate.

The Centennial Celebration of the Hoosier Line centered on a four-day festival at New Albany, hometown of New Albany & Salem founder James Brooks. From July 27 through July 30, 1947, New Albany held festivities— Homecomers' Day, Exhibitors' Day, Youth Day, and finally, Transportation Day. Concurrently, the Monon began a four-day celebration of its own—a Centennial Train Show that stopped in 20 Indiana towns starting at Hammond and ending at New Albany.

To re-create the era of the Hoosier Line's origins, Baltimore & Ohio 4-4-0 *William Mason* and two period passenger cars were borrowed and ran from Hammond to

New Albany. Supported by the all-male "Monon quartet," female singers dressed in period costumes, songstress Marie Lawler, and, of course, John Barriger, Monon's traveling train show made its way to New Albany for an extravagant finale during New Albany's Transportation Day. Along the way, the *William Mason's* train employed loudspeakers to fill Hoosier towns with music. The director of the Centennial Celebration, John A. McGee, had written eight Monon songs for the event.

At New Albany on Transportation Day, the city held a parade (complete with Monon float), draped Monon red banners across its streets, and hosted dignitaries (including Indiana Governor Ralph Gates). The *William Mason* and its train were joined by Monon's new streamlined *Hoosier*, and by Southern Railway's ancient "Best Friend of Charleston," which had steamed with two open coaches across the K&IT bridge from Louisville.

At the end of the festivities, it was estimated that more than 100,000 people had come to trackside to join in John Barriger's biggest party—Monon's Centennial Celebration.

Facing page: John Barriger is at the engineer's cab window of the *William Mason* as Monon's Centennial Special passes down 5th Street in Lafayette, bound for New Albany in July 1947. *(JIM BENNETT COLLECTION)* **Above:** White flags fly atop Monon RS-2 No. 21 as the Alco leads a passenger extra that accompanied the Centennial Special to New Albany. Crowds have filled the station platform at Bloomington; along the Monon, more than 100,000 people came to trackside. *(J. F. BENNETT, FRANK VAN BREE COLLECTION)* **Left:** For New Albany's Transportation Day, which concluded Monon's Centennial Celebration, Southern Railway contributed the *Best Friend of Charleston*, which steamed with two cars across the K&IT bridge from Louisville to James Brooks' hometown. *(FRANK VAN BREE COLLECTION)*

Above: Monon's *Tippecanoe* provides a Hoosier Christmas card scene as it loads passengers and baggage at Monticello. *(LINN H. WESTCOTT; COLLECTION OF KALMBACH PUBLISHING CO.)*
Right: Hoosier Line RS-2s and rider car mark the arrival of a Monon local in the streets of New Albany. *(JACK FRAVERT)*

CI&L carried 6.3 million tons of freight and earned $15.6 million in revenue that year. But then, in 1950, traffic rebounded—and Monon toted 6.9 million tons of freight in its boxcars and hoppers and gons, and marked $17.4 million in freight revenue into its ledger books. In 1951 freight climbed to 7.7 million tons, and revenue to $19 million, then in 1952—despite a decline to 7.1 million tons hauled—freight revenue reached an all-time record: $19.5 million.

During the period of growth, the mixture of commodities carried on Hoosier Line freights changed only slightly; Monon's tonnage increases were coming from nearly all traffic sectors. Coal originating on the I&L branch remained in decline, but coal originating on other lines and moving over the Monon was increasing; stone traffic, after floundering during World War II, began a rejuvenation that would bring it back to 1930's levels; grain remained a strong Hoosier Line tonnage commodity; and the most rapid growth—not

surprising, given Monon's improved freight schedules and sales efforts—was in the movement of time-sensitive manufactured products.

Despite the passenger problem, the corporate news was good: From 1946 to 1952, Monon's annual operating revenues grew from $11.4 million to $21.8 million. Net operating revenue grew from a deficit of $595,000 in 1946 to $2.1 million in the black in 1950, then eased back to $1.9 million in 1952. In 1950 through 1952, the Monon's "bottom line"—net income—showed profits of more than $1 million each year. John Barriger had, indeed, pulled the Chicago, Indianapolis & Louisville out of bankruptcy for good.

Merger Ideas and Farewell

In December 1952, Monon Chairman Arthur Leonard announced the resignation of John Barriger, to be effective December 31. Barriger, age 53 and never one

The White River flows silently in the background as 4500-horsepower in Monon F-3's rattle a freight north through Gosport in a fitting testament to John Barriger's style of railroading on the Hoosier Line. *(J. F. BENNETT, JIM BENNETT COLLECTION)*

to linger before seeking new challenges, was bound for the New Haven Railroad, a passenger-heavy, financially troubled eastern carrier. Barriger would serve as vice president under NYNH&H President Buck Dumaine.

In parting, Barriger publicly advocated merger as the Monon's long-term key to prosperity—and suggested the Chicago & Eastern Illinois as the Monon's natural partner. The C&EI, larger than the Monon at 868 route miles but similar in structure to the Hoosier Line, ran from Chicago to Evansville, Ind., and a link with the L&N, and also had lines extending deep into southern Illinois' coal fields and, via trackage rights on the New York Central, a line to East St. Louis. "The Monon makes two fingers of a hand and the C&EI the other three fingers," noted Barriger. During his tenure

on the Monon, Barriger had made several merger contacts with the Chicago & Eastern Illinois (and he even proposed a lease of the Monon to C&EI in 1952). But C&EI was only mildly interested and the possibility of a merger between the two midwestern roads never reached serious consideration.

Following his departure from the Monon, John Barriger would serve the New Haven, as president of the Pittsburgh & Lake Erie, as chairman of the Missouri-Kansas-Texas (Katy), as chief executive officer of the Boston & Maine, as a consultant to the Federal Railroad Administration, and as a special traffic representative for the Rock Island. On December 9, 1976, John Walker Barriger III died at age 77, and only then did this most remarkable railroad career come to its end.

Sporting an antenna for the television inside, Warren Brown's legacy to the Monon—the business car *Lynne*—carries the markers of the southbound *Thoroughbred* crossing Monon Creek at Monon, Ind., April 4, 1959. *(J. PARKER LAMB)*

5

TRANQUIL TIMES, TROUBLED TIMES

The Hoosier Line, 1953-1959

THE MAN with the formidable task of following John Barriger as president of the Monon was Warren Brown. Brown had, of course, served Barriger as the CI&L's vice president-traffic. He was elected to the Monon presidency by the board of directors on December 29, 1952, and took his new position January 1, 1953. Before being hired by Barriger in 1947, Brown had worked for the Nickel Plate Road. On the NKP during the years 1924-1947, Brown had risen from a freight representative to Nickel Plate's general freight agent at St. Louis, Mo.

As Barriger's chief deputy during the barnstorming sales and publicity tours of the late 1940s and early 1950s, Warren Brown knew the Hoosier Line literally foot by foot, its customers and employees name by name, and he was destined to continue Barriger's methods of hands-on traffic sales and management. He would also continue Barriger's penchant for providing the Hoosier Line with publicity. And Brown would use the Monon's presidency as a pulpit from which to preach that American railroading needed to be freed of its regulatory harness if it was to prosper in the second half of the 20th century.

In retrospect, it can be said that the tenure of Warren Brown as president of the Hoosier Line was one first of tranquility, then of troubled declines in profitability. Warren Brown's era was a time of intrigue with piggyback service, a time when noticeable advances were made in attracting tonnage from factories and farm fields—but not necessarily enough to offset the ever slow, but certain, decline in coal tonnage originating on the CI&L.

When Brown served his final day as Monon's president on December 31, 1958, the Hoosier Line was physically not unlike it had been six years earlier. Freight car purchases during the Brown years were adequate but not extraordinary. Not a single new diesel locomotive purchase had been required. The *Thoroughbred* and *Hoosier* and *Tippecanoe* still rolled (although all were endangered).

Operating revenues changed little from the last season of Barriger rule (1952) through 1958—first modestly increasing, then modestly decreasing (*i.e.*, $21.8 million in 1952; $22.6 million in 1956; $20.0 million in 1958). But operating costs were on a persistent rise, and the Hoosier Line's net operating revenue thus was in decline (from $5.3 million in 1952 to $3.7 million in 1958). From 1952 to 1958, Monon's operating ratio climbed from 75.7% to 83.1%.

1953: Year of the Stations

For the trackside observer of the Hoosier Line, the first year of Warren Brown's presidency could perhaps best be recalled by the opening of three new passenger stations. That a railroad the size of the CI&L would construct three new stations in a single year during the passenger-depressed 1950s was surely uncommon, but then the circumstances behind two of the new stations' construction were also uncommon.

The new stations were opened at Monon, Lowell and Hammond. Both the Monon and Lowell stations were snug, brick structures built for the same reason—to replace stations flattened in train accidents. Monon, of course, had been the site of the *Thoroughbred* runaway

Although not as famous as boxcar CIL 1, Monon's legion of boxcars with a white band and THE HOOSIER LINE along the top was noted among train-watchers. CIL 861 at left was one of nine 50-ton boxcars purchased in 1953. *(FRANK VAN BREE COLLECTION)*

in September 1951, and following the clean-up a retired passenger combine had served as Monon's depot. Then, on June 10, 1953—with Warren Brown, Indiana Public Service Commission Chairman Warren Buchanan, and the 60-piece Monon High School band in attendance—the new, bunting-draped Monon station was dedicated.

Tiny Lowell, Ind., population 1,600, had been the site of the derailment of freight No. 71 on May 22, 1952. The resulting fire from alcohol-filled tank cars did considerable damage, including destruction of the downtown depot. But in August 1953, Monon turned on its publicity flair once again, opening a new station amid a celebration that included releasing balloons, singing Monon songs, handing out Monon engineer's caps and chocolate bars, and finally, a dedication speech by Warren Brown.

The final station opening of 1953 occurred at Hammond, where in October, Monon and Erie dedicated a new joint station, a diminutive stone structure. Perhaps because the new Hammond station was born of economic convenience rather than from a catastrophic event, the opening was not cause for an "event" of the scope of the Monon and Lowell station openings. Nonetheless, the new Hammond station did play host to a special exhibition train.

The year 1953 also marked the purchase of a creation that would grow synonymous with the Warren Brown years: the business car *Lynne*. On August 18, 1953, the Monon purchased from Pullman an aged sleeper/observation, the *Great Spirit*, built in 1924 and used primarily on Great Northern's *Oriental Limited* and *Empire Builder*. When purchased, the car was stored in Chicago and was then moved by the CI&L to Lafayette Shops for conversion to a business car.

Recast in Monon red and gray outside, and with all the accouterments of a business car inside (including staterooms, kitchen, dining room and office desk), the *Lynne*—named for Warren Brown's granddaughter,

Lynne Marie Chambers—made its maiden run (to Wallace Junction) on April 6, 1954.

Golden Spike for the Monon

Just as John Barriger had found reason in 1947 to celebrate the 100th anniversary of the chartering of the New Albany & Salem, Warren Brown found cause for a celebration of Monon history during his tenure. In Brown's case, the celebration occurred on the 100th anniversary of the completion of the New Albany & Salem's main line from New Albany to Michigan City. At 4:00 p.m., on June 24, 1954—100 years to the minute after the NA&S's final spike was driven—Warren Brown and Indiana Senator Homer Capehart stood at the historic site near Greencastle and drove a "golden" spike. Following the ceremony, the spike was removed and presented to Capehart along with a plaque for display in his Washington office.

Yet another notable Monon promotion occurred in 1954: "Operation Kiddie." Starting on October 26, 1954, and operating every Tuesday, Wednesday and Thursday through November 18, Monon ran special passenger trains from Indianapolis to Sheridan and return, all carrying Indianapolis-area school children. The idea, presented by president Brown to the Indianapolis school district, was to introduce children to railroad operations. During the 12 days the special trains operated, Monon's red-and-gray trains carried more than 10,000 students.

While the Monon was putting on its "public face" at the likes of Greencastle and Indianapolis, there were other activities ongoing, more mundane, perhaps, but more vital to the road's operations—and profit/loss ledger as well. On May 1, 1954, Monon opened a new freight house at South Hammond. The two-story stone structure, with a 50x500' main floor, cost $320,000. With the new freight station, Monon ended its lease of downtown Chicago space from Chicago & Western Indiana. The Hoosier Line hoped to save $90,000 a

Fairbanks-Morse and Electro-Motive switchers converge at the north end of Lafayette Shops yard as the Monon veterans shuffle cars. For FM No. 18, Shops was home for virtually its entire career. (DAVE FERGUSON'S PHOTO ART)

year by ending its Chicago operation, and also expected to speed up its handling of less-than-carload (LCL) freight, which could be unloaded from freight cars when they arrived at South Hammond rather than waiting for a transfer job to take the freight cars to downtown Chicago.

Another effort at improving operations on the Monon undertaken in 1954 was the installation of a train radio system. A radio broadcasting and receiving station was placed in service at Lafayette Shops, and 12 diesels and six cabooses were equipped with train radios. Also, train crews began receiving hand-held

radios for switching operations (installation of Monon's train radio system continued throughout the late 1950s).

For the traffic department of the Monon, 1954 was largely devoted to two words—coal and piggyback. For the coal-producing I&L branch, 1954 was a very bad year. At year end, only 233,360 tons of bituminous coal had been originated on the Monon (less than half that originated as late as 1951). But for once there seemed hope. By the end of the year, the S&A Coal Corp. had completed a new coal washer and tipple, to be fed by strip mines, on the Monon at Victoria. And

BL-2 33 and a local navigate between a pair of Monon's classic semaphores on the Indianapolis line. The Electro-Motive diesel arrived on the Monon in 1948 and would be traded to Alco as credit for C-420s in 1966. *(DAVE FERGUSON'S PHOTO ART)*

Above: The 1953 opening of the joint Monon/Erie passenger station at Hammond, Ind., was marked by the visit of a display consist which included Monon F-3A 81B, diner 53 and an Erie sleeper; behind that stood various other rolling stock contributed by the two roads.

Equipment is on the Monon main; Erie's main line is left of the F-unit. *(DAVE FERGUSON'S PHOTO ART)* **Top:** Monon's two-story freight house at South Hammond was built at a cost of $320,000 and was opened on May 1, 1954. *(FRANK VAN BREE COLLECTION)*

plans were under way for a second new washer and tipple—on leased Monon land near Midland—for the Ax Coal Co.

In anticipation of new business, Monon took delivery in 1954 of 150 new coal hoppers. The results appeared in 1955, when coal tonnage originated on the I&L rebounded to 432,875 tons (unfortunately, only to begin a renewed decline in 1956).

Piggyback: In October 1954, Monon announced plans to inaugurate overnight piggyback service between its terminal cities, and ramps were built at South Hammond, New Albany, and Indianapolis. An

employee contest was held to name the service, and Walter Hecht, a car inspector at South Hammond, penned the winner—"Trailer Maid" service. Piggyback operations were begun on January 11, 1955, with 10 38-foot, converted flatcars, 14 black-and-gold trailer vans, eight open-top vans, and one flatbed trailer devoted to the effort. The service was accommodated with existing train schedules. Trailer flats were handled from South Hammond to New Albany on train 71 and vice versa on train 70. South Hammond-Indianapolis trailers departed on train 71 and at Monon were cut out and placed in train 91. Indianap-

Reason for renewed hope on the I&L branch in 1954 was S&A Coal Corporation's construction of a new coal washer and tipple—to be fed by strip mines—at Victoria. In January 1955, Monon hoppers stood for loading at the new facility. (FRANK VAN BREE COLLECTION)

olis–South Hammond movements were handled by trains 90/70. Some trailers were also handled on Monon's other South Hammond–New Albany trains. Yard jobs at South Hammond, Monon, Indianapolis and New Albany handled the necessary switching. Generally, the piggyback flats were placed in trains immediately behind the locomotives. Over-the-road cartage was provided to downtown Chicago and Louisville. In the first nine months of 1955, Monon handled 1,100 trailer loads, and by the end of the year its fleet had grown to 20 converted flatcars, 19 vans, eight

open-top vans, and three flatbeds. Limited piggyback interchange with the Chicago & North Western (to CN&W's Proviso freighthouse) and the Nickel Plate (at Linden, Ind.) had also started.

A "New" Name

On January 10, 1956, the 10-year stock trust agreement set up at the Monon's 1946 reorganization ended. The stock trustees—Arthur Leonard, Homer Livingston and John Barriger (who had replaced John Dwyer upon his death in 1951)—issued a lengthy "final report." Paramount among all the facts presented in the 26-page document was one simple sentence: "The current financial position of the Company is better than at any time in its 108-year history."

But while the stock trustees predicted a good immediate future for the Hoosier Line, their conclusion was

Maiden run: On April 6, 1954, Monon's new business car, Lynne, made its first shakedown run from Lafayette to Wallace Junction and back. (DAVE FERGUSON'S PHOTO ART)

102

With head-end caboose 81222 snuggled behind, Alco RS-2 21 makes a charge through Crawfordsville in June 1958 with northbound local No. 42. (*J. PARKER LAMB*)

On the afternoon of May 29, 1958, Monon F-3A 84B is in charge of train 6, the northbound *Thoroughbred*, approaching State Line tower, Hammond. From State Line, where Monon track ends, train 6 will make the final 19.8 miles of its journey to Dearborn Station on Chicago & Western Indiana rails. (*J. PARKER LAMB*)

Above: Crossing its namesake river at Monticello, Ind., the *Tippecanoe* behind F-3A 82B is but weeks away from its April 9, 1959, discontinuance. Single coach on the rear implies the lack of patronage that killed the train. *(J. PARKER LAMB JR.)* **Left:** The spirit of the Hoosier Line is shared with a new generation as veteran Monon crewmen reveal their art to a pair of young boys. Monon's "Operation Kiddie" in the fall of 1954 introduced more than 10,000 Indianapolis-area school children to railroading. *(DAVE FERGUSON'S PHOTO ART)*

Facing page: On the tracks of the Chicago & Western Indiana, train 5, the *Thoroughbred*, leaves Chicago's skyline behind on September 13, 1959. Ahead for F-3A 84A and its three-car consist lies an 8-hour, 324-mile journey to Louisville. *(JIM WOZNICZKA)*

In 1959, Monon vacated its 1902-built station in Lafayette. Interim replacement (until a small brick structure was opened in 1960, which by 1987 was serving as a feed store) was retired grill-coach 67, sans trucks. View looks northward; station site was at the north end of the street-running. *(RON STUCKEY)*

tempered: "The difficulties of small-scale operation in the railroad business are well recognized, and Monon's isolated and unsupported position as a small independent carrier is somewhat unique and not always comfortable. Consolidation with a complementary railroad system, or even with a partially competing system, could be highly advantageous to both parties, and should ultimately be achieved."

Thus in their parting, the stock trustees had seconded John Barriger's 1952 recommendation that the Monon find a merger partner. In fact, in the middle 1950s, the railroad that Barriger had earmarked as his choice as a Monon merger mate—the Chicago & Eastern Illinois—showed signs of warming to a Monon-C&EI partnership, but solid progress was never made on the marriage.

As a fitting celebration to the end of the last vestiges of its reorganization, the Hoosier Line assumed a "new" name the day after the stock trustee agreement ended. On January 11, 1956, the Chicago, Indianapolis & Louisville name ceased to exist. Instead, the railroad's longtime nickname—Monon—finally became its official corporate title.

At the close of the stock trustee era, another event occurred which would change a number of the faces in Monon's board room. In December 1955, Ben W. Heineman and his associates sold their Monon holdings of some 73,000 stock shares. Heineman, who was chairman of the executive committee of the Minneapolis & St. Louis Railway, sold stock to the firms of Sutro Brothers & Co. and Gruss & Co., both of New York. This allowed Walter D. Floersheimer, who was senior partner of Sutro Brothers & Co., to become chairman of the board of the Monon in 1956, replacing stock trustee Arthur Leonard. But the immediate effect of the change in control was minimal, with Warren Brown remaining as president.

Text continued on page 108

As it should have been: On December 12, 1947, train 5 slowly swings around the 9-degree curve at Monon for its station stop. When train 5 of September 17, 1951, ran amuck, the 1916-built limestone depot would be flattened. (JOHN F. HUMISTON)

THE DAY had not gone well. As Monon train No. 5—the southbound *Thoroughbred*—departed Rensselaer, on the afternoon of September 17, 1951, the train was running half an hour late. Its tardiness was due to several unscheduled, uncommon stops. Monon F-3As 85B and 85A were on the point of No. 5, with a second set of F-3s—81B and 82A—tucked in behind, being ferried to Lafayette. Both sets of F units had engine crews on board. The leading F-3's overspeed control (which automatically applies the brakes if a prescribed speed is exceeded) was set at 69 mph, and 50 miles north of Rensselaer No. 5's engineer had allowed the train to top 70 mph, the brakes had set, and the *Thoroughbred* had ground to a halt. Then, as No. 5 restarted, the rear flagman noted that the brakes were sticking on the rear passenger car and he stopped the train.

After the second unscheduled stop—and restart—the engineer aboard the second set of F-3s ventured through the bowels of the leading F units and entered the cab of 85B to ask about the unusual events. There, he noted that the engineer in charge—65-year-old Herbert H. Dickerson—acted unusual, perhaps ill, and offered to take over. Dickerson said no.

As the train rolled on toward Rensselaer, twice more Dickerson allowed No. 5 to exceed 70 mph and the overspeed control had taken over. But during the station stop at Rensselaer, the engineer of the second set of Fs, despite the numerous overspeed incidents, decided that Dickerson was not ill, and returned to his trailing unit.

At 3:14 p.m., still 28 minutes off schedule, No. 5 raced at 68 mph toward its station stop at Monon. As the *Thoroughbred* passed signal 86.1—only two miles from the Monon depot—Dickerson's fireman, Charles Henriott, called the signal, then, noticing that the train had passed the spot where engineers usually made a brake application, reminded Dickerson to close the throttle and apply the brakes.

Dickerson made only a light brake application and the fireman told him he thought their speed was excessive. Dickerson responded that he'd operate the train—and proceeded to release the brakes and reopen the throttle. At that, the fireman tried to take over the controls, but Dickerson pushed him away. In the rear units, the other engine crew realized No. 5 was in trouble, and threw the train into emergency. But it was too late.

At 3:16 p.m., moving at 64 mph, the *Thoroughbred* hit the nine-degree, 15-mph curve at Monon, derailed, and plowed head-on into the stone depot. The station was turned to rubble, the F units scattered like toys. But miraculously, only the rear truck of the first mail car derailed and no passengers aboard the *Thoroughbred* were seriously injured. There was only one fatality: Engineer Dickerson. The other engine crewmen, the train's conductor, and the head brakeman were injured, but all recovered. On the ground, two girls waiting on the platform were seriously injured, as was the Monon's 16-year-old telegrapher at Monon, Mahlon (Cookie) Eberhard.

In the aftermath of the Monon wreck, the ICC could

The Monon station sign hangs precariously above limestone rubble as F-3A 85A, which had been second unit on the southbound *Thoroughbred* of September 17, 1951, lies on its side awaiting help. *(HULCE MARTIN COLLECTION)*

only take note of the unusual events leading to the catastrophe and ruled the obvious—that "excessive speed on curve" was the cause. The reasons for the bizarre actions of Dickerson, an employee of the Monon for 45 years and an engineer since 1920, could only be guessed. The railroad recovered. The main line was open nine hours after the accident; the four F-3s were repaired; and, on June 10, 1953, the railroad ceremoniously opened a new brick Monon depot that stands to this day. And the mysterious events of September 17, 1951, forever entered into Hoosier Line lore.

Facing page: Black-and-gold F3A 85A and red-and-gray 81B (third unit of train 5) rest askew after the accident. Locomotive 81B stopped literally atop the crossing of the Monon's two routes. *(HULCE MARTIN COLLECTION)* **Left:** Nearly the same photo angle as in the facing page wreck photo is evident in this view of the new Monon depot, draped with bunting for its opening dedication on June 10, 1953, as the southbound *Tippecanoe* makes its arrival. *(DAVE FERGUSON'S PHOTO ART)*

For the Monon, 1956 proved a year of contrasts. The piggyback experiment continued to show promise and, in fact, agreements were in place with 15 other railroads for handling trailer movements. Welded rail made its debut on the Hoosier Line. Operating revenue reached a record $22.6 million, loads handled topped 217,000, total tonnage exceeded 7.2 million tons. But net revenue and net income declined because of rising operating costs. Then, in 1957 the operating revenue dropped modestly to $22.2 million, loads handled dropped to 195,000, tonnage to 6.5 million tons. Operating costs, nonetheless, still increased—to $18.4 million. The Monon remained profitable, but its returns were growing more modest.

With John Barriger's interest in passenger business ever more distant, in mid-1957 the Monon's management took aim at its varnish as one way to lower operating costs. In June 1957, Warren Brown announced to the Indianapolis Traffic Club that the Hoosier Line was considering asking out of the passenger business. Brown stated that Monon had lost $1.2 million on its red-and-gray conveyances in 1956 (on revenues of $1.8 million and expenses of $3 million).

To control costs, Monon stripped away the last remnants of food service on the *Thoroughbred* in early 1957, then with the fall schedules of 1957, discontinued parlor car and diner service on the *Hoosier* and *Tippecanoe*. The news came on April 26, 1958: Monon petitioned to the Indiana Public Service Commission to discontinue all its passenger trains.

The year 1958 was not progressing well in general. Freight traffic nationally was down and the Monon was no exception. At year end, Monon had carried only 174,822 loads (5.8 million tons); total revenue dropped to $20.2 million. Net revenue from operations totaled only $3 million, and when one worked all the way down to the Monon's bottom line, only $99,702 remained to separate it from red ink. As recently as 1955, the bottom line profit had been $1.3 million.

Given the stagnation of traffic and decline in profits, what was perhaps inevitable occurred in December 1958. Citing the pressures of his job and concerns for his health, Warren Brown announced his resignation effective December 31. Brown would leave the Monon to take a new position with the Western Pacific. At the same time, Monon's vice president-traffic, C.E. Ragland, resigned to go to the New Haven, and H.C. Greer, vice president-finance, retired.

The Brief Tenure of Carl Bick

Following the resignation of Warren Brown, the Monon's presidency was for a short time left vacant. However, Carl A. Bick, the road's vice president-operations, was promoted to chief executive officer (and then president in April 1959). Bick had come to the Monon from the Burlington Route during John Barriger's tenure in 1950. Bick first served the Monon as comptroller and had been promoted to vice president-operations when Warren Brown became president. Like Barriger and Brown, Carl Bick was another traffic-oriented man, a man who openly dreamed of expanding Monon's piggyback service, strengthening its traffic base, and even moving Monon toward diversification into the trucking industry.

A Hoosier Line crewman watches his charge pass as BL-2 No. 33 eases toward switchpoints at Crawfordsville on June 9, 1958. The train is southbound local No. 43. (*J. PARKER LAMB JR.*)

Above: In the afternoon shadows of May 31, 1960, an A-B-A set of F-3's heads train 73 toward a crossing of the 600-foot-long Wabash River bridge north of Lafayette. *(J. PARKER LAMB JR.)* **Left:** End of an era—On April 9, 1959, train 15, the southbound *Hoosier*, calls in the dusk for the final time at Hammond. When F-3A 83A pulled this train into Indianapolis Union Station some four hours later, scheduled Monon passenger service to the Hoosier capital ended forever. *(JIM WOZNICZKA)*

By happenstance, though, one of Carl Bick's first duties would not be an expansion move, but rather to preside over the death of Indianapolis passenger service. Following Monon's April 1958 petition, the Indiana Public Service Commission held hearings through 1958, then ruled that the Hoosier Line could, indeed, discontinue trains 11/12 and 14/15, the *Tippecanoe* and *Hoosier* on the Chicago–Indianapolis route.

However, the PSC also ruled that the Monon should continue operating the *Thoroughbred* between Chicago and Louisville. On April 9, 1959, the final runs of the *Tippecanoe* and *Hoosier* were made. Last of the Indianapolis line trains was the southbound *Hoosier*, No. 15, scheduled to depart Chicago at 5:30 p.m., and arrive Indianapolis at 9:30 p.m. With No. 15's arrival at darkened Indianapolis Union Station, more than half a century of Monon passenger service to the Hoosier capital ended.

In another event related to passenger service during the Bick era, the elegant old Lafayette station, which dated to 1902, was sold in 1959, and temporarily replaced with ex-grill-coach 67 which sat, *sans* trucks, along the line at 5th and Salem Sts. In 1960, a new combination freight/passenger station replaced the grill-coach.

Exactly what changes and accomplishments Carl Bick, with his schooling under both Barriger and Brown, might have brought to the Hoosier Line will never be fully known. Because little more than a year into Bick's term as president, stock control of the Monon again passed to a new group of men. The Monon soon had a new, strong-willed chairman of the board, a man with his own unique vision for a "new" Monon. A man named William C. Coleman. In the decade of the 1960s, the ideals of John Barriger and his men would become passe on the Hoosier Line.

RS-2 29 with northbound local 42 stands on the siding at Linden, Ind., as northbound freight 72 in tow behind F-3A 62A sweeps past on the main line on May 31, 1960. *(J. PARKER LAMB)*

With the great brick bastille—Lafayette Shops—atop the hill and FM H-10-44 No. 18 standing at the yard lead, the northbound *Thoroughbred* accelerates under the exhaust of F-3A's 84A and 83A on May 31, 1960. *(J. PARKER LAMB)*

Switching at Francesville, Ind., C-
420 506 and U23B 602 point train
56 toward Michigan City on July
29, 1971. (ROBERT P. OLMSTED)

6

THE NEW MONON, THE LAST MONON

The Hoosier Line, 1960-1971

IT WAS in August 1960 that William C. Coleman's investment group took working control of the Monon, holding more than 14% of the Hoosier Line's voting securities. Carl Bick remained as the Monon's president, but Coleman took over the chairman's seat from Walter Floersheimer—and as Chairman of the Board, Coleman began his drive toward a "New Monon." And what was the Monon that Coleman inherited? The "old" Monon that he presumed to replace?

At the close of 1959, the Hoosier Line employed 1,635 men and women, operated 58 diesel locomotives, rostered 27 headend and passenger cars (and two business cars), and handled tonnage in 3,163 company-owned freight cars. The Hoosier Line's F-3s and BL-2s and RS-2s, *et al.*, had rolled up 868,914 freight train miles and toted more than six million tons in trains that averaged 56 cars. Monon's traffic was diverse, and 65% originated off-line. Coal remained Monon's single most important commodity, but it now accounted for only 16% of the Hoosier Line's tonnage (and only a third of that coal originated on Monon's I&L branch). Stone was still a distant second in tonnage. Overall, Monon handled an average of 499 loads of freight per day.

Passengers? Monon's varnish spun off 325,149 miles and hauled 74,000 passengers, averaging 39 passengers per train. The Hoosier Line's total operating revenue—freight and passenger—in 1959 was $20.2 million, its net operating income $1.1 million. The numbers seemed acceptable if not reason for rejoicing —unless you recalled that as few as four years earlier,

with little more tonnage, the Monon's net operating income had been more than double that of 1959.

A little Indiana railroad chugs along its friendly way. Year after year, it keeps on going . . . making some progress—making friends—making mistakes, too— just a small railroad that gets there.
—Monon Annual Report, 1963

That was how the "new" Monon's management would come to assess the Hoosier Line's recent history. Obviously a dry-eyed lot, apparently not overwhelmed with, or at least willing to forget, the rather uncommon accomplishments of Barriger and his men little more than a decade before. But to William Coleman and company, the bottom line was suffering. An investment had to be protected; there was a transformation to be done. But the transformation would take time—in 1960 and 1961 the slow decline in profitability that had afflicted the Monon since 1956 turned to red ink. In 1960, Monon posted its first net operating deficit since 1946, and in 1960-1961, the road would lose $2.1 million.

William Coleman's vision for the Hoosier Line centered on two points. First, streamline and rationalize the property, cutting or controlling costs along the way. And second, increase Monon's traffic base. In the first instance, Coleman made immediate progress—in 1960-1961, the Monon closed seven on-line agency stations, restructured the Hoosier Line sales staff, cut overall employment by 62, trimmed freight train miles, and leased rather than purchased new freight equipment (in these two years, Monon leased more than 300 additional freight cars, but purchased only 35 new covered hoppers).

Monon's traffic increases were not so immediate—in fact, by 1961 traffic had declined to 5.7 million tons (versus six million tons in 1959). Average loads handled per day was down to 456 (from the 499 of 1959). But Coleman's plan for improving the traffic base of the Monon—with bituminous coal—was a longer term proposition.

King Coal

It was, perhaps, natural that William Coleman would look to coal as the Monon's savior. Although he came to the Monon as a transit executive, having held vice president positions on the Milwaukee & Suburban Transportation Corp. and Indianapolis Transit System, Coleman had been born in McEwen, Tenn., and had spent 30 years with the coal firms, Koppers Co. and Eastern Gas & Fuel Associates.

The first step by the Monon toward fulfilling Coleman's plan—for a coal-unloading facility on the Ohio River and a Great Lakes dock at Michigan City—came in the spring of 1961, when the Monon applied for a $3.5 million federal-guaranteed loan. The amount was soon increased to $5 million—with roughly $4 million earmarked for construction of the docks. In August 1961, the loan was guaranteed by the Interstate Commerce Commission, and in October the Monon applied to the ICC for permission to build new trackage necessary at Louisville (the barge facility was to be on the south side of the Ohio River, linked to the Monon via the Kentucky & Indiana Terminal) and Michigan City.

Coleman's intent was that the Monon would haul Appalachian coal—transported from West Virginia down the Ohio by barge—north from Louisville to waiting Great Lakes steamers at Michigan City, and to power plants in the Chicago region. But opposition from eastern coal-hauling roads fearful of lost traffic soon appeared at the ICC's door. The Monon would have to fight.

A second, less visible plan of Coleman's to increase Monon's coal tonnage was to revitalize traffic on the I&L branch. In 1960, the Hoosier Line—through subsidiary Chicago & Indianapolis Coal Co.—began leasing land around Clay City, Ind., with the idea of developing new coal sources on the I&L.

On January 1, 1962, Coleman strengthened his control of the Hoosier Line, taking over the presidency from Carl Bick (who retired on December 31, 1961), and retaining his position as chairman of the board. Planning of the coal facilities on the Ohio and Lake Michigan proceeded, but any meaningful progress was stalled while the subject went under consideration by the ICC.

Meanwhile, some progress was made elsewhere. Coleman's Monon was trying to attract new industrial development along its line and completed 56 leases or track agreements to serve on-line firms. A new company-owned warehouse was opened adjacent to McDoel Yard in Bloomington. Monon was starting to capture movements of new autos to the southeast and purchased six trilevel auto racks. Total coal tonnage did increase slightly over the level of previous years (to one million tons carried in 1962 versus 950,000 tons in 1960), but the increase was fueled entirely by loaded

hoppers coming off the L&N and the Southern Railway. Coal tonnage originating on the Monon's own I&L branch actually continued its decline—rapidly—to only 193,000 tons in 1962.

Overall, Monon's business rebounded modestly—back to six million tons carried (the equal of the Hoosier Line's 1959 business). And Coleman's cost control measures, coupled with increased freight rates, put the Hoosier Line back in the black—in 1962 net operating income stood at $1,063,000.

For William Coleman's Hoosier Line, the year 1963 did not begin smoothly. The ICC held hearings on the Monon's proposed barge and dock facilities and its request for a "Certificate of Convenience and Necessity" for the project. The hearings closed on April 19, by which time no fewer than eight railroads—the Illinois Central, Chicago South Shore & South Bend, Chesapeake & Ohio, Norfolk & Western, Baltimore & Ohio, New York Central, Pittsburgh & Lake Erie, and Pennsylvania—had protested. And at virtually the

same time, Coleman faced a proxy challenge from stockholders who did not share his idea of the Monon's future. The stockholders' insurgency failed. In a mid-April vote for seats on the board of directors, Coleman's compatriots handily won by more than 2 to 1.

With improvements in Monon's financial condition continuing in 1963, the "new Monon" for the first time made major equipment purchases. Orders were placed for another six trilevel auto racks, for boxcars, and for covered hoppers. The biggest of the freight car purchases was a $700,000 order for 50 "Big John" covered hoppers numbered in the 44000 series. But the most remarkable order Monon placed in the books in 1963 would be for locomotives.

On October 15, 1963, an ICC hearing examiner issued his report from the April hearings on Monon's proposed coal facilities on the Ohio River and Lake Michigan. The report recommended approval of the Monon's plan. And even before the report was formally issued, Monon—in September 1963—placed its order for the diesels that would lug coal between the Ohio River and Lake Michigan—the burly, 2,750-hp, six-motored Alco C-628s.

At the time Monon ordered its nine C-628s, the six-motor Alco was nothing more than lines on blueprint paper at Alco's Schenectady (N.Y.) plant. The C-628 had been announced by Alco in January 1963, and Monon's order was the second taken for the model,

behind only the Atlantic Coast Line. The first C-628 off Alco's production line—a unit for the Atlantic Coast Line—would debut on January 17, 1964.

Monon's nine C-628s were scheduled for delivery in February and March 1964. The specifications of Monon's C-628 order would equip the big Alcos ideally for unit train service: Dual controls would negate any need to turn the units, 4,000-gallon fuel tanks would allow the beasts three round trips over the length of the Hoosier Line without refueling. At 399,950 pounds, the Alcos would weigh in at more than 1½ times the weight of any previous Monon diesel, and would exert 80,000 pounds of tractive effort (the equal of a booster-equipped Hoosier Line J-4 2-8-2).

Troubled Plans for Expansion

In January 1964, William Coleman made another move—a major one. Monon, quietly until it hit the trade press, acquired 20% of the stock of the Chicago South Shore & South Bend Railroad. The move was cloaked at first as merely an "investment" for the Monon, but discussions of joint operations—and the addition of the South Shore to the map of the Hoosier Line in Monon's 1963 Annual Report—left limited doubt about the long-term goals of Coleman.

At first glance, the CSS&SB seemed a peculiar addition to the Monon. After all, the 90-mile South Shore was the last of America's major interurban lines and was saddled with electric passenger service from Chicago to its end point at South Bend, Ind. But for Coleman's plans to entrench Monon around the base of Lake Michigan, the CSS&SB was a prime acquisition. Not the least important attribute of the South Shore was that it served Indiana's Burns Ditch lakefront, where various steelmakers were expected to expand mill operations. And it should be recalled that among the protesters of Monon's coal dock plans was the South Shore.

With appeals to the hearing examiner's approval of Monon's plan due to be filed with the ICC in early 1964, it made sense to bring CSS&SB into the Monon family, thus removing the railroad that perhaps had the most to lose by Monon's expansion in Michigan City. Unfortunately for the Monon, the CSS&SB proved a hostile merger partner.

The South Shore did want a merger partner—but a different one. In its 1963 Annual Report, South Shore

had gone so far as to show with maps how it would fit into three major eastern roads. CSS&SB wanted a large mate—a partner more secure than it viewed the Monon. In March 1964, South Shore refused a bid from the Hoosier Line to seat a Monon director on its board, and in June, South Shore filed in U.S. district court for a restraining order to prevent Monon from adding to its holdings until the ICC could rule on the legality of Monon's stock purchases. South Shore suggested that in addition to Monon's 20% ownership, parties "friendly" to the Hoosier Line held another 20%. Legal maneuvering continued through the summer of 1964, as the ICC refused to intervene.

Meanwhile, at the likes of Lafayette and Mitchell and New Albany, the more immediate business of moving tonnage (and passengers) was carried on. The Alco C-628s (Nos. 400-408) arrived in March 1964 and were put to work on Monon's mainline freights. Coal originated on the I&L was still in general decline (to 144,000 tons in 1964), while coal from off-line increased modestly (to 977,000 tons). The combined coal figures represented 17.4% of the Hoosier Line's tonnage. Long strings of loaded trilevel auto carriers became common sights behind Monon's C-628s, as the Hoosier Line

forwarded 184,650 tons of motor vehicles—and earned revenues of $1.2 million doing so. Total freight tonnage totaled 6.4 million tons—Monon's best showing since 1957.

The passenger story was far different: Since 1960 (the first full year the *Thoroughbred* was Monon's lone varnish), revenues from Nos. 5/6 had dropped from $743,000 to $655,000, the number of passengers carried from 57,000 to 43,000, the count of passengers per train from 40 to 29. Late in 1964, Monon made a cost-cutting move, revising the *Thoroughbred's* schedule to one that could be accommodated with a single consist. Train 6 departed Louisville at 6:30 a.m. and arrived Chicago at 1:05 p.m.; then train 5 departed Chicago at 5:25 p.m., and arrived Louisville at 2:10 a.m. Since the Hoosier Line by this time carried few passengers south of Bloomington, the uncomfortable hours of departure and arrival at Louisville mattered little.

In an unusual move, considering the general decline of the *Thoroughbred*, in 1964 Monon announced it would consider revival of its Chicago–Indianapolis passenger service—if it could obtain mail and express business, and if the ICC would agree to consider the

A trio of RS-2's—27, 21 and 24—slowly propel a Monon transfer run from South Hammond to Clearing Yard (Belt Railway of Chicago) through Pullman Junction at 95th Street, Chicago, on March 9, 1963. F's or BL-2's were more common on this run, which operated via the Chicago & Western Indiana, and it was also a haunt for the big Alco Century 628's. (JIM WOZNICZKA)

service experimental. The idea had been promoted to the Monon as early as March 1962 by the Indianapolis Chamber of Commerce, but after 1964 it was left to die quietly.

End of the Dreams

It was but a month into 1965 that William Coleman's dreams for the Monon began to turn into a nightmare. On January 28, 1965, the ICC ruled on Monon's proposed water-to-rail-to-water shipments of coal, and in a 6-to-5 decision, turned thumbs down on the Hoosier Line. The ICC's decision indicated that "public convenience and necessity" had not been shown and indicated that competitive service over all-rail routes was readily available.

The decision was a controversial one. In fact, one ICC commissioner, Virginia Mae Brown (the first woman member of the ICC), issued a stinging rebuttal to the six members who voted down the Monon proposal. Also among the votes *for* the Monon proposal was that of ICC Chairman Charles A. Webb. The following March, the Monon would issue a request for reconsideration of the ICC's decision, but the Monon's

plan for coal facilities on the Ohio River and Lake Michigan was forever dead.

In March, matters worsened: Chesapeake & Ohio Railway proclaimed itself a major stockholder of the South Shore, and applied to the ICC for control of the railroad. Having found the large parent it had envisioned, the South Shore board immediately backed C&O's proposal. Yet another battle awaited the Monon.

With word out that C&O owned 30% of South Shore's stock—and with C&O offering $42.50 per share to buy more—Monon reacted by calling for an investigation of C&O's purchases. Monon noted to ICC Chairman Webb that Chessie was being allowed to buy stock while the Hoosier Line was barred from further purchases by legal action brought by the South Shore. By April, the whole CSS&SB stock matter—and the purchases of both Monon and C&O—was under investigation by the ICC. Stock buying by both roads had stopped, and it appeared that, in reality, Monon owned approximately 60,000 shares—and C&O owned 154,000. In May, to counter C&O's request for control of the South Shore, Monon issued its own petition to the ICC requesting control of the CSS&SB.

A touch of snow is pasted to the pilot of F-3A 203 (ex-82A) as it stands at Bedford depot with the southbound *Thoroughbred* on March 29, 1964. When the new *Thoroughbred* schedule would take effect later in the year, it would no longer be possible to photograph No. 5 here in daylight. *(J. DAVID INGLES, COLLECTION OF LOUIS A. MARRE)*

As the South Shore matter stood before the ICC, all parties positioned themselves. South Shore President W.P. Coliton embraced C&O control. "Being a part of a strong system like C&O-B&O [Baltimore & Ohio, also under control of the C&O] is our only solution," said Coliton.

Monon management stressed its own needs: "Monon is in need of additional traffic and such traffic would be made available if, through control of the South Shore, it were enabled to improve its access to the industries along the southern end of Lake Michigan." The Hoosier Line also noted that it stood to lose traffic and revenue (as much as $1.8 million) from Louisville & Nashville's impending purchase of the Chicago & Eastern Illinois' Evansville-Chicago line. Alluding to the South Shore's electrified commuter operation, Coleman went so far as to point out that "certain of the executives and directors of the Monon have had long and successful experience in operating transit systems." South Shore, at least, was unimpressed with Monon's arguments—by the end of May 1965,

CSS&SB had asked the ICC to reject Monon's bid for control.

In the end, a truce was called between Monon and C&O, and an agreement reached. The Hoosier Line, no doubt, realized the odds were firmly against it. Not only was it battling a railroad many times its size, but also a truly hostile South Shore.

By year end 1965, Monon had agreed to withdraw its bid for control of the South Shore in exchange for trackage rights on the CSS&SB into Burns Harbor and between Michigan City and the Illinois-Indiana state line (pending C&O control). Monon also agreed to sell Chessie its 60,000 shares of stock if and when the ICC approved C&O control of the South Shore. The C&O did take control of the CSS&SB in 1967 and

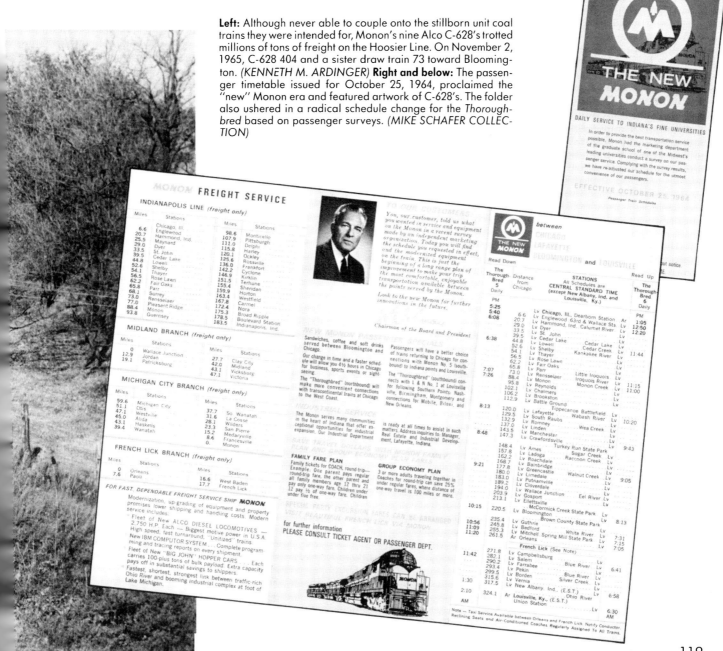

Left: Although never able to couple onto the stillborn unit coal trains they were intended for, Monon's nine Alco C-628's trotted millions of tons of freight on the Hoosier Line. On November 2, 1965, C-628 404 and a sister draw train 73 toward Bloomington. *(KENNETH M. ARDINGER)* **Right and below:** The passenger timetable issued for October 25, 1964, proclaimed the "new" Monon era and featured artwork of C-628's. The folder also ushered in a radical schedule change for the *Thoroughbred* based on passenger surveys. *(MIKE SCHAFER COLLECTION)*

Monon sold its stock to Chessie, but Monon's trackage rights on the railroad were never significantly employed.

One final sting awaited Monon in 1965: On December 31, Railway Post Office service was discontinued on train 5/6. Given that two-thirds of the *Thoroughbred's* operating revenues were generated by RPO and bulk mail, the train could ill afford the loss.

At the end of 1965, the mood at Monon's headquarters in Chicago's McCormick Building could understandably have been dour. But there was reason to rejoice as well: For while the Monon had suffered setbacks in its quest for expansion, its day-to-day operations, its C-628s and RS-2s, its engineers and station agents and signal maintainers, had melded to turn an operating income of $2.3 million. The Hoosier Line was again comfortably in the black.

Toward Transition

Following the turmoil of 1965, the Monon moved toward transition. Thoughts of expansion, and takeover bids, would soon change to thoughts of the Monon itself finding a larger merger partner. Leadership would soon change. But in the interim would be a year of refinement—and pleasing profits: 1966.

With the arrival of the Alco C-628s back in 1964, Monon had begun storing, and eventually retiring, a number of its Barriger-era freight-service F-3s. But aside from that—and Lafayette Shops' 1960-1961 repowerings of the Monon's three Fairbanks-Morse diesels with EMD power plants—little else had changed in Monon's motive power pool.

However, starting in 1965 and extending into 1966, Monon undertook a program to upgrade its Alco RS-2s. Popular with enginemen (except perhaps for their tendency to bounce when running long-hood first), the RS-2s were yeomen creatures able to serve

virtually any duty the Monon required. But, by 1965, the diesels were all over 15 years old—average lifespan for a diesel by first-generation standards.

Rather than look to replacements, the Monon rebuilt the RS-2s. The upgrading included new Alco 244-series V-16 engines rated at 1,600 hp, standardization with General Electric 752E6 traction motors, addition of roller bearings to units not already so equipped, general standardization of components, and renumbering—from Nos. 21-29 to 51-59. With the rebuilding, the veteran Alcos would serve for the remainder of the Hoosier Line's existence.

Aside from the RS-2 rebuilds, there was greater need for new road power on the Monon. The remaining F-3s had accumulated heavy mileage figures and the EMD BL-2s (really little more than F-3s with semi-road-switcher carbodies) were likewise growing expensive to operate and maintain. Monon's response was an order to Alco Products—in May 1966—for six C-420s. Funds from the loan Monon had obtained in the early '60s for building its now-dead coal facilities were used to purchase the diesels.

Four-axled, 2,000-hp, equipped with turbocharged Alco 251-series V-12s, 59 feet, 9 inches long—the Alco C-420 was very much a modern-day RS-2, and thus seemed ideally suited to the Monon. A pair of the C-420s was ordered with steam generators (and thus required high front hoods) for use on the *Thoroughbred*. Patronage on train 5/6 was actually improving slightly in 1966 and Monon expected that any train-off petitions it might make on the *Thoroughbred* would be met with an ICC decision to continue operations north of Bloomington. And at any rate, if the *Thoroughbred* did come off in future years, the hi-nosed C-420s would be easily transferred into full-time freight service.

The half-dozen C-420s (Nos. 501-506) arrived in August 1966—and it was perfect timing. The Hoosier

Under a funnel of black exhaust fully befitting a CI&L J-4 Mikado, C-628 403 carries green flags as she and a sister depart McDoel Yard, Bloomington, southbound on Halloween 1965. Dual-control 628's often ran long-hood first. (KENNETH M. ARDINGER)

Above: Despite the differences in carbodies, the same sounds are pouring from F-3A 208 (ex-84B) and EMD-re-engined FM H-15-44 No. 46 as they work together at South Hammond on July 13, 1965. *(J. DAVID INGLES, COLLECTION OF LOUIS A. MARRE)* **Right:** Reborn at Lafayette in January 1966 with an Alco-supplied 244-series 1600-horsepower power plant, RS-2 58 (ex-28) stands for its portrait beside the red brick shops. All nine of Monon's RS-2's were rebuilt at Lafayette in 1965-66. *(DAVE FERGUSON'S PHOTO ART)*

Line's freight traffic was heavy, and the new C-420s were needed to assist their bigger C-628 sisters. By the end of 1966, Monon had moved 6.6 million tons of freight, the road's best year since 1956. Both freight originating on the Monon and bridge traffic improved, this despite a decrease in coal tonnage. Movement of new autos south reached an all-time peak at 251,039 tons. Compared to 1965, total freight train mileage increased by 14,096 miles, average freight train load by 181 tons. Average revenue loads handled per day reached 464. It all translated to $21.1 million in operating revenue—and $2.8 million in net operating income.

"We will devote special and professional attention to the potentials and implications of railroad merg-

ers."　　Monon President and Chairman Samuel T. Brown's message to stockholders, March 15, 1967

Early in 1967, William Coleman decided to resign as president and chairman of the Monon. His resignation became effective on February 20, 1967, and on that same day Samuel T. Brown was elected to both positions. Although William Coleman would remain on Monon's Board of Directors and Executive Committee through 1968, his era on the Hoosier Line was over.

Samuel Brown, a native of Roanoke, Va., had come to the Monon's Board of Directors in 1956, at a time when he was president of Virginia Iron, Coal & Coke Co., and he had been a member of the road's Executive Committee throughout the Coleman era. Now, it fell to

121

Delivery of Monon's second order of Alco C-420's (Nos. 507-518) in 1967 sounded the death knell for C-628's on the Hoosier Line. On August 20, 1967, C-628 407 (**right**) was moving dead on the Erie Lackawanna through Huntington, Ind., bound back to Alco. Six days later, on August 26, brand-new C-420 514 (**above**) was at Binghamton, N.Y., en route from Alco to the Monon. The C-628 and its sisters would be resold to Lehigh Valley and eventually serve Conrail. (C-628 PHOTO, LOUIS A. MARRE; C-420 KEN DOUGLAS, COLLECTION OF LOUIS A. MARRE)

Brown to take Monon to its finale. Brown's long-term goal for the Hoosier Line was merger—but he also considered proper operating practices, cost control, and maintenance of property vital.

Quickly, under Samuel Brown's hand, Monon made two important moves. On March 27, 1967, the Hoosier Line filed for the discontinuance of its *Thoroughbred* effective May 8. The ICC opened its investigation of the Monon's petition on April 25 and hearings were subsequently held at Chicago, Rensselaer, Lafayette, Crawfordsville, Greencastle, Bloomington and Louisville. In the investigation, Monon showed that it had lost $174,000 on the train in 1965, $321,000 in 1966, and $107,506 in the first four months of 1967. Loss of the RPO at the end of 1965 had cost the Monon approximately $140,000 in annual mail revenue. The average number of passengers using train No. 5 in

1966-1967 was 64. Train No. 6 averaged 66 passengers. Of all the *Thoroughbred's* intermediate stations, only Bloomington and Lafayette averaged more than 10 patrons for the *Thoroughbred* per train. Passenger counts south of Bloomington represented about a third of those on the north end.

The ICC considered—as the Monon feared—requiring continuation of the *Thoroughbred* between Chicago and Bloomington, and also considered requiring three-day-per-week (Friday-Saturday-Sunday) service. But in the end, the ICC concluded that the burden of the *Thoroughbred's* loss was too great for a road the size of the Hoosier Line, and on August 20, 1967, gave its permission for the discontinuance of Monon's last passenger train.

The Monon agreed to operate the *Thoroughbred* through the end of September in a gesture to accom-

In August 1966, Monon received its first half-dozen Alco C-420's (501-506). Among them, a pair—Nos. 501 and 502—were equipped with steam generators (and thus wore high noses) for use on the *Thoroughbred*. On April 30, 1967, No. 502 brings the *Thoroughbred* north through the rain-soaked streets of Bedford. *(WILLIAM H. HUSA JR.)*

Thoroughbred finis: On September 30, 1967, Monon's last scheduled passenger train, No. 6, the northbound *Thoroughbred*, approaches Pullman Junction on Chicago's south side. Within a half hour, when No. 6 ends its journey at Dearborn Station, Monon's passenger era will be at its end. This final *Thoroughbred* departed Louisville behind high-nosed C-420 502, but was swapped with backward-running C-420 510 at Shops Yard where last No. 6 met a southbound football special (itself powered by C-420's 517 and 501) which needed the 502. *(JIM WOZNICZKA)*

Top: With the demise of scheduled passenger service, Monon's high-nosed C-420's spent the majority of their time in general freight use. On February 22, 1968, the pair worked train 56 north on the Michigan City line at Haskells, Ind. *(ROBERT P. OLMSTED)* **Above:** Bound for Louisville with train 73 in July 1971, U23B 606 and kindred sweep past limestone scrap used to reinforce right-of-way embankment near Diamond, Ind. Appropriately, the scene is on the portion of the Monon built as the Indiana Stone Railroad. *(GARY W. DOLZALL)*

modate returning college students. But on September 29, train 5 made its last southbound journey, and on the following day—September 30, 1967—train 6 made its last run. The Monon had said farewell to its *Thoroughbred.*

The second of Monon's moves under Samuel Brown concerned motive power. In June 1967, the Hoosier Line placed an order with Alco for a dozen C-420s. It was for this order that Monon's three-year-old C-628s would serve as trade-ins. With Monon's plan for hauling coal from river to lake now dead, there seemed little reason to retain the massive, heavy C-628s (only Norfolk & Western owned C-628s that were heavier than Monon's). The Alco C-420 was far better suited to the Hoosier Line, being able to serve in any duty from yard switcher on up, and the C-628s had actually proved rather troublesome creatures. Early on, piston and turbocharger failures had been epidemic on the C-628s (not only on Monon, but all roads) and, in fact, Lafayette Shops played a major role in developing steel-capped pistons that solved the C-628's power plant problems.

By late summer, the fallen C-628s—grimy, forlorn, stripped of headlights—moved dead to the north end of the Monon where they were sent east on the Erie-Lackawanna, bound back to Schenectady, N.Y. There they would be rebuilt and resold by Alco to the Lehigh Valley. Meanwhile, in the summer of 1967, Alco built Monon's 12 new C-420s, and in August the units (Nos. 507-518) went to work on the Hoosier Line.

When Samuel Brown's first year as president and chairman of the Monon concluded, the Hoosier Line showed well, if not up to the standards of 1966. Tonnage hit 6.3 million tons, total operating revenue $19.8 million, net operating income $1.5 million. The Hoosier

Line was ever more becoming a bridge carrier and deliverer of goods: In 1967, 69% of Monon's total tonnage originated off-line.

Signs of Merger

During the first months of 1967 following Samuel Brown's rise to the top of the Monon, the matter of merger had received limited *public* attention. But the matter was being actively pursued. For the Monon there were two prime merger prospects—its major Louisville connections, the Louisville & Nashville and the Southern Railway. On paper at least, the Southern seemed a likely candidate. L&N was at the time finalizing its entry into Chicago via purchase of Chicago & Eastern Illinois' Evansville–Chicago route (while the remainder of the C&EI was headed toward merger into Missouri Pacific*). Southern, on the other hand, had made no inroads north, and Brown approached the Southern first regarding merger. But the Southern, then under the stewardship of W. Graham Claytor, Jr., chose to remain in its traditional territory and not risk offending its friendly northern connections by venturing to Chicago via the Monon. That left the Louisville & Nashville.

Even though L&N was close to a Chicago entry via the C&EI, the Hoosier Line did offer it advantages. The Monon could provide L&N direct access to Chicago from Louisville itself, and from L&N's coal lines in eastern Kentucky and Tennessee. Bringing Monon into the L&N fold would also protect the Louisville & Nashville from any last-minute attempts by Monon to block its purchase of the C&EI's line. And, L&N's

*Actually, the C&EI main line north from Woodland Junction, Ill., to Dolton, Ill. (Chicago), would be shared by L&N and MoPac.

Above: In May 1970, new U23B 606 and a trio of C-420's burrow under the Indiana highway 37 bridge at Harrodsburg with train 72. Portrait is a latter-day view of the Hoosier Line at one of several locations made famous by J. F. Bennett's photography (see also page 64). **Below:** The White River valley at Gosport is filled with the throaty exhaust of Alcos as C-420 516 and sisters grind southbound with train 73 in July 1971. (BOTH PHOTOS, GARY W. DOLZALL)

During Monon's final month—July 1971—Alco and General Electric diesels head a northbound freight slapping over the diamond of the old Indianapolis & Vincennes line of the Pennsylvania Railroad (Penn Central at the time of this photo) at Gosport Junction. Had James Brooks' plans of 1852 been fulfilled, this location would instead have been the junction of the New Albany & Salem's branch to Indianapolis. (GARY W. DOLZALL)

merger with the Monon would effectively block Southern from direct access to Chicago from Louisville, should Southern change its mind about venturing north.

By the early months of 1968, Monon and Louisville & Nashville executives were near agreement on merger terms, and then, in April 1968, it became public, as Monon and Louisville & Nashville directors agreed in principle on merger. On August 28, 1968, shareholders of the Hoosier Line and L&N were asked to vote on the matter. Each Monon shareholder would receive a one-for-one exchange of new L&N $35 par value preferred stock for each share of Monon common stock held. The L&N preferred stock would be convertible at any time following merger to L&N common on a basis of three preferred shares for one common share. Samuel Brown put his muscle behind merger: "We believe that the competitive position of the Monon is such that it is necessary to affiliate with a large railroad such as the L&N. . . ." The shareholders approved (98% voted in favor of merger), and Monon and L&N jointly applied to the ICC for merger of the 541-mile Monon into the 5,800-mile L&N. The ICC convened merger hearings on April 3, 1969.

Considering the difficulty of moving a merger proposal through the ICC of the 1960s, the L&N-Monon marriage went smoothly—and relatively quickly. The major hurdle was put in place by the Milwaukee Road, which as protection asked for trackage rights over the Hoosier Line from Bedford to Louisville. Together with Milwaukee's Chicago-Terre Haute-Bedford line, these trackage rights would allow Milwaukee to compete for Louisville–Chicago business—and connect with the Southern Railway.

Southern backed Milwaukee's proposal, then, in May 1969, went one step further. Southern stated that if the L&N canceled its merger plans with Monon due to

Milwaukee's conditions (or any other reason), it stood ready to make an offer for the Hoosier Line. President Graham Claytor admitted that Southern had "reassessed" its position on the Monon. But Southern's too-little, too-late rhetoric had little effect on the merger. L&N retained its interest in Monon and fought the Milwaukee trackage rights provision (eventually all the way to the U.S. Supreme Court) before begrudgingly accepting the terms.

As Samuel Brown's management moved the Hoosier Line toward merger, it could not dismiss the requirements of operating the Monon. Indeed, the Monon in its final years maintained its right-of-way in good condition, made several large equipment purchases, and moved substantial tonnage. In 1968, 1969 and 1970, Monon hauled 6.9 million tons, 7.2 million tons and 7 million tons, respectively. Coal traffic was again on the increase, with movements totaling over one million tons each year. Virtually all was carried in L&N hoppers, though, because Monon's I&L branch production had dropped as low as 86,000 tons (in 1969). Operating revenues remained above $20 million per year (and peaked in 1970 at $23.4 million); net operating income concluded at $1.1 million in 1970.

The company's final notable equipment purchases came in 1969. The Hoosier Line purchased 100 new boxcars and 100 new covered hoppers (and rebuilt 100 gondolas and 200 boxcars). And in June 1969, Monon ordered its final locomotives—eight U23Bs from General Electric. The GEs—2,250-hp, four-axle units powered by turbocharged 12-cylinder engines—were comparable to Monon's C-420s in size, performance and ability. More C-420s were, unfortunately, out of the question, because in 1969 Alco was ending locomotive production. The U23Bs (Nos. 601-608) arrived on the Monon in April 1970 and went to work in general service.

Finale: Five miles south of Monon, Ind., on July 30, 1971, U23B 602 and C-420 506 draw train 57 from Michigan City toward Lafayette. The following day, the railroad would become a division of the Louisville & Nashville. *(ROBERT P. OLMSTED)* **Right:** The face of second-generation Alco diesels came to symbolize the Monon in its final years. *(GARY W. DOLZALL)*

The Finale

It was on January 23, 1970, that Samuel Brown received the news that he and his stockholders so wanted. ICC Examiner James E. Hopkins issued his report favoring the Monon-L&N merger. "The competitive situation from the southeast will not be substantially changed," Hopkins wrote of the merger.

Included in the ICC's condition was Milwaukee Road's requested trackage rights, and an option for Milwaukee Road to purchase Monon's share of the Kentucky & Indiana Terminal. On September 18, 1970, the full ICC approved the Monon-L&N merger, retaining Milwaukee Road's conditions (over the further protests of Monon and L&N) and discounting a protest from Penn Central that it would lose traffic to the combined Monon-L&N. On February 10, 1971, the ICC reaffirmed its findings over final arguments.

The merger was on, the date was set for July 31, 1971. On that date, 124 years to the day after the New Albany & Salem had been proclaimed as organized by Indiana Governor James Whitcomb, the Monon passed to history.

Wooden doors and red bricks frame F-3A 63 as it stands at Lafayette Shops on May 16, 1948. *(JOHN F. HUMISTON)*

7

THEY CALLED IT SHOPS

The Heart of the Hoosier Line:
Lafayette Shops

IT WAS more than a century ago—in the spring of 1882—that talk first began of a new shop for the Louisville, New Albany & Chicago. The railroad was simply outgrowing the diminutive New Albany shops that had been founded by the New Albany & Salem. Lafayette, 118 miles southeast of Chicago, in Tippecanoe County, Ind., snuggled along the Wabash River, was a popularly proposed site, and reports indicated that the city would grant the LNA&C 30 acres of land and $25,000 in cash for the privilege of being home to the railroad's new main shop.

But in the following months, rumors swirled. Before the end of 1882, Jeffersonville (an unlikely off-line location), Lafayette and Monon had all been "confirmed" in the railroad trade press as the future home of the Hoosier Line's new shops. As for Lafayette, there were reports that the LNA&C was negotiating for purchase of the buildings of the Lafayette Car Works. By 1883, the competition narrowed, to Lafayette or Monon, and both cities were reported to be offering handsome subsidies to the LNA&C. Then, all talk of a new shop suddenly fell quiet—and remained so for just short of a decade.

The idea of a new LNA&C shop was reborn at the start of the 1890s, and—in 1892—the voters of Fairfield Township, Tippecanoe County, voted to donate $100,000 and 45 acres of land to the LNA&C for construction of a new shop. Lafayette had won. LNA&C's legendary general manager, W.H. McDoel, rejoiced in the selection: "This new location for the shops will be of great advantage to the company, as it is practically the center of the system and will enable us to do more

work at less expense than we can with the present facility."

For construction of the new shops, a new company —wholly owned by the LNA&C—was created. It was the Lafayette & Monon Railway Co. The building of Lafayette Shops started in 1894, and in October 1895 the Hoosier Line began use of its new facility. When the edifice was fully completed and equipped in 1896, it had cost $398,852.

The Hoosier Line's new shops stood on a hilly perch, red brick buildings capped with stone trimmings, overlooking the main line north of the city of Lafayette. When the shops opened there were two main structures. One building held a 210-foot-long machine shop and 90-foot boiler shop, with adjoining blacksmith shop, engine and dyno room, and boiler room. The second building was a car shop—95 x 300 feet in size. The buildings rested on either side of a 70-foot transfer table, which was powered by two General Electric streetcar motors. Smaller buildings held a paint shop, oil house, storeroom, and offices. A 20-stall roundhouse, with 70-foot turntable, and a coal chute were built nearby.

In the years that followed Lafayette Shops' opening, the Hoosier Line would with regularity improve its great bastille. Between 1919 and 1921, a new car shop was built; in 1927, a major addition—brick and glass in form, complete with 200-ton overhead crane—was melded to the old locomotive shop. But it was not only the lathes and forges and presses of Lafayette Shops that would prove worthy, but its men. Time and time again, the men of "Shops" would be called upon to perform an uncommon task—and succeed.

In the years 1921-1926, Lafayette Shops took the tired hulks of two 4-4-0s, a dozen 4-8-0s, and five 4-6-0s and rebuilt them with such fervor that "CIL Shops" could be cast upon new builder plates. In the case of the 4-4-0s and Ten-Wheelers (the latter built as early as 1890), the job was one of taking dismantled remains and rebuilding them into living, steaming, useful locomotives.* Throughout the steam era, Lafayette tended to the heavy, dirty, necessary jobs demanded by the iron horse: fitting new tires, replacing flues, reboring cylinders. And the shops modernized its steam flock—adding superheaters and mechanical stokers and power reverse gear to aged veterans. To Monon's biggest and best 2-8-2s—J-4s 570-579—Lafayette Shops added Franklin trailing truck boosters (only No. 570 had been so equipped by its builder) and roller bearings.

It was in the Barriger era, of course, that Lafayette made the transition from caretaker of steam locomotives to keeper of diesels. And the transition cost the

Monon $200,000. Ceremoniously opened at 10:00 a.m. on March 23, 1948, a new Lafayette diesel shop occupied the west end of the aged, locomotive shop. Heavy repairs would still take place in the east end, but the 170x65-foot, three-level diesel shop meant the learning of new skills for its men—and destruction for Lafayette's grand old roundhouse.

The most cherished accomplishments of Lafayette's locomotive and car shops are documented: the rebuilt ex-Army streamlined passenger cars of 1947-1948; the "bay-window cupola" cabooses built new in 1956-1957; the repowered Fairbanks-Morse diesels in 1960-1961; the veteran Alco RS-2s rebuilt in 1965-1966. And there were more, less noted examples of Lafayette's skills: Pullman tourist cars turned to baggage cars in the late 1940s; 69 aged hopper cars rebuilt in 1949; flatcars transformed for Monon's new piggyback service in the mid-1950s; scores of boxcars and gons rebuilt anew in the 1960s.

And, always, there was the nearly unnoticed, yet most important of Shops' toil, keeping a fleet of diesels and boxcars and hoppers and coaches rolling. To measure that contribution, consider the role of Lafayette Shops in the Barriger era, when, massive new car purchases notwithstanding, Monon's freight

*The 19 locomotives rebuilt in the 1921-1926 rebuilding program were: 4-4-0s 80-81 (ex-111-112) rebuilt in 1924; 4-8-0s 220-231 (ex-200-211) rebuilt during 1923-1926; and 4-6-0s 107-111 (ex-88-90, 120-121) rebuilt during 1921-1923.

Right: Mikado 522 rests sans drivers and with her smokebox door opened in the cathedral-like locomotive shop at Lafayette on June 30, 1946. Retirement for the 2-8-2 would come a year later. **Middle right:** Venerable Monon 4-8-0 229, born in 1900 (as 209) and rebuilt at Shops in 1923, stands in Lafayette roundhouse, also on June 30, 1946. The 4-8-0 would share honors with 0-6-0 95 as the last Monon steam locomotive officially retired—on September 14, 1949. (BOTH PHOTOS, MALCOLM D. McCARTER)

equipment begged attention. In 1947, Lafayette turned heavy repairs on 222 freight cars; in 1948, 381 more; in 1950, "Shops" and its men ran 467 cars through the old brick car shop for heavy repairs.

Glamorous or no, uncommon or ever so common, Lafayette Shops did the job of keeping the Hoosier Line whole.

Left: Aerial view of Shops during the diesel era reveals the heart of the Hoosier Line. At far right is the 500-ton concrete coal tipple built in 1927. Nearby, the turntable remains, but the roundhouse is already demolished. The locomotive shop is prominent in this view (left of brick chimney stacks); peaked-roof building to the left is the old car shop, with larger, newer car shop to extreme left. **Above:** Symbolic of the countless freight-car rebuildings and repairs that Shops accomplished through the years is a string of 10100-series boxcars rebuilt at Lafayette in 1969 with roof hatches for grain-hauling. (BOTH PHOTOS, FRANK VAN BREE COLLECTION)

Photographed in the twilight of the steam era, the Lafayette machine shop—housed in the locomotive shop building—reflects the standards established by Monon craftsmen. Visible in the shops are a variety of lathes, boring mills, presses and bending rolls. Awaiting installation are tender wheels and locomotive siderods. Neatly stacked at the rear are new locomotive driving wheels. (*DAVE FERGUSON'S PHOTO ART*)

After its final class III shopping, K-5A 4-6-2 No. 444 rides the turntable at Lafayette on April 12, 1946. (*DAVID W. CHAMBERS, COLLECTION OF RICHARD J. COOK*)

Below: At Lafayette Shops in 1947, one of Monon's dining-bar-lounge cars is created from an ex-Army hospital car. Interior appointments, windows and Hoosier Line red and gray paint are yet to be applied by Shops workmen. **Bottom:** First baggage-mail car (No. 11) and first coach (No. 21) to be completed in Lafayette Shops' Barriger-era rebuilding program stand proudly at the complex after their completion in the summer of '47. *(BOTH PHOTOS, DAVE FERGUSON'S PHOTO ART)*

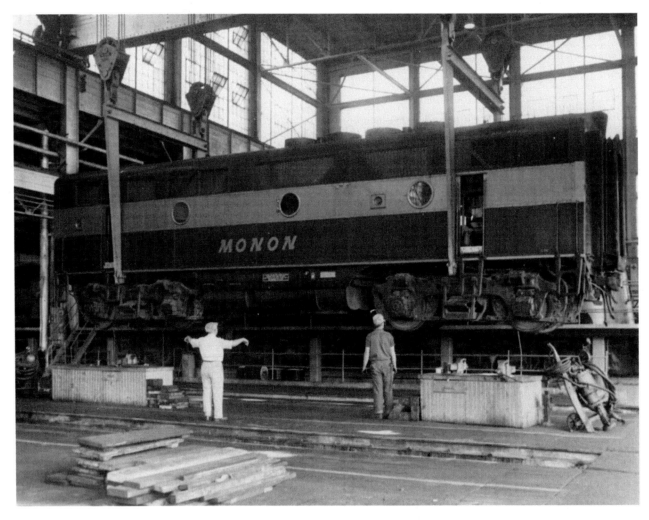

Workmen oversee the lifting of F-3B 63C by the locomotive shop's 200-ton overhead traveling crane. Multiple-level platforms of the diesel shop are visible behind the airborn unit. *(DAVE FERGUSON'S PHOTO ART)*

"Bay window cupola" was the moniker Monon gave the eight 81525-series cabooses Lafayette's workmen constructed in 1956-57. *(DAVE FERGUSON'S PHOTO ART)*

Facing page: Lafayette masterwork: An Electro-Motive 567-series V-16 power plant stands atop the frame of one of Monon's FM H-15-44's, replacing the unit's original opposed-piston FM engine. DATE: May 31, 1960. *(J. PARKER LAMB)*

F-3's in freight and passenger colors and a single RS-2 occupy the locomotive shop at Lafayette in 1960. Overhead crane is visible at the far end of the shop. (J. PARKER LAMB)

The days of workmen applying red-and-gray passenger colors to Monon F-3's were numbered as a veteran shopman touched up the lettering of F-3 82 on May 31, 1960. (J. PARKER LAMB)

The siding south of Harrodsburg is empty as train 6, the northbound *Thorough-bred*, glides toward Bloomington. A cook in the kitchen section of the dining-parlor-observation car on the rear is leaning out for some fresh air. *(J. F. BEN-NETT, JIM BENNETT COLLECTION)*

8

RED-AND-GRAY THROUGH THE HOOSIER STATE

A Recollection of Monon Passenger Trains, 1946-1967

THE TRAINS, the dreams, the failures of Monon's postwar romance with the passenger train already have been documented in this book's pages. But in this chapter we invite you to join in a closer look at the special nature of Hoosier Line varnish, of trains named *Hoosier, Tippecanoe, Thoroughbred, et al.* We invite you to recall heavyweight, Pullman green trains tugged by aging Pacifics in their final days; to remember newborn red-and-gray streamliners headed by EMD F-3s; to witness aging coaches repainted black and gold rolling behind Fs and RS-2s and, finally, Alco C-420s.

The Monon trains born of the Barriger era changed faces through the years. Colors changed, of course, and so did motive power. But changed as well was the makeup of the trains, the consists that were spliced together in coach yards at Chicago and Indianapolis and Louisville. What follows is a brief summation of each train's history and the equipment assigned* the trains in the years 1946-1967.

Train 1/2: The *Varsity,* as described in Chapter 4, was a short-lived train that ran from Bloomington to Chicago on Friday evenings only and from Chicago to Bloomington on Sundays. Its purpose was to serve the weekend travels of college students—at Purdue University (Lafayette), Wabash College (Crawfordsville),

DePauw University (Greencastle), and Indiana University (Bloomington). Thus, train 1/2 operated only during school sessions. It was equipped with coaches and a grill-coach. The *Varsity* was inaugurated on January 6, 1950, was discontinued in June 1950, then made a curious, but brief, return in the spring of 1953.

Train 3/4: Traditionally Monon's Chicago–Louisville night train, it had been shifted to a morning operation at the end of 1945. Barriger reestablished train 3/4 on an overnight scheduled on September 29, 1946, and the nocturnal train took the name *Night Express.* It carried heavyweight coaches and Pullman sleepers, with through cars to and from French Lick operating on trains 23/24 (see below). Rechristened the *Bluegrass* on February 15, 1948, the train soon carried red-and-gray painted heavyweight sleepers and ex-Army rebuilt coaches. But it never found enough passengers to fill its coach seats or sleeper berths, and on September 24, 1949, it was discontinued.

Train 5/6: Monon's venerable day train 5/6 between Chicago–Louisville had been killed in 1945. But the train—and train numbers—were brought back to life by Barriger when he returned train 3/4 to night operation. The new Nos. 5/6 began with morning departures from Chicago and Louisville. Given the name *Day Express* while still equipped with old heavyweights (coaches and a lounge car, plus a diner operating between Chicago and Bainbridge), train 5/6 was renamed *Thoroughbred* on February 15, 1948. At the same time, train 5/6 was given an altered schedule, with early afternoon departures from Chicago and

*On virtually all railroads, Monon included, passenger train equipment assignments were subject to short-term changes for a myriad of reasons. Assigned equipment could be in the shops for repair and other cars substituted, heavy holiday traffic or special events could swell consists, light patronage could reduce consists, etc. Thus, equipment assignments, while they reflect the nature of a given train in a given era, should not be considered "cast in stone."

Combined train 3-31 (Chicago-Indianapolis/Louisville) strings out 10 cars behind burly K-6 Pacific No. 452 as it rolls over the Chicago & Western Indiana at 89th Street, Chicago, on Sunday, June 9, 1946. John

Barriger's expansion of passenger service the following month would put an end to the railroad's practice of combining the two trains as far as Monon, Ind. (*JOHN F. HUMISTON*)

Louisville. The train employed newly rebuilt red-and-gray coaches and an old dining-parlor car until ex-Army rebuilt dining-parlor-observation cars Nos. 58-59 were issued from Lafayette in mid-1948. Unfortunately, the flat-ended observations endured on the *Thoroughbred* only into late 1951 and were replaced with grill-coaches. In 1956, the *Thoroughbred* went coach only.

During the cost-cutting of the early 1960s, Alco RS-2s were frequently used on the *Thoroughbred* on the far north end of the run, between South Hammond and Dearborn Station. The reason for this was that by substituting an RS-2 for an F-3A on the run into Chicago, the Monon avoided unit-turning charges on the C&WI. On occasion, the RS-2s ran as far south as Lafayette. In 1964, the *Thoroughbred's* schedule was revised so the train could be operated with a single train set. This set departed Louisville as No. 6 in the wee hours of the morn, arrived Chicago midday, departed Chicago as No. 5 in the evening, and arrived

back at Louisville well after midnight (see Chapter 6). The *Thoroughbred* was destined to be Monon's last passenger train. Train 5 made its last southbound run on September 29, 1967; train 6 operated northbound for the last time on September 30, 1967.

Train 11/12: The name *Tippecanoe* had been synonymous with Monon's Chicago–Indianapolis morning trains since the 1920s, but it disappeared at the start of World War II. John Barriger brought the name back for Monon's postwar morning train on the Indianapolis line (although early plans called for the morning and evening trains to be called the *Morning Hoosier* and *Afternoon Hoosier*, a la the Burlington's Chicago-Minneapolis *Morning* and *Afternoon Zephyrs*). Equipped with heavyweight parlor, diner-lounge, and coaches until the new streamlined equipment arrived, the *Tippecanoe* shared the first set of streamlined equipment (coaches, dining-bar-lounge, and parlor-observation) with the *Hoosier* beginning August 17, 1947. However, because of a lack of parlor patrons on

Striding into Greencastle in August 1946, Monon's *Day Express* presents a mix of green heavyweights behind veteran K-3-class 4-6-2 No. 420. The following year, red-and-gray diesels will silence the 4-6-2. *(HAROLD STIRTON)*

The reborn *Tippecanoe*, which returned to Monon's timetables in July 1946, overtakes Erie 2-8-2 3146 at the Rock Island overpass at 79th Street, Chicago, on August 19, 1946. *(JIM SCRIBBINS)*

Seldom-photographed train 23 stands at Bedford at 6:25 a.m. in the summer of 1947 midway on its Blooming-ton-French Lick journey. RS-2 No. 24 was regular power on trains 23 and counterpart 24, which carried a Chicago-French Lick sleeper, coach and sundry head-end cars. In the siding adjacent to the Bedford freight house is Monon boxcar No. 1 on display. *(GEORGE W. HOCK-ADAY)*

Public timetable "corrected to August 17, 1947" revealed the new expanded passenger services implemented by Barriger. At this time, only trains 12 and 15 were advertised as being streamlined. *(COLLECTION OF MIKE SCHAFER)*

the morning train, the parlor-observations (Nos. 71-72) were dropped from the *Tippecanoe* in 1949 to be replaced with dinette-coaches Nos. 81-82 (see Chapter 4). On the other hand, the ex-*Thoroughbred* dining-parlor-observation cars Nos. 58/59 came to be used on the *Tippecanoe* in the early and mid-1950s, although they were never advertised as "observations" in *Tippecanoe* service.

In 1956, to cut equipment usage, the *Tippecanoe* and *Hoosier* began sharing reduced train sets. The set which was assigned to the southbound *Tippecanoe* (train 11) and northbound *Hoosier* (train 14) consisted of coaches and one of the ex-*Thoroughbred* dining-parlor-observations, while the northbound *Tippecanoe* (train 12) and southbound *Hoosier* (train 15) carried coaches, a dining-bar-lounge, and parlor-observation. This practice continued until all Indianapolis trains were stripped to coaches only in September 1957. On April 9, 1959, the *Tippecanoe* was discontinued.

Train 14/15: The postwar history of the *Hoosier*, Monon's famed evening Chicago–Indianapolis train (it operated as a morning train only at the end of World War II) followed closely that of its morning sister, the *Tippecanoe*. Before receiving Monon's first streamlined train set in August 1947, the *Hoosier* operated with heavyweight parlor cars, diner, and coaches. After introduction of Monon's red-and-gray equipment, the *Hoosier* was the better patronized of Monon's two Indianapolis line trains, and thus it kept its original streamlined equipment assignment— coaches, dining-bar-lounge, and parlor-observation— until the equipment cuts of 1956 mentioned above. Like the *Tippecanoe*, the *Hoosier* went coach-only in September 1957 and was discontinued April 9, 1959.

Train 23/24: This was John Barriger's postwar French Lick train. It connected with train 3/4 and carried through cars to and from French Lick. When originated in 1946, it operated from Bloomington to French Lick on a schedule of 5:40 a.m.–7:45 a.m. (southbound) and 9:30 p.m.–11:30 p.m. (northbound). After the *Bluegrass* was born in 1948, train 23/24 was carded only between Orleans and French Lick. An Alco RS-2 was standard power, pulling coaches and, of course, the heavyweight sleepers. Train 23/24 died with the *Bluegrass* on September 24, 1949, and with it scheduled Monon passenger service to French Lick.

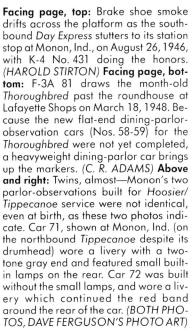

Facing page, top: Brake shoe smoke drifts across the platform as the southbound *Day Express* stutters to its station stop at Monon, Ind., on August 26, 1946, with K-4 No. 431 doing the honors. *(HAROLD STIRTON)* Facing page, bottom: F-3A 81 draws the month-old *Thoroughbred* past the roundhouse at Lafayette Shops on March 18, 1948. Because the new flat-end dining-parlor-observation cars (Nos. 58-59) for the *Thoroughbred* were not yet completed, a heavyweight dining-parlor car brings up the markers. *(C. R. ADAMS)* Above and right: Twins, almost—Monon's two parlor-observations built for *Hoosier/ Tippecanoe* service were not identical, even at birth, as these two photos indicate. Car 71, shown at Monon, Ind. (on the northbound *Tippecanoe* despite its drumhead) wore a livery with a two-tone gray end and featured small built-in lamps on the rear. Car 72 was built without the small lamps, and wore a livery which continued the red band around the rear of the car. *(BOTH PHOTOS, DAVE FERGUSON'S PHOTO ART)*

In a superb coming-and-going sequence by John Humiston, Monon's north-bound *Tippecanoe* glides along the shore of Cedar Lake on October 10, 1948. F-3 84 is on the point; parlor-observation 71 is carrying the train's rear markers. (BOTH PHOTOS, JOHN F. HUMISTON)

Unique power lashup of RS-2 25 and F-3 81 draw the southbound *Thoroughbred* across the Paisley trestle at 2:48 p.m.—virtually on time—on Sunday, June 20, 1948. *(JOHN F. HUMISTON)*

The ancient stone piers and steel girders of Monon's bridge over the White River at Gosport, Ind., tremble under the weight of the *Thoroughbred* as train 6 rolls north behind dual-service black-and-gold F-3 85 circa 1948. *(J.F. BENNETT, JIM BENNETT COLLECTION)*

Right: Monon public timetable of January 1949 showed the road's new streamliner fleet completely in place; as it were, the *Bluegrass* was discontinued later in the year. *(COLLECTION OF MIKE SCHAFER)* **Below:** At one of Chicago's fabled train-watching locations, 21st Street, the southbound "Tip" swings across the Pennsylvania main line riding C&WI rails on the first lap of its 183.5-mile journey to Indianapolis. The date is October 4, 1950, and the train is operating without its parlor-observation. *(WALLACE W. ABBEY, COLLECTION OF KALMBACH PUBLISHING CO.)*

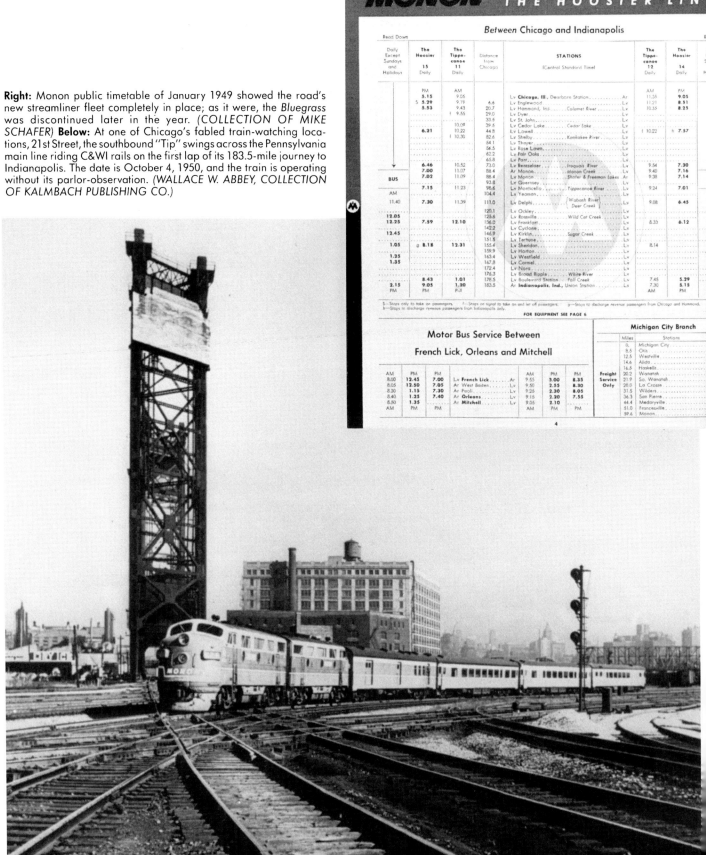

MONON THE HOOSIER LINE

Between Chicago and Indianapolis

Daily Except Sundays and Holidays	The Hoosier 15 Daily	The Tippe-canoe 11 Daily	Distance from Chicago	STATIONS (Central Standard Time)	The Tippe-canoe 12 Daily	The Hoosier 14 Daily
PM 5.15	AM 9.06		Lv **Chicago, Ill.**, Dearborn Station ... Ar	AM 11.35	PM 9.05
S 5.29	9.19	6.6	Lv Englewood ... Lv	11.21	8.51
5.53	9.43	20.7	Lv Hammond, Ind. ... Calumet River ... Lv	10.35	8.25
	f 9.55	29.0	Lv Dyer ... Lv		
		33.5	Lv St. John ... Lv		
	10.09	39.5	Lv Cedar Lake ... Cedar Lake ... Lv		
6.21	10.22	44.8	Lv Lowell ... Lv	f 10.22	h 7.57
	f 10.30	52.6	Lv Shelby ... Kankakee River ... Lv		
		54.1	Lv Thayer ... Lv		
		56.5	Lv Rose Lawn ... Lv		
		62.2	Lv Fair Oaks ... Lv		
		65.8	Lv Parr ... Lv		
6.46	10.52	73.0	Lv Rensselaer ... Iroquois River ... Lv	9.54	7.30
7.00	11.07	88.4	Ar Monon ... Monon Creek ... Lv	9.40	7.16
7.02	11.09	88.4	Lv Monon ... Shafer & Freeman Lakes ... Ar	9.38	7.14
		93.8	Lv Guernsey ... Lv		
7.15	11.23	98.6	Lv Monticello ... Tippecanoe River ... Lv	9.24	7.01
		104.4	Lv Yeoman ... Lv		
AM 11.40	7.30	11.39	111.0	Lv Delphi ... {Wabash River / Deer Creek} ... Lv	9.08	6.45
		120.1	Lv Ockley ... Lv		
12.05		128.6	Lv Rossville ... Wild Cat Creek ... Lv		
12.25	7.59	12.10	136.0	Lv Frankfort ... Lv	8.33	6.12
		142.2	Lv Cyclone ... Lv		
12.45		146.9	Lv Kirklin ... Sugar Creek ... Lv		
		151.5	Lv Tartune ... Lv		
1.05	g 8.18	12.31	155.4	Lv Sheridan ... Lv	8.14	
		159.9	Lv Horton ... Lv		
1.25		163.4	Lv Westfield ... Lv		
1.35		167.8	Lv Carmel ... Lv		
		172.4	Lv Nora ... Lv		
		176.3	Lv Broad Ripple ... White River ... Lv		
2.15	8.43	1.01	178.5	Lv Boulevard Station ... Fall Creek ... Lv	7.45	5.29
PM	9.05	1.20	183.5	Ar **Indianapolis, Ind.**, Union Station ... Lv	7.30	5.15
	PM	P.M			AM	PM

S—Stops only to take on passengers.   f—Stops on signal to take on and let off passengers.   g—Stops to discharge revenue passengers from Chicago and Hammond.   h—Stops to discharge revenue passengers from Indianapolis only.

FOR EQUIPMENT SEE PAGE 6

Motor Bus Service Between
French Lick, Orleans and Mitchell

AM	PM	PM		AM	PM	PM
8.00	12.45	7.00	Lv French Lick ... Ar	9.55	3.00	8.35
8.05	12.50	7.05	Ar West Baden ... Lv	9.50	2.55	8.30
8.30	1.15	7.30	Ar Paoli ... Lv	9.26	2.30	8.05
8.40	1.25	7.40	Ar Orleans ... Lv	9.15	2.20	7.55
8.50	1.35		Ar Mitchell ... Lv	9.05	2.10	
AM	PM	PM		AM	PM	PM

Michigan City Branch

	Miles	Stations
	0.	Michigan City
	8.5	Otis
	12.5	Westville
	14.6	Alida
	16.8	Haskells
Freight	20.2	Wanatah
Service	21.9	So. Wanatah
Only	28.0	La Crosse
	31.5	Wilders
	36.3	San Pierre
	44.4	Medaryville
	51.0	Francesville
	59.6	Monon

4

MONON THE HOOSIER LINE

Between Chicago, French Lick and Louisville

Read Up

The Bluegrass 3 Daily	The Thorough- bred 5 Daily	Distance from Chicago	STATIONS (Central Standard Time)	The Thorough- bred 6 Daily	The Bluegrass 4 Daily	The Bluegrass 4-24 Daily
PM	PM			PM	AM	AM
11.05	1.45		Lv Chicago, Ill., Dearborn Station .... Ar	7.45	7.40	7.40
11.19	1.59	6.6	Lv Englewood Lv	7.31	7.26	7.26
11.43	2.23	20.7	Lv Hammond, Ind. .... Calumet River ... Lv	7.03	7.01	7.01
		29.0	Lv Dyer Lv			
		33.5	Ls St. John Lv			
		39.5	Lv Cedar Lake .... Cedar Lake ... Lv			
	2.53	44.8	Lv Lowell Lv	6.21	6.25	6.25
		52.6	Lv Shelby .... Kankakee River ... Lv	g 6.12		
		54.1	Lv Thayer Lv			
		56.5	Lv Rose Lawn Lv			
		62.2	Lv Fair Oaks Lv			
		63.8	Lv Parr Lv			
12.38	3.20	73.0	Lv Rensselaer .... Iroquois River ... Lv	5.52	5.51	5.51
12.55	3.36	88.4	Ar Monon .... Monon Creek ... Lv	5.38	5.34	5.34
12.59	3.38	88.4	Lv Monon ... Shafer & Freeman Lakes Ar	5.36	5.29	5.29
		95.8	Lv Reynolds Lv			
1.47	4.25	120.0	Lv Lafayette .... Wabash River ... Lv	4.53	4.43	4.43
		132.9	Lv Romney Lv			
2.12	4.52	137.0	Lv Linden Lv	f 4.25	4.15	4.15
2.32	5.07	147.3	Lv Crawfordsville ... Sugar Creek ... Lv	4.11	3.59	3.59
		148.4	Lv Ames Lv			
	5.20	157.8	Lv Ladoga Lv			
2.53	5.26	162.2	Lv Roachdale Lv	3.52	3.36	3.36
		168.7	Lv Bainbridge Lv			
3.10	5.47	177.8	Lv Greencastle Lv	3.35	3.10	3.10
		189.2	Lv Cloverdale Lv			
		194.0	Lv Wallace Junction ... Eel River ... Lv			
		213.1	Lv Ellettsville Lv			
4.21	6.43	220.3	Lv Bloomington .... Ar	2.41	2.02	11.55
		221.5	Lv McDoel Yards Lv			
5.05	7.19	245.8	Lv Bedford .... White River ... Lv	2.00	1.06	11.17
5.22	7.33	255.3	Lv Mitchell Lv	1.43	12.51	10.55
5.35	7.50	261.5	Ar Orleans Lv	1.32	12.39	10.40
	M8.05	269.1	Ar Paoli .... Paoli Trestle ... Lv	M 1.15		10.20
	M8.30	278.1	Ar West Baden Lv	M12.50		
	M8.35	279.2	Ar French Lick Lv	M12.45		10.00
	M7.00	279.2	Lv French Lick .... Ar	M 3.00		
	M7.05	278.1	Lv West Baden Lv	M 2.55		
	M7.30	269.1	Lv Paoli Lv	M 2.30		
5.35	7.50	261.5	Lv Orleans .... Ar	1.32	12.39	
		271.8	Lv Campbellsburg Lv			
5.59	8.12	282.1	Lv Salem .... Blue River ... Lv	1.12	12.19	
		290.2	Lv Farrabee Lv			
		293.4	Lv Pekin Lv			
		299.5	Lv Borden Lv			
6.57	8.57	317.5	Lv New Albany, Ind. ... Ohio River ... Lv	12.28	11.28	
7.30	9.25	324.1	Ar Louisville, Ky., Union Station ... Lv	12.01	11.00	
AM	PM			PM	PM	

f—Stops to take on and let off passengers. g—Stops on signal Sundays only to take on passengers. M—Via Motor Bus, tickets reading via C.I. & L. Ry. will be honored on Motor Bus.

For connecting service to and from **New York** and **St. Louis** see page 6.

FOR EQUIPMENT SEE PAGE 6

5

Below: From the darkened, brick train shed of Indianapolis Union Station, the *Tippecanoe* emerges behind F-3A 85A in August 1949. A New York Central steam switcher is barely visible at right. *(TOM RANKIN COLLECTION)* **Bottom:** Monon's brick New Albany depot stands vigil as the southbound *Thoroughbred* invades the streets of Hoosier Line founder James Brooks' hometown on July 14, 1949. *(WILLIAM J. HUSA JR.)*

Hammond trio: Three scenes of the northbound *Thoroughbred* at the joint Erie-Monon station at Hammond, Ind., show the train's varied consists during its last few years. **Top left:** In the dusk of April 9, 1959, a red-and-gray No. 6 arrives behind the 84A. For the photographer, this shot was a bonus—he had come to Hammond to photograph the last run of the *Hoosier* (see page 110). *(JIM WOZNICZKA)* **Middle left:** Early in the 1960's, No. 6 pauses in a scene unique to the north end of the railroad. Use of an RS-2 rather than a single F-3A north of South Hammond yard negated the need to turn units at Dearborn Station, Chicago. *(JIM WOZNICZKA)* **Bottom left:** Steam whispers from the pilot of aged but still stylish F-3 pair leading the *Thoroughbred* on a snowy January 19, 1965. *(ROBERT P. OLMSTED)*

Above: Uncommon indeed is this motive-power combination on the southbound *Thoroughbred* of August 19, 1962, as BL-2 34 and an F-3A team up. The veteran BL-2 was called in when an F-3A failed. Scene is at Pullman Junction, Ill., on C&WI trackage. *(JIM WOZNICZKA)* **Left:** A malfunctioning C-420 put BL-2 37 in command of the *Thoroughbred* departing Dearborn Station on June 3, 1967; ailing C-420 trailed at rear. *(MIKE SCHAFER)*
Below: A not-ailing C-420 casts out of Chicago with the *Thoroughbred* near 16th Street on September 3, 1967. Before the month is out, the *Thoroughbred* will be history and high-nose Century 420 No. 501 will be relegated to freight duties. *(JIM WOZNICZKA)*

In October 1946, CI&L 4-6-2 432 draws a Monon presidential inspection special south across the steel trestle at Paoli, Ind., on the French Lick branch. Soon, the fortunate guests on board will be treated to a night's stay at the French Lick Springs Hotel. *(LINN H. WEST-COTT, COLLECTION OF KALMBACH PUB-LISHING CO.)*

Heavyweight Pullmans and RS-2 No. 21 crowd the house tracks at the French Lick Springs Hotel on Kentucky Derby weekend 1948. For Monon varnish, no weekend exceeded the glory of Derby weekend, and for rail travelers, French Lick Springs was *the* place to stay the night before the "Run for the Roses." *(GEORGE W. HOCKADAY)*

A Railroad of

FOR A RAILROAD of its size, the Monon was host to special passenger trains of seemingly endless variety. Monon ran specials for employees, for railfans, for college students, for football and baseball games, and for a fabled horse race.

With the Monon's strong bond to its on-line colleges (witness the *Varsity* experiment), "back-to-school" specials were regular fare on the Monon in the fall, the spring, and during the holidays. Football specials (most notably Indiana-Purdue trains for the "Old Oaken Bucket" football rivalry) endured into the final years of the Monon. The Hoosier Line's last football special—which operated from Lafayette to Bloomington and return using C-420s 501-502 and coaches of Monon, B&O, Santa Fe, Grand Trunk, and other origins—ran in the fall of 1967. The game, at Bloomington, was won by Indiana and sent the Hoosiers to their first and only Rose Bowl appearance.

Virtually all railroads operate special trains for their executives and friends of the railroad, but the Monon—during the Barriger era—took the art to high form, running "barnstorming tours" to visit on-line shippers, and operating annual "inspection trains" over every mile of the railroad. With shippers, bankers, press, and Monon officials on board, the Hoosier Line inspection trains typically departed Chicago in the morning and journeyed to Indianapolis on day 1. That night, the train would turn north, to arrive Michigan City early in the morning of day 2. By the end of day 2, the train would have journeyed from Michigan City to Lafayette, and from Lafayette to Bloomington (with a turn on the I&L branch thrown in). On day 3 the train galloped from Bloomington to Louisville, then back north to Orleans and down the French Lick branch. After a night in the French Lick Springs Hotel, passengers boarded the train on day 4 for the journey back to Chicago.

But of all Monon's specials, certainly there is no doubt of the most famous. That fell to the Hoosier Line's "Derby trains," which each May funneled toward Louisville Union

Special Occasions

Specials were prolific on the Monon early in the Barriger era. Take, for example, RS-2-powered Michigan City-Lafayette excursion train for the Railway & Locomotive Historical Society. Behind RS-2 25 is Monon business car 1. (JOHN F. HUMISTON)

Station to carry passengers bound for Churchill Downs and the running of the Kentucky Derby. While Monon's Derby trains operated from as far as Chicago, it was the French Lick Springs Hotel—but 80 miles from Louisville by rail—that was the favorite haunt of the horse players, and it was there that special consists crowded the house tracks the eve before the "Run for the Roses." For the Monon train-watcher, Derby trains meant sightings of business cars—Monon's own and other roads'—and rainbow consists of cars ranging in ownership from Monon to Atlantic Coast Line.

The long tradition of Derby trains on the Monon survived until the very end; the last Hoosier Line Derby train—C-420 503, a coach, and Monon business car—operated in May 1971. It was a fitting, proper conclusion to Monon's passenger train era.

Above: Near Boulevard Station, Indianapolis, on April 25, 1954, dual-service F-3A's 85A&B draw a 14-car troop train through the north side of the Hoosier State capital. (RON STUCKEY COLLECTION) **Left:** Fairbanks-Morse H-15-44's 36 and 37 provide motive power for an employee's excursion over the Michigan City branch on July 25, 1948. Note "run through" Michigan City depot. (PERRY F. JOHNSON)

In the twilight of Monon's independent existence, the trackside experience is made unforgettable by a pair of aged but able Alco RS-2's leading the south-end local southbound at Thornton, Ind., in July 1971. (GARY W. DOLZALL)

9

TONNAGE ON THE HOOSIER LINE

A Pictorial of Monon Freight Operations After World War II

YOU'RE standing at ballast's edge, on the Monon main line near Thornton. It is summer—July 1971—amid the twilight of the Hoosier Line's independent life. Here, deep in the Salt Creek valley of southern Indiana, less than five miles north of Bedford, you're surrounded by fields of corn and gently rolling hills dressed with aged trees. It is quiet, calm, a gentle summer wind whispering through branches and corn stalks. Quiet. Until from the north, the blat of a single-note airhorn demands your attention. You gaze ahead at the curve, at tracks that slip behind a wooded hill, waiting, listening to the growing sound of diesel power plants issuing an uneven but confident cadence.

And then, the machines appear around the curve and are before you—a pair of black-and-gold Alco RS-2s bathed in their own charcoal exhaust. Atop the lead RS-2, white flags—for "extra"—flap at the train's 35-mph gait. Behind the bouncing Alcos, the train sweeps by you—a dusty red crew car, a chord of empty gondolas bound for Bedford's quarries, boxcars and mixed freight bound beyond. The train is the south end local out of McDoel Yard, Bloomington, a yeoman-duty turn that will make calls all the way to K&IT's Youngtown Yard in Louisville before the day is done.

Quickly, too quickly, the train is out of sight, and quiet returns to rural southern Indiana. But you leave trackside with an experience not likely forgotten—of the Hoosier Line and how it moved its tonnage.

For the train-watcher of Monon freight operations during the Hoosier Line's final quarter century, the experience was first of black, aged steam locomotives living their final days, then black-and-gold diesels

issued from diesel-makers' plants at La Grange, Ill., and Schenectady, N.Y., and Beloit, Wis., and Erie, Pa. It was the experience of scheduled mainline freights seconded by locals and extras.

The scheduled Chicago–Louisville trains established early in the Barriger era—Nos. 70-75—were the backbone of Hoosier Line freight operations, although with the Coleman-era cost controls, trains 72/73 were dropped north of Lafayette (the flat territory north of there allowed combining tonnage) and in 1962 trains 74/75 were dropped altogether. It was not uncommon, however, to see the remaining trains carrying green flags—*i.e.,* running in multiple sections—when business was heavy.

The trains Barriger established on the Michigan City and Indianapolis lines also saw change, although much earlier. The Michigan City line was originally served by train 56/57 which ran the distance between Michigan City and Louisville; the Indianapolis trains—Nos. 90/91—operated South Hammond–Indianapolis. But by 1950, both these operations were shortened—Nos. 56/57 to Michigan City–Lafayette, and Nos. 90/91 to Indianapolis–Monon. In that form, they would remain through the Monon's existence. Very briefly, beginning in 1947, the Michigan City line was also served by train 58/59, which ran Monon–Michigan City, but available tonnage did not dictate their continued operation.

When the Barriger-era through-freight schedules were established, a network of locals was also created. As was Monon tradition, the locals carried 40-series train numbers. By 1947, these local trains were carded:

Monon J-1-class 2-8-2 No. 514 and its crew pose atop the bridge over Indiana highway 37 at Clear Creek in a post-World War II J. F. Bennett classic. The photo was taken on the old Smithville line, which was by this time reduced to a spur to limestone quarries. *(J. F. BENNETT, JIM BEN-NETT COLLECTION)*

40/41 (McDoel–Louisville); 42/43 (Lafayette–McDoel); 44/45 (Lafayette–South Hammond); 46/47 (Monon–Indianapolis); and 48/49 (Michigan City–Monon). The 40-series trains originally operated on daily-except-Sunday frequencies. All the locals survived through the late 1950s; however, Nos. 44/45 and 46/47 were reduced to three times a week (in each direction) by that time. The Indianapolis local (46/47) was killed as a scheduled train by 1960, and all locals were deleted from timetables during the early part of the Coleman era. Nonetheless, the local network remained intact, for the most part, through the final days of the Monon, with all locals operating as extras.

Freight operations on the French Lick and I&L branches, and into the Monon's stone district, were never formally scheduled after World War II—all trains operated as extras. The French Lick branch was worked with turns from McDoel Yard, Bloomington. Alco RS-2 road-switchers (or occasionally the F-M road-switchers) were regular fare on the French Lick locals, but on at least one occasion in the early 1960s—when the Southern Railway delivered a trainload of coal to French Lick via its branch from Huntingburg, Ind.—a trio of Monon's C-628s was sent to French Lick to lug the coal off the branch. It was, undoubtedly, the greatest test the lanky Paoli trestle would ever endure!

McDoel Yard was also the point from which extras to work the southern Indiana stone district originated. Turns (often at night) were sent to serve quarries and mills as far as Bedford, 25 miles south.

The I&L branch was operated in several fashions. During its glory days before WWII, Midland had been a crew station (in 1922, 12 crews were based there) with trains working the branch and dropping coal loads at Wallace Junction and Bainbridge on the main line. But with the ever-constant decline in coal traffic, operations on the branch likewise declined. In the Barriger era and beyond, a train and crew would be called at

On August 10, 1947, Hoosier Line 2-8-2 530 draws through Wanatah, Ind., working a local on the Michigan City line. In the siding waiting for the Mikado and its tonnage to clear is Monon's *Hoosier* traveling on its exhibition tour. (MALCOLM D. McCARTER)

Facing page: Under a lazy trail of coal smoke, Monon 2-8-0 No. 283 drifts past the station platform at Monticello, Ind., and into the town's streets in this recollection of the Barriger-era Monon before diesels arrived. (W. A. AKIN JR., COLLECTION OF KALMBACH PUBLISHING CO.) **Right:** Two eras of Monon motive-power—the old embodied by J-1 2-8-2 525, the new by NW-2 diesel switcher DS-3—cross paths at McDoel Yard. The Mike is leading a northbound extra; the NW-2 is working as the yard switcher. (HAROLD J. STIRTON)

An elderly wooden caboose is tucked behind Monon 551 as the 2-8-2 ducks through the rock cut and across Clear Creek one mile north of Harrodsburg with a local freight. This area, immediately north of Harrodsburg, was perhaps the most remote, and beautiful, portion of the entire Hoosier Line. (J. F. BENNETT, JIM BENNETT COLLECTION)

Shops when a train of coal had accumulated at Midland. The train would take whatever empties were on hand at Shops for the southbound run to Midland, and return to Lafayette with loaded hoppers. In the final years of the Monon, the I&L branch was also regularly served from the south—from McDoel. A train would make a McDoel-Midland-McDoel turn; coal bound north would be dropped in a siding on the main line for the next northbound train to pick up.

Another important Monon freight operation to not ever appear in timetables was the transfer service north of South Hammond, which took Monon power and transfer freights onto the Chicago & Western Indiana at State Line Tower and, indeed, as far north as the Belt Railway of Chicago's Clearing Yard (Monon owned one-fifth interest in the C&WI and one-twelfth interest in the Belt Railway of Chicago). At the south

end of the railroad, Monon trains operated directly into the Kentucky & Indiana Terminal's Youngtown Yard on the north side of Louisville (Monon's ownership of the K&IT was one-third).

Not to be forgotten were Monon's maids-of-all-work, the yard switchers. Traditionally, Monon yard job assignments were at South Hammond, Monon, Belt Junction (Indianapolis), Lafayette, McDoel, Bedford, and New Albany. Michigan City was worked by locomotives off train 56; Midland was not regularly assigned, but was worked as coal demands dictated. Monon's switching requirements at Louisville were handled by K&IT's yard engines, which through the Monon's postwar era ranged from pinstriped 0-8-0s to blue-and-white Baldwin, F-M and EMD diesels.

In the pages of this chapter, we explore with photographs Hoosier Line scenes that exist no longer.

Traditionally chronicled for its passenger trains to "the Springs," the French Lick branch nonetheless was a source of tonnage for CI&L, as evidenced by 2-8-2 No. 518 stepping across the trestle over Lost River north of Paoli, Ind. *(LINN H. WESTCOTT, COLLECTION OF KALMBACH PUBLISHING CO.)*

Right: At South Hammond on August 12, 1948, Monon NW-2 12 (renumbered from DS-2 in 1947) has been repainted from its original black-and-white livery into the equally short-lived black-and-yellow scheme. Another trip to Lafayette's paint shop waits—to apply the black-and-gold colors the NW-2 will wear for two decades. *(COLLECTION OF LOUIS A. MARRE)*
Below: Wearing the short-lived black/yellow livery it wore when delivered, RS-2 21 challenged snow and tonnage as it works southbound at 10th Street, Michigan City, on January 19, 1948. *(PERRY F. JOHNSON)*

Above right: Flying white flags, Class J-4 Mikado 573 leads a coal extra, originating at Midland, o[f] the I&L branch and onto the main line at Wallace Junction, Ind., in 1946. *(LINN H. WESTCOT[T] COLLECTION OF KALMBACH PUBLISHING CO.)* **Above left:** On August 3, 1948, Monon moved [a] 53-car train of coal from Midland to Chicago (for shipment over the Great Lakes). Wearing whit[e] flags, F-3 62 stands on the north leg of the wye at Wallace Junction as the train prepares to mov[e] onto the main toward Lafayette. *(DAVE FERGUSON'S PHOTO ART)*

Above: Landmarks of Bloomington in the late 1940's—the limestone Monon depot, the Hotel Graham and the Monroe County Courthouse (prominently cameoed in the 1979 movie *Breaking Away*)—are evident in this J. F. Bennett photo of A-B-A F-3's pulling train 74 northward through downtown on May 17, 1947. *(J. F. BENNETT, JIM BENNETT COLLECTION)* **Right:** Utilizing the McDoel switcher as a pusher to assist northbound freights out of Bloomington was common practice throughout Monon's diesel era. In 1947, NW-2 16 applied its 1000 horsepower to the rear of a wooden caboose as a freight climbed the grade toward Hunters, Ind. *(J. F. BENNETT, FRANK VAN BREE COLLECTION)*

Early in its career, Monon BL-2 No. 32 slaps across the Pennsylvania at La Crosse, Ind., working tonnage on the Michigan City branch. (MALCOLM D. McCARTER)

Lafayette Junction, the Hoosier Line's crossing of the Big Four (New York Central) and Lake Erie & Western (Nickel Plate), is enlivened on May 29, 1949, by the arrival of Fairbanks-Morse H-15-44 No. 46 heading a string of freight. (ELLIOTT KAHN)

Bound for South Hammond from the Belt Railway of Chicago's Clearing Yard, a Monon transfer encounters an Erie Lackawanna RS-3 at State Line tower on May 11, 1963. (JIM WOZ-NICZKA)

With the rear of its train still strung over the K&IT bridge and the Ohio River, F-3A 64 and mates pass VI tower and dive into the streets of New Albany with a northbound freight. (JACK B. FRAVERT)

Facing page: Local No. 42 (McDoel-Lafayette) works at Crawfordsville, Ind., on June 9, 1958, as it journeys northward with smokey Alco RS-2 21 providing the muscle. (J. PARKER LAMB) Above: In 1948, year-old RS-2 No. 27 and a sister lead local No. 40 through the trackwork at New Albany. (JACK B. FRAVERT) Right: In the latter years of Monon's life, the I&L branch was operated variously from Lafayette and from Bloomington. In June 1963, RS-2 27 prepares to push a train bound for Midland out of McDoel Yard. Ancient wooden cabooses were a fixture on the Midland turn. (KENNETH M. ARDINGER)

Above: Departing Hammond with a southbound local, C-420 No. 510 eases under the Kingery Expressway and across the Little Calumet River bridge on March 25, 1971. *(ROBERT P. OLMSTED)*
Right: A familiar sight on Monon's post-World War II locals were the "head-end cabooses" or crew cars, such as that shown in use in the photo above. Built to carry crew members and l.c.l. (less-than-carload) shipments, the cars in later years were also used to carry spare knuckles, tools and sundry. Four head-end cabooses (C211-C214, later 81211-81214) were built at Lafayette in 1945; another four (81222-81225) were built at Lafayette in 1956. *(KENNETH M. ARDINGER)*

Top: Re-enacting a tradition dating to New Albany & Salem days, C-420 516 pushes a string of freight cars into the "run-through" depot at Gosport, Ind. Train is No. 73 bound south for Bloomington and Louisville; date is July 1971, amid the Monon's final weeks. *(GARY W. DOLZALL)* **Left:** Dragging train 72 north toward Bloomington, U23B 607 head GE and Alco kindred through the rocky cut at Diamond, Ind., in July 1971. *(GARY W. DOLZALL)* **Above:** The last Monon train on the I&L branch before the L&N merger stands at Midland, Ind., in July 1971, with engineer R. E. Prien at the throttle of C-420 515. *(R. E. PRIEN COLLECTION)*

Above: On July 29, 1971, train 56 for Michigan City works the Penn Central interchange at San Pierre, Ind. *(ROBERT P. OLM-STED)* **Left:** Pride of the Monon's caboose fleet were the 8 "bay window cupola" cabooses (Nos. 81525-81532) built at Lafayette Shops in 1956-57. Original colors were caboose red, with white lettering, black roofs and undergear, silver steps and railings. Along with 9 cabooses built by International Railway Car Co. in 1952 (Nos. 81501-81509), the Lafayette-built cabooses covered the Monon's primary trains. *(DAVE FERGUSON'S PHOTO ART)*

Bound for Bedford: Highway sign pointing the way to Bedford seems appropriate for Louisville & Nashville U23B 2722 as it leads a southbound freight on ex-Monon rails at Harrodsburg in March 1976. Today, the tracks here have vanished. *(GARY W. DOLZALL)*

10

EPILOGUE

The Hoosier Line After July 31, 1971

WHEN THE Monon ceased to exist as an independent railroad, its routes, its equipment, its men did not simply disappear, but rather carried on under a new owner's name—Louisville & Nashville. At merger, the Hoosier Line became the Monon Division of the L&N, then later the Monon Subdivision of L&N's Louisville Division.

Now, more than thirty years removed from the merger, great change has come to the Hoosier Line. The Monon's locomotives are, except for a few survivors, retired (see "Rosters"); the grounds of South Hammond yard lie quiet; many stations are demolished; Lafayette Shops no longer tends locomotives; even significant portions of the railroad itself have been abandoned. But there remains, too, along much of the old Monon the continued passage of trains.

Following the Monon-L&N merger, the Milwaukee Road began utilizing its hard-won trackage rights from Bedford to Louisville. Typically, Milwaukee Road operated two trains a day in each direction on the ex-Monon. Milwaukee's Chicago-Louisville service survived the cutbacks that followed Milwaukee's bankruptcy in 1977 (although most of Milwaukee's Chicago-Terre Haute trackage was abandoned in favor of Conrail trackage rights). On January 1, 1986, the Milwaukee was merged into the Soo Line, which, in turn, in 1990 was integrated into its parent, Canadian Pacific. Today, CP continues to draw tonnage over ex-Monon rails between Bedford and Louisville.

Just as the Monon was merged into a larger entity, so has the L&N itself since been absorbed. In the mid-1970s, the L&N began to lose much of its identity, when parent Seaboard Coast Line created the "Family Lines," comprised of SCL, L&N, Clinchfield, Georgia Railroad, At-

lanta & West Point, and Western Railway of Alabama. Then, on December 29, 1982, members of the "Family Lines" were fully merged to form Seaboard System Railroad. In 1986, the short-lived Seaboard System was, in turn, folded into its parent, eastern transportation giant CSX, which also included the ex-Baltimore & Ohio, Western Maryland, and Chesapeake & Ohio. CSX grew into a far more massive system in 1999 when Conrail was divided between CSX and Norfolk Southern.

And what of the old Monon today under giant CSX? Not surprisingly, the Monon's branch lines fared worst and disappeared most quickly. Gone is the French Lick branch (Paoli to French Lick abandoned in May 1977; Orleans to Paoli in 1981). Gone is Monon's I&L branch, abandoned in August 1981. The last remnant of the Bedford & Bloomfield—from Bedford to Dark Hollow—was cast away in February 1980. The Michigan City line exists only from Monon to Medaryville, 14.8 miles, with trackage north of Medaryville abandoned in April 1981 (except for a short stretch of trackage in Michigan City utilized by the South Shore). The Indianapolis line is operated by CSX only between Monon and Monticello. Seaboard System continued to operate the entire Indianapolis line into the early 1980s, and as late as 1986 the south end of the route was operated (as far north as Sheridan) by Indiana Hi-Rail Corp. But the old Hoosier Line northward out of Indiana's state capital is now only a bike and walking trail, albeit one named in honor of the Monon. Just before its demise, the Indianapolis line saw a dramatic return of red-and-gray diesels, when in 1985 the Indiana Transportation Museum repainted into Monon passenger livery two ex-Milwaukee Road F units for use on its Carmel-Indianapolis "Fairtrain" (in addition to ITM's F's, another diesel in

Monon livery, Monon BL–2 32 restored by the Kentucky Railway Museum, made excursion appearances on the Hoosier Line's south-end in 1974 and 1975).

When the original edition of this book was released in 1987, it could be reported that the Monon's main stem—from Chicago to Louisville—was intact and in service. Only the northern six miles of the railroad between the Grand Trunk (Canadian National) crossing at Maynard and State Line Tower were no longer active (Hammond-State Line Tower trackage was abandoned in April 1985). And, remarkably, in addition to those of CSX, the trains of two modern entities—Conrail and Amtrak—could be regularly found on ex-Monon rails. Conrail's blue diesels began appearing on a portion of the ex-Monon in 1986 when Conrail's Indianapolis-Lafayette tonnage started operating Indianapolis-Crawfordsville via Conrail's ex-Peoria & Eastern line, and from Crawfordsville to Lafayette via CSX (ex-Monon) trackage rights.

What was undoubtedly the most remarkable event of the post-Monon era occurred when regularly scheduled passenger service returned to Hoosier Line rails. In March 1975, Amtrak's Chicago-Florida train, the *Floridian,* was transferred to the ex-Monon Chicago-Louisville line because Penn Central trackage through Indiana was in terrible condition. Passenger stops were established at Lafayette and Bloomington. Originally a night train over the old Monon, the *Floridian* changed to a daylight operation on the Hoosier Line before meeting its demise in October 1979. Despite the death of the *Floridian,* passenger service did not disappear from the Hoosier Line for long. In October 1980, Amtrak's Chicago-Indianapolis *Hoosier State* was inaugurated, using the ex-Monon main from Maynard to Crawfordsville, where it swung onto the ex-P&E toward Indianapolis. Today, the *Hoosier State* operation has been incorporated into longer-distance trains, the Chicago-Washington *Cardinal* and Chicago-Jeffersonville (Ind.) *Kentucky Cardinal,* utilizing the same ex-Monon segment.

While the north end of the ex-Monon remained rich in traffic, including Amtrak service, and the far southern end continued to witness Soo and CSX tonnage, the middle section of the Hoosier Line's main witnessed declining traffic into the early 1990s, through service was discontinued in 1992, and abandonment loomed. On Au-

In 1975, Milwaukee Road Geeps walk at 8 miles per hour south through the downtown square of Bedford, utilizing the hard-won trackage rights on the ex-Monon MILW gained in the ICC's approval of the Monon/L&N merger. (GARY W. DOLZALL)

Left: Milwaukee's trackage rights over the south end of the post-merger Monon resulted in orange-and-black diesels trodding unfamiliar ground. On May 31, 1975, Milwaukee Road-rebuilt EMD Geep 994 leads a trio of sisters off the K&IT bridge at New Albany, Ind. (GARY W. DOLZALL) **Below:** A quartet of L&N units swings through Orleans, Ind., southbound on a spring day in 1977. The brick depot was of similar style and vintage to the ancient Gosport station; it sat between the Orleans passing track and the main. The French Lick branch is aside the base of the water tower. (MIKE SCHAFER)

gust 17, 1993, nature decided the matter, forever slicing the ex-Monon's main. More than 12 inches of rain fell around Cloverdale and Owen County, feeding flash floods that washed out sections of the ex-Monon between Gosport and Cloverdale. With the line broken, abandonment proceedings followed, with Cloverdale-Gosport formally abandoned in March 1994; Bloomington-Bedford in July 1996; and Gosport-Elletsville in September 1997 (although service had ceased well before such dates). Another short, but notable, section of the ex-Monon mainline—its route through the streets of Lafayette—was abandoned in May 2000 when a long-envisioned plan to utilize Norfolk Southern (trackage to bypass the city's congested streets) was completed.

With the middle of the Hoosier Line's main line now gone, tonnage operations today are far different than in the Monon era, but still significant. On the north end of the ex-Monon, CSX trains move from Chicago's Clearing Yard and from the Burlington Northern Santa Fe in the Windy City, via Maynard and Crawfordsville, to Indianapolis. CSX locals operate between Avon and Hawthorne yards in Indianapolis to Lafayette, where a yard job remains active 24 hours a day. Locals also continue to operate out of Lafayette and Monon serving remaining sections of the Monon, and CSX operates a Lafayette-Evansville freight service, which travels on the ex-Monon as far south as Greencastle, where it uses a connector installed in 1992 with the ex-Conrail St. Louis mainline (now also part of CSX).

The south end of the Hoosier Line continues to see CP trains (usually one in each direction daily) between Bedford and Louisville, and, in fact, these are the only trains that operate between Bedford and Mitchell. The ex-Monon between New Albany and Mitchell has, meanwhile, evolved into a segment of CSX's Louisville-St. Louis route, with as many as six trains a day weaving through the old Monon-B&O interchange at Mitchell. Further north, McDoel Yard at Bloomington, although isolated, is still utilized. The Indiana Rail Road, which

operates the ex-Illinois Central line through Bloomington (and is a subsidiary of CSX), uses the yard to serve the industries located on ex-Monon trackage around Bloomington, and then routes this traffic via its ex-IC line.

It is surely true that much of the Monon, now three decades after its merger into L&N, is only to be found in history, and in the hearts and minds of those who cherished this Indiana institution. But for the curious, there remain many familiar places where the call of air horns and the roll of steel wheels still can be witnessed along the Hoosier Line.

The engineer of Louisville-bound tonnage has 9000 horsepower bridled as his charge eases down 15th Street in New Albany on June 26, 1984. The first two units—U30C 1493 and SD-40 1238—wear Family Lines livery; the trailing unit, SD-40-2 3575, carries the Seaboard System name. *(BOTH PHOTOS, DONALD R. KAPLAN)*

Above: Hoosier Line tradition: Although the diesels are gray and yellow, the Monon tradition of serving the stone business of southern Indiana continued in September 1974 as GP-18 902 and a GP-35 work a mill spur near Clear Creek, Ind. *(GARY W. DOLZALL)*
Right: Louisville & Nashville U23B 2739, a GP-30 and two first-generation Geeps slide under Milwaukee Road's Bedford stone quarry line as they work southward to Louisville in 1975. *(GARY W. DOL-ZALL)*

In 1972, L&N suffered a shortage of motive power and consequently leased or borrowed Seaboard Coast Line, Clinchfield, Chesapeake & Ohio and other diesels, providing some undreamed of variety on the former Monon. In March 1972, a matched A-B-B-A set of Clinchfield F units climb the "Knobs" northbound between Pekin and Borden, Ind., recalling in spirit the black-and-gold F's that battled this hill for more than two decades. (GARY W. DOLZALL)

Although L&N did not use any of the Monon F-3A's it inherited at the merger, Louisville & Nashville's own F units made occasional appearances on the old Monon. In August 1972, a fascinating lashup of L&N GP-40, Seaboard Coast Line GP-30, two L&N F-7A's and ex-Monon RS-2 260 draw around the curve at Hunters north of Bloomington with a southbound freight. (GARY W. DOLZALL)

175

The dome car is undoubtedly a fine place to view the scenery of the old Monon's Southern Division as Amtrak's *Floridian* rolls downgrade at Sand Pit, south of Bedford, on September 10, 1977. On the point: EMD F-40PH 238. *(RICHARD KOENIG)*

Ghost of the *Bluegrass*: Like a specter in the night, Amtrak's *Floridian* pauses in Bloomington to load passengers on a snowy eve in January 1976 during the train's overnight trek between Louisville and Chicago. The husky SDP40F is a far cry from Monon's F-3's of past days. *(GARY W. DOLZALL)*

History repeating itself: On June 23, 1984, some 17 years after the final run of the *Thoroughbred*, Amtrak's daily Indianapolis-Chicago *Hoosier State* cruises north on 5th Street, Lafayette, past the 1902-built Monon passenger station. The rear end of the train is actually nearer to what is Amtrak's passenger station, the Lahr House Hotel in downtown Lafayette. In 1986 the train was renamed the *Cardinal* after it was combined with triweekly Chicago-Cincinnati-Washington-New York service that had been rerouted via Indianapolis. So for the first time in over half a century, the old Monon was once again part of a Chicago-Cincinnati passenger route. *(DONALD R. KAPLAN)*

Above: After two seasons of wearing a wine-colored paint scheme, Indiana Transportation Museum's two ex-Milwaukee Road F's were repainted in the time-honored Monon red-and-gray scheme for Fairtrain's 1985 operation. "Monon" FP-7 96C stands at Carmel, Ind., on the ex-Monon Indianapolis branch as fairbound passengers load. One F is at each end of the consist. **Right:** Reborn Monon BL-2 No. 32, donated by L&N to Kentucky Railway Museum, skirts Clear Creek as it heads south near Diamond, Ind., with a May 11, 1975, Louisville-Bloomington round trip excursion. *(BOTH PHOTOS, GARY W. DOLZALL)*

Above: New faces in Bedford's streets: Canadian Pacific and Soo Line diesels draw tonnage south through the streets of Bedford, bound for Louisville on March 12, 1999. Soo Line, then parent Canadian Pacific, were the successors to Milwaukee Road and its trackage rights operations on the south end of the ex-Hoosier Line. *(ERIC POWELL)* **Right:** Amid the waning years of tonnage venturing down Lafayette's 5th Street, CSX 6528, still dressed in the livery of the Chessie System, draws Train R591 carefully through the heart of the city, bound from Lafayette to Evansville on May 21, 1994. *(ERIC POWELL)*

Above left: In a scene that no train-watcher could have even imagined in the Monon era, Burlington Northern Santa Fe GE Dash 8-40BW #730, dressed in the famous "Warbonnet" red-and-silver livery of the Santa Fe, leads tonnage near Lafayette on the ex-Hoosier Line on March 5, 2000. The train is a CSX run-through from the BNSF in Chicago to Avon Yard in Indianapolis, and it often employs BNSF motive power. *(ERIC POWELL)* **Above right:** On the Fourth of July, 1996, CSX train R591, with SD40–2 8144 on the point, slowly navigates the new connection at Greencastle between the ex-Monon and CSX's mainline to St. Louis (which CSX acquired with Conrail; it was originally New York Central's St. Louis route). This train operates from Lafayette to Greencastle on the ex-Monon, Greencastle to Terre Haute on the ex-NYC, and Terre Haute to Evansville on CSX's ex-Chicago & Eastern Illinois line. *(ERIC POWELL)* **Left:** Nature sealed the fate of the middle section of the ex-Monon's Chicago-Louisville main line when, on August 17, 1993, storms and the resulting flash floods caused washouts such as this on the ex-Hoosier Line main in Owen County. *(SPENCER EVENING WORLD)*

Right: Track crews pull up rails at one of the ex-Monon's most visited and photogenic sites—Harrodsburg Curve—in 1994. The dean of Monon photographers, J. F. Bennett, made this location famous, and scores of Hoosier Line train-watchers followed in his footsteps. Views of this location in happier times appear in this book on pages 2, 64, 77, 125, and 170. *(DAVID A. McKALIP)* **Below left:** CSX tonnage rolls over the south end of the ex-Monon at Salem on February 23, 1997, passing classic Hoosier Line semaphores, still guarding the right-of-way. The ex-Monon between New Albany and Mitchell (and the ex-B&O line west of Mitchell) evolved into part of CSX's routing for traffic between Louisville and St. Louis. *(ERIC POWELL)* **Below right:** Although Bloomington's McDoel Yard became isolated by abandonment of the ex-Monon main both north and south of the city in the 1990s, the yard continued to see use. Reached via the Indiana Rail Road's ex-Illinois Central line through Bloomington, the yard continued to serve as a focal point of Indiana Rail Road's switching of Bloomington industries. In May 2001, Indiana Rail Road power congregated near the ex-Monon station and yard office. *(DAVID A. McKALIP)*

ACKNOWLEDGMENTS

WORKING on this new edition of *Monon: The Hoosier Line,* we were pleasantly reminded, as during the preparation of the original, of the truth in the phrase "Hoosier hospitality." A book of this kind is the cooperative accomplishment of many—the authors, the publishers, and most importantly, scores of contributors who see the value of sharing their resources and collections with others. We were blessed with aid and enthusiastic support from many such willing and gracious Monon enthusiasts, who thus helped in an important and meaningful manner to document the Monon, its personality, and its history.

As might be expected with a work about "The Hoosier Line," the majority of contributions came from Hoosiers—thus our reference to "Hoosier hospitality." But if there was one lesson learned in this process, it was that there are Monon followers across this country, from Florida to Washington State. At the risk of leaving out someone, we'd like to issue some special thanks:

Frank Van Bree provided an important selection of photos and an unmatched research source of Monon corporate records and documents when the book was first written—and offered continuing and much appreciated support as this new edition evolved. We are pleased to include Frank's own "Afterword" on the Monon in this revised edition.

We thank and remember the late Lloyd Kimble, a long-time Monon employee and friend, for his contribution of rare, old photos—and for his company during all the days we spent as youngsters hanging around the Mitchell depot watching the trains of the Hoosier Line.

If there is one special delight we take in this book, it is in our presentation of a thorough selection of photos taken by the late J. F. Bennett. Bennett was a career Monon man—a telegrapher who hired on at Shelby in the 1920s and spent most of his years at McDoel—and he was the consummate Monon photographer as well. We thank J. F. Bennett's nephew Jim Bennett for providing his uncle's remarkable photos, as well as some of his own work.

Dave Ferguson of Ferguson's Photo Art in Lafayette provided us with scores of Monon company photos. While we've credited such photos in this volume to Ferguson's Photo Art, Dave would want us to mention that the majority represent the expert camera work of Gil Hutton.

Another superb photographic record of the Monon in the Barriger years came from *Trains* magazine (Kalmbach Publishing Co.). We thank the late David P. Morgan, long-time editor of the magazine, and retired Kalmbach president James J. King, for allowing our use of the Monon photos taken by the late Linn H. Westcott and other company staffers.

Before leaving the subject of photographic contributions, we also wish to thank two other studios—J. C. Allen & Sons (Chester Allen) of Lafayette and Roberts' Studio (Bruce Roberts) in Bedford—for their assistance. For his darkroom artistry, we extend our utmost thanks to Paul A. Erler for his long hours and superb work in printing many of the photos reproduced in this book. And, for his contemporary photographs appearing in this edition, we thank Eric Powell, whose expert camera work proves there is still much drama to be recorded along the Hoosier Line.

For contributions and continued support we also wish to mention the following individuals: J. Parker Lamb, Malcolm D. McCarter, John F. Humiston, William Schnaiter, David A. McKalip, Kenneth Ardinger, Harold J. Stirton, Robert P. Olmsted, Jim Wozniczka, Denny Wozniczka, Richard Baldwin, Don Dover, Dan Dover, Louis A. Marre, C. R. Adams, Robert Stacy, Perry F. Johnson, Jack B. Fravert, Hulce Martin, William J. Husa, Jr., Elliot Kahn, Ron Stuckey, Jim Scribbins,

Bob Lorenz, Stephen P. Davidson, Fred Cline, Thomas Keane, Ken Atkinson, Richard Bowen, Montford Switzer, Scott Pandorf, John M. Taylor, James M. Guthrie, J. David Ingles, J. Anthony Koester, Dave Randolph, R. E. Prien, Robert Wheeler, Robert Conyer, James W. Smith, Warren L. Smith, Ken Marsh, Richard J. Cook, George W. Hockaday, Donald Kaplan, Tom Smart, and George Yater. And we thank the following organizations: CSX Corp. (Charles B. Castner, Joseph Beckman, and R. Lyle Key); the Indiana Rail Road (Thomas Hoback); the Indiana Department of Transportation (Tom Beck); the *Spencer Evening World;* Electro-Motive Division of General Motors; Chrome Locomotive, Inc.; Union Tank Car Co.; the Elgin, Joliet & Eastern; Alco Historic Photos; and the Monon Railroad Historical-Technical Society.

Finally, we recognize that this book would not exist without the confidence, commitment, and enthusiasm of the publishing professionals with whom we have worked. We thank Mac Sebree, then of Interurban Press, for originally bringing this volume to fruition, and Roberta Diehl of Indiana University Press for being so instrumental in the development of this new edition. We also thank Mike Danneman for so skillfully creating the dustjacket painting for this book and, in the process, capturing so much of the Monon's magic on canvas.

And we especially thank our families—particularly our wives, Donnette and Lana—for living through the tribulations of this book's creation.

Gary W. Dolzall
Stephen F. Dolzall

AFTERWORD

Frank Van Bree, President
Monon Railroad Historical-Technical Society, Inc.

A GENERATION of Hoosiers has grown to maturity since the Monon ran its historic route from the hills of southern Indiana through the cornfields of the heartland to the shores of Lake Michigan. Tell someone under 40 that you worked on the Monon and you'll be asked, "What's that?" Yet there is continuing interest in this railroad which was limited in its ability to compete even before the days of the mega-carriers. Today it would be looked at as too small to be spun off as a mom-and-pop regional feeding business to its former owner. In the late 1960s, however, it was a property that added real value to the L&N.

The Southern Railway regretted that it refused the opportunity to buy the Monon. Southern's traffic department wanted to retain its traditional north-south gateways and did not want to offend friendly carriers with whom it interchanged at those locations. Later, second thoughts caused Southern to change its position and offer to equal the proposal the L&N had made to Monon shareholders if for any reason L&N decided not to consummate the merger.

L&N was unhappy with the condition imposed by the Interstate Commerce Commission that allowed the Milwaukee Road to be a tenant line of the Kentucky & Indiana Terminal Railroad rather than buy Monon's one-third ownership interest from L&N. Ultimately, of course, L&N decided that it would accept the ICC condition. And it acquired a quality railroad. The main line track and road bed required only maintenance, not substantial rebuilding or upgrading, for more than ten years. The road motive power was modern and served the L&N well as did the small but relatively new car fleet.

The real treasure that the L&N acquired were the Monon employees. It was said by more than a few L&N officials that a Monon man could railroad with anybody.

He was proud of where he came from, the training he had, and the knowledge he brought to the merged company. "You could always tell one of 'em by the way he talked, the way he walked, and the way he did his job," is what one L&N manager told me. I think that manager meant that a Monon man had a quiet sort of assurance and the self confidence that he was up to the task even though he now worked for a railroad ten times larger.

There are very few working railroaders today at CSX who have a Monon seniority date prior to July 31, 1971. The Monon man is passing into history just as his company has.

Why the continuing interest in the Monon? A lot of reasons make the short list: The availability of documents from which its history can be studied; a convenient size to model with accuracy, and the ability to render a complete replica of the modeler's favorite time period and location; the legacy of the super railroad that John Barriger envisioned; and access to Monon people who like to talk about their railroad.

This is one of only three books that have been written about the history of the Monon. Each book seems to have whetted the appetites of the readers for more knowledge and in-depth study of some particular item of personal interest. Source material is readily available in the archives of the University of Louisville, the Indiana Historical Society, and the Monon Railroad Historical-Technical Society, and is not of such magnitude as to intimidate the inquirer.

Modeling the Monon is not a daunting challenge. Information and photographic evidence are available on track layout, industries served, motive power, and rolling stock for almost any period and locale the modeler chooses. For those whose attention to detail and accuracy are the hallmarks of their hobby, the size of the

Monon is inviting. You don't need three rooms and a garage to do the whole railroad if that's your ambition. There are people in other countries who have never set foot on the property, but they model it too.

Most people probably became aware of the Monon through the publicity that John Barriger's vision of a super railroad brought to it. Monon neither was nor could it have ever been a super railroad. But Barriger took what he had to work with and maximized every publicity opportunity so that everyone in the Midwest at least—and nationally to some degree—thought that the Super Monon was just around the curve. Even today, national railroad journals publish pictures and articles often enough to keep its memory alive and generate a little more interest.

The Monon today lives largely through books like this and the efforts of its historical society. The Monon Society has a voracious appetite for photographs, historical records, and anecdotal evidence of what life on the Monon was like. With a small but enthusiastic membership, it is attempting to acquire, restore, and display what little rolling stock remains, all within the constraints of an inadequate treasury. Its headquarters at Linden, Indiana, contain the archives, and adjacent land is the final home of a restored caboose, boxcar, and eventually a heavyweight passenger car which will contain photographs and other memorabilia. Nearby, CSX rolls by with freight and Amtrak with passengers on the former main line between Crawfordsville and Lafayette. To satisfy the appetites of its members for history and models, it publishes a quarterly journal, one issue of which is entirely photographs combined with an annual calendar. It annually commissions an HO kit that precisely replicates a piece of Monon rolling stock. A Web site and electronic mailing list have been added so that anyone who wants to inquire or talk about the Monon can do so electronically.

While the Monon Railroad corporation no longer exists, rail operations continue over about half of the Monon's trackage and its fans keep the Monon alive in memory, model, and exchange of information. To borrow a phrase from Mahlon "Cookie" Eberhardt, employee, collector, and historian, "Long live the Monon."

ROSTERS
MONON STEAM LOCOMOTIVE ROSTER
AS OF MAY 1, 1946
(BY CLASS)

Heading codes:
R/n = Road number
B/d = Builder date
C/n = Construction number
P/n = Previous Monon road number(s)

Class B-8/0-6-0, Alco-Brooks

R/n	B/d	C/n	P/n	Disposition
30	2/05	30704	18	Retired 1946.
35	1/08	45088	23	Retired 1949.

Notes:
1. Monon 35 renumbered 95 in 1947. Last Monon steam in service.

Class B-9/0-6-0, Alco-Brooks

R/n	B/d	C/n	P/n	Disposition
37	10/23	64888	—	Retired 1947.
38	10/23	64889	—	Retired 1947.
39	10/23	64890	—	Retired 1946.

Notes:
1. Monon 37 renumbered 97 in 1947 before retirement.
2. Monon 38 renumbered 98 in 1947 before retirement.

Class E-1a/4-8-0, Alco-Brooks/Lafayette Shops

R/n	B/d	C/n	P/n	Disposition
224	6/98	2966	204	Retired 1947.
229	4/00	3495	209	Retired 1949.

Notes:
1. Monon 224 was originally E-1, rebuilt to E-1a at Lafayette 1925.
2. Monon 229 was originally E-1, rebuilt to E-1a at Lafayette 1923.

Class E-1b/0-6-0, Alco-Brooks, Lafayette Shops

R/n	B/d	C/n	P/n	Disposition
222	6/98	2964	202	Retired 1947.
225	6/98	3191	205	Retired 1947.
227	4/99	3193	207	Retired 1946.
230	4/00	3496	210	Retired 1947.

Class J 552 shuffles about at Monon, Ind., in August 1946—the twilight of the steam era on the Chicago, Indianapolis & Louisville. (HAROLD STIRTON)

R/n	B/d	C/n	P/n	Disposition
231	4/00	3497	211	Retired 1949.

Notes:
1. Monon 222, 225, 230 originally E-1, rebuilt at Lafayette 1925.
2. Monon 227 originally E-1, rebuilt at Lafayette 1926.
3. Monon 231 originally E-1, rebuilt at Lafayette 1924.

Class G-2b/4-6-0, Alco-Brooks/Lafayette Shops

R/n	B/d	C/n	P/n	Disposition
111	4/00	3501	121/141	Retired 1948.

Notes:
1. Monon 111 originally Class G-6, rebuilt at Lafayette 1923.

Class H-6/2-8-0, Alco-Brooks

R/n	B/d	C/n	P/n	Disposition
281	5/11	44938	286	Retired 1947.
283	5/11	49940	288	Retired 1948.
285	5/11	49942	290	Retired 1948.
286	5/11	49943	291	Retired 1948.

Class J-1/2-8-2, Alco-Brooks

R/n	B/d	C/n	P/n	Disposition
501	3/12	50703	—	Retired 1948.
509	8/12	51658	—	Sold to Tennessee Railroad (No. 40), 1946.
510	8/12	51659	—	Retired 1948.
511	8/12	51660	—	Retired 1946.
514	8/12	51663	—	Sold to Tennessee Railroad (No. 41), 1946.
517	8/12	51666	—	Retired 1946.
518	8/12	51667	—	Retired 1947.
520	8/12	51669	—	Retired 1946.
521	8/12	51670	—	Retired 1948.
522	8/12	51671	—	Retired 1947.
523	8/12	51672	—	Retired 1947.
524	8/12	51673	—	Retired 1948.
525	5/18	58631	—	Retired 1949.
527	5/18	58633	—	Retired 1947.
528	5/18	59134	—	Retired 1946.
529	5/18	59135	—	Retired 1946.

Class J-1a/2-8-2, Alco-Brooks

R/n	B/d	C/n	P/n	Disposition
530	1/23	63823	—	Retired 1948.
531	1/23	63824	—	Retired 1946.
532	1/23	63825	—	Retired 1947.

Class J-2/2-8-2, Alco-Schenectady

R/n	B/d	C/n	P/n	Disposition
550	10/18	59680	—	Retired 1948.
551	10/18	59681	—	Retired 1948.
552	10/18	59682	—	Retired 1947.
553	10/18	59683	—	Retired 1947.
554	10/18	59684	—	Retired 1949.

Class J-3/2-8-2, Alco/Richmond

R/n	B/d	C/n	P/n	Disposition
560	10/26	67085	—	Retired 1949.
561	10/26	67086	—	Retired 1948.
562	10/26	67087	—	Retired 1947.
563	10/26	67088	—	Retired 1947.
564	10/26	67089	—	Retired 1948.
565	10/26	67090	—	Retired 1949.

Class J-4/2-8-2, Alco/Schenectady

R/n	B/d	C/n	P/n	Disposition
570	10/29	68051	580	Sold 1947 to Pittsburgh & Shawmut, No. 570.
571	10/29	68042	—	Sold 1949 to Pittsburgh & Shawmut, No. 571.
572	10/29	68043	—	Sold 1949 to Pittsburgh & Shawmut, No. 572.
573	10/29	68044	—	Sold 1947 to Pittsburgh & Shawmut, No. 573.
574	10/29	68045	—	Sold 1947 to Pittsburgh & Shawmut, No. 574.
575	10/29	68046	—	Sold 1947 to Pittsburgh & Shawmut, No. 575.
576	10/29	68047	—	Sold 1948 to Tennessee, Alabama & Georgia, No. 402.
577	10/29	68048	—	Sold 1947 to Pittsburgh & Shawmut, No. 577.
578	10/29	68049	—	Sold 1948 to Tennessee, Alabama & Georgia, No. 401.
579	10/29	68050	—	Sold 1949 to Pittsburgh & Shawmut No. 579.

Notes:
1. Monon No. 570 delivered number 580, immediately renumbered 570.

Class K-2a/4-6-2, Alco/Brooks

R/n	B/d	C/n	P/n	Disposition
410	5/06	39594	354	Retired 1947.
412	5/06	39596	356	Retired 1947.
413	5/06	40110	357	Retired 1947.

Class K-3/4-6-2, Alco/Brooks

R/n	B/d	C/n	P/n	Disposition
420	8/09	46234	403	Retired 1947.

Class K-4/4-6-2, Alco/Brooks

R/n	B/d	C/n	P/n	Disposition
430	5/11	49934	403	Retired 1947.
431	5/11	49935	404	Retired 1947.
432	5/11	49936	405	Retired 1947.

Class K-5/4-6-2, Alco/Brooks

R/n	B/d	C/n	P/n	Disposition
440	9/12	51674	—	Retired 1948.
442	9/12	51676	—	Retired 1948.

Class K-5a/4-6-2, Alco/Brooks

R/n	B/d	C/n	P/n	Disposition
443	1/23	63827	—	Retired 1949.
444	1/23	63828	—	Retired 1948.
445	1/23	63829	—	Retired 1948.

Class K-6/4-6-2, Alco/Brooks

R/n	B/d	C/n	P/n	Disposition
451	10/16	56395	—	Retired 1947.
452	10/16	56397	—	Retired 1947.

Class L-1/2-10-2, Alco/Brooks-Schenectady

R/n	B/d	C/n	P/n	Disposition
604	11/14	54893	—	Retired 1946.
606	11/16	56398	—	Retired 1947.
607	11/16	56399	—	Retired 1946.

Notes:
1. Monon 604 was built at Alco/Schenectady.
2. Monon 606, 607 was built at Alco/Brooks.

MONON
DIESEL-ELECTRIC ROSTER
(BY BUILDER AND MODEL)

Roster heading codes:
R/n = Road number
D/d = Delivery date
C/n = Construction number
S/n = Subsequent Monon road number(s)
A/B = A (cab unit); B (cabless booster)

American Locomotive Co.
(Alco-GE, Alco Products)

RS-2/1500-horsepower, B-B road-switcher

R/n	D/d	C/n	S/n	Disposition
21	1/47	74993	51	To L&N 260 at merger. Retired 1972.
22	3/47	75142	52	Rebuilt to L&N slug 2063 in 1972.
23	4/47	75144	53	L&N trade-in to General Electric, 1972.
24	8/47	75261	54	Rebuilt to L&N slug 2064 in 1972.
25	10/47	75394	55	L&N trade-in to General Electric, 1972.
26	10/47	75395	56	L&N trade-in to General Electric, 1972.
27	10/47	75396	57	L&N trade-in to General Electric, 1972.
28	8/47	75143	58	L&N trade-in to General Electric, 1972.
29	8/47	74992	59	Rebuilt to L&N slug 2065 in 1972.

RS-2 notes:

1. RS-2's 21, 22, 24, 25, 28, 29 built with steam generators.
2. RS-2's 24, 25 built with Timken roller bearing journals.
3. All RS-2's rebuilt to 1600-horsepower at Lafayette 1965-66 and renumbered into 51-59 series.
4. RS-2 28 built as Alco demonstrator 1501 in 1/47; demonstrated on Canadian National, Ontario Northland in April and May 1947. Delivered to Monon as No. 28 in 8/47.
5. RS-2 29 built as Alco demonstrator 1500 in 1/47; demonstrated on Canadian National and Ontario Northland in April and May 1947. Delivered to Monon as No. 29 in 8/47.

C-628/2750-horsepower, C-C, heavy road-switcher

R/n	D/d	C/n	S/n Disposition
400	3/64	84903	— To Alco 1967 for C-420's. Resold to Lehigh Valley 633, to Conrail 6729. Retired 1978.
401	3/64	84904	— To Alco 1967 for C-420's. Resold to Lehigh Valley 634, to Conrail 6730. Retired 1978.
402	3/64	84905	— To Alco 1967 for C-420's. Resold to Lehigh Valley 635. To Conrail 6731. Retired 1978.
403	3/64	84906	— To Alco 1967 for C-420's. Resold to Lehigh Valley 636. Assigned CR 6732. Retired 1978.
404	3/64	84907	— To Alco 1967 for C-420's. Resold to Lehigh Valley 637. To Conrail 6733. Retired 1978.
405	3/64	84908	— To Alco 1967 for C-420's. Resold to Lehigh Valley 638. To Conrail 6734. Retired 1978.
406	3/64	84909	— To Alco 1967 for C-420's. Resold to Lehigh Valley 639. To Conrail 6735. Retired 1979.
407	3/64	84910	— To Alco 1967 for C-420's. Resold to Lehigh Valley 640. To Conrail 6736. Retired 1981.
408	3/64	84911	— To Alco 1967 for C-420's. Resold to Lehigh Valley 641. To Conrail 6737. Retired 1979.

C-420/2000-horsepower, B-B, road-switcher

R/n	D/d	C/n	S/n Disposition
501	8/66	3448-05	— To L&N 1318, retired 1/82, sold to Chrome Crankshaft.
502	8/66	3448-06	— To L&N 1319, retired 7/82, sold to Chrome Crankshaft.
503	8/66	3448-01	— To L&N 1320, retired 4/82, sold to Chrome Crankshaft.
504	8/66	3448-02	— To L&N 1321, retired 7/82, sold to Chrome Crankshaft.
505	8/66	3448-03	— To L&N 1322, retired 10/81, sold to Chrome Crankshaft.
506	8/66	3448-04	— To L&N 1323, retired 4/82, sold to Chrome Crankshaft.
507	8/67	3490-01	— To L&N 1324, retired 4/82, sold to Chrome Crankshaft, resold to Arkansas & Missouri. Renumbered A&M 68.
508	8/67	3490-02	— To L&N 1325, retired 4/82, sold to Chrome Crankshaft.
509	8/67	3490-03	— To L&N 1326, retired 4/82, sold to Chrome Crankshaft.
510	8/67	3490-04	— To L&N 1327, retired 5/82, sold to Chrome Crankshaft.
511	8/67	3490-05	— To L&N 1328, retired 4/82, sold to Chrome Crankshaft.
512	8/67	3490-06	— To L&N 1329, retired 7/82, sold to Chrome Crankshaft.
513	8/67	3490-07	— To L&N 1330, retired 7/82, sold to Chrome Crankshaft. Leased to Iowa Railroad, resold to Naples Terminal, still numbered 1330.
514	8/67	3490-08	— To L&N 1331, retired 7/82, sold to Chrome Crankshaft. Resold to Arkansas & Missouri for parts.
515	8/67	3490-09	— To L&N 1332, retired 7/82, sold to Chrome Crankshaft. Resold as Indiana Hi-Rail 332. Leased to Delaware-Lackawanna Railroad.
516	8/67	3490-10	— To L&N 1333, retired 11/79. Rebuilt by GE-Hornell as Apache Railway 83.
517	8/67	3490-11	— To L&N 1334, retired 4/82, sold to Chrome Crankshaft. Resold as Indiana Hi-Rail 334. Leased to Delaware-Lackawanna Railroad.
518	8/67	3490-12	— To L&N 1335, retired 7/82, sold to Chrome Crankshaft.

C-420 notes:
1. C-420's 501, 502 built with high nose and steam generator.

Electro-Motive Division, General Motors

SW-1/600-horsepower, B-B, switcher

R/n	D/d	C/n	S/n	Disposition
DS-50	2/42	1597	1 (2)	Sold 1948 to United Electric Coal Co. Preserved as CI&L DS-50 at Indiana Transportation Museum.
5	8/49	8423	—	To Bulk Terminal No. 5 in 1964.
6	8/49	8424	—	To Union Tank Car Leasing No. 200, 1963.

SW-1 notes:
1. DS-50 was Monon's first diesel. Renumbered No. 1 (as second unit to carry that number) in 1947.

NW-2/1000-horsepower, B-B, switcher

R/n	D/d	C/n	S/n Disposition
DS-1	4/42	1598	11 Sold 1970. Became Elgin, Joliet & Eastern 447 in 1972. Extant but stored.
DS-2	4/42	1599	12 To L&N 2202. Retired 1983.
DS-3	4/42	1600	13 To L&N 2203. Retired 1982.
14	1/47	4445	— Sold 1970. Became EJ&E 446 in 1971. Stored.
15	1/47	4446	— To L&N 2204, retired 1977. To Southern Pacific slug 1013.
16	1/47	4447	— To L&N 2205. Retired 1983.
17	1/47	4448	— To L&N 2206. Retired 1977, to SP slug 1011.

NW-2 notes:
1. DS-1 through DS-3 renumbered 11-13 in 1947.

F-3/1500-horsepower, B-B, streamlined cab unit

R/n	A/b	D/d	C/n	S/n	Disposition
Original 16 freight units					
51A	F-3A	12/46	3663	64A/101	Retired 1966.
51B	F-3A	12/46	3664	64B/110	Scrapped.
52A	F-3A	12/46	3665	65A/111	Scrapped.
52B	F-3A	12/46	3666	65B/112	Scrapped.
61A	F-3A	12/46	3669	103	Traded to Alco for C-420's 1966.

61B	F-3A	12/46	3670	104	Scrapped.
61C	F-3B	12/46	3677	301	Scrapped.
62A	F-3A	12/46	3671	105	Scrapped.
62B	F-3A	1/47	3672	—	Wrecked at Ash Grove, Ind., 6/3/47, scrapped after wreck.
62C	F-3B	12/46	3678	302	Scrapped.
63A	F-3A	1/47	3673	107	Scrapped.
63B	F-3A	1/47	3674	108	Scrapped.
63C	F-3B	1/47	4067	303	Scrapped.
64A	F-3A	1/47	3675	—	Wrecked at Ash Grove, Ind., 6/3/47, scrapped after wreck.
64B	F-3A	1/47	3676	Notes	Scrapped.
64C	F-3B	1/47	4068	—	Wrecked at Ash Grove, Ind., 6/3/47, scrapped after wreck.

Original 8 Passenger units

81A	F-3A	5/47	4453	201	Scrapped.
81B	F-3A	5/47	4454	202	Scrapped.
82A	F-3A	5/47	4455	203	To L&N, traded to EMD 1972.
82B	F-3A	5/47	4456	204	To L&N, traded to EMD 1972.
83A	F-3A	5/47	4457	205	Scrapped.
83B	F-3A	5/47	4458	206	Scrapped.
84A	F-3A	5/47	4459	207	Sold 1970, scrapped.
84B	F-3A	5/47	4460	208	Traded to Alco 1966 for C-420's, resold to L&N No. 805. Retired.

Ex-Electro-Motive demonstrators

85A	F-3A	8/47	4065	209	Scrapped following L&N merger.
85B	F-3A	8/47	4066	210	Sold before merger to L&N (via Precision). To L&N 554. Retired.
65C	F-3B	8/47	3373	305	Traded to Alco, scrapped.

Replacement units

62B (3)	F-3A	3/48	7416	106	Scrapped.
64A (3)	F-3A	3/48	7417	109	Scrapped.
64C (2)	F-3B	9/47	5194	304	Scrapped.

F-3 notes:

1. F-3A No. 51A was renumbered 64A (2nd) from mid-1947 to 3/48, then renumbered back to 51A.
2. F-3A No. 51B was renumbered 64B (2nd) in mid-1947.
3. F-3A 52A was renumbered 65A in late 1947.
4. F-3A 52B was renumbered 65B in late 1947.
5. F-3A 64B was renumbered 62B (2nd) in mid-1947, renumbered 51B (2nd) in 3/48.
6. During 1963, all F-3's were renumbered, freight F-3A's into the 100-series; passenger F-3A's into the 200-series; F-3B's into the 300-series (individual renumberings indicated in roster above).
7. F-3A 62B delivered new in 3/48 was third unit to carry that number.
8. F-3A 64A delivered new in 3/48 was third unit to carry that number.
9. F-3B 64C delivered in 9/47 was second unit to carry that number.
10. F-3A's 81A/B through 85A/B were built with steam generators.

BL-2/1500-horsepower, B-B, semi-streamlined road-switcher

R/n	D/d	C/n	S/n	Disposition
30	4/48	4449	—	Sold for trade-in to Pennsylvania-Reading Seaboard Line in 1970
31	4/48	4450	—	Sold for trade-in to L&N in 1967.
32	4/48	4451	—	Donated by L&N to Kentucky Railway Museum and restored to operable condition.
33	4/48	4452	—	Trade-in to Alco for C-420's, 1966.
34	4/48	5243	—	Trade-in to Alco for C-420's, 1966.
35	4/48	5244	—	Sold for trade-in to PRSL in 1970.
36 (2)	4/49	8420	—	Sold 1970.
37 (2)	5/49	8421	—	Sold for trade-in to PRSL 1970.
38	5/49	8422	—	Traded to Alco for C-420's, 1966.

BL-2 notes:

1. Monon 30 was first BL-2 delivered by EMD. Monon 38 was last BL-2 built.
2. BL-2 36 was second unit to carry that number (following F-M H-15-44).
3. BL-2 37 was second unit to carry that number (following F-M H-15-44).

Fairbanks-Morse

H-10-44/1000-horsepower, B-B, switcher

R/n	D/d	C/n	S/n	Disposition
18	11/46	L1020	—	To W. R. Grace No. 102, 1963. Scrapped, 1968.

H-10-44 notes:

1. Re-engined with Electro-Motive 567 12-cylinder 1000 h.p. power plant at Lafayette Shops in 1961.

H-15-44/1500-horsepower, B-B, road-switcher

R/n	D/d	C/n	S/n	Disposition
36	9/47	L1198	45	Cannibalized 1968; scrapped 1970.
37	12/47	L1199	46	Scrapped 1970.

H-15-44 notes:

1. Monon 36-37 (renumbered 45-46 in 1949) were first H-15-44's built by FM.
2. Monon 45-46 re-engined with Electro-Motive 567 16-cylinder 1500 h.p. power plants at Lafayette Shops in 1960.

General Electric

U23B/2250-horsepower, B-B, road-switcher

R/n	D/d	C/n	S/n	Disposition
601	3/70	37293	—	To L&N 2700, SBD 2700, SBD 3230, CSX 3230, retired 4/90.
602	4/70	37294	—	To L&N 2701, SBD 2701, SBD 3231, CSX 3231, retired 3/93.
603	4/70	37295	—	To L&N 2702, SBD 2702, SBD 3232, CSX 3232, retired 2/92.
604	4/70	37296	—	To L&N 2703, SBD 2703, SBD 3233, CSX 3233, retired 11/91.
605	4/70	37297	—	To L&N 2704, SBD 2704, SBD 3234, CSX 3234, retired 11/91.
606	4/70	37298	—	To L&N 2705, SBD 2705, SBD 3235, CSX 3235, retired 4/91.
607	4/70	37299	—	To L&N 2706, SBD 2706, SBD 3236, CSX 3236, retired 5/95.
608	5/70	37300	—	To L&N 2707, SBD 2707, SBD 3237, CSX 3237, retired 5/91.

U23B notes:

1. Monon 604 (L&N 2703) was first Monon diesel painted L&N gray/yellow.

MONON PASSENGER EQUIPMENT ROSTER

(POST WORLD WAR II)

R/N	Type	Original Builder	Year Built	Monon Acqu'd	Monon Retired	Notes
1	Business	TCRR	1925	1946	1963	1
2	Business	Pullman	1924	1953	1971	2
3	Business	AC&F	1926	1963	1968	3
11	Mail-baggage	AC&F	1944	1947	1964	4
12	Mail-baggage	AC&F	1944	1947	1964	5
13	Mail-baggage	StLC	1942	1942	1968	6
14	Mail-baggage	StLC	1942	1942	1968	6
17	Mail-express	B&S	1913	1913	1949	7
18	Mail-express	B&S	1913	1913	1953	8
19	Mail-baggage	StLC	1942	1942	1968	6
21	Coach	AC&F	1944	1947	R/B	9
22	Coach	AC&F	1944	1947	1960	10
23	Coach	AC&F	1944	1947	R/B	11
24	Coach	AC&F	1944	1947	1960	12
25	Coach	AC&F	1944	1947	1968	13
26	Coach	AC&F	1944	1947	R/B	14
27	Deluxe coach	AC&F	1944	1959	1959	15
28	Deluxe coach	AC&F	1944	1948	1959	16
29	Deluxe coach	AC&F	1944	1948	R/B	17
30	Deluxe coach	AC&F	1944	1948	1959	18
31	Deluxe coach	AC&F	1944	1948	1959	19
32	Deluxe coach	AC&F	1944	1948	1959	20
33	Deluxe coach	AC&F	1944	1948	1959	21
34	Deluxe coach	AC&F	1944	1949	R/B	22
41	Coach	AC&F	1944	1956	1968	23
42	Coach	AC&F	1944	1959	1968	24
43	Coach	AC&F	1944	1960	1968	25
44	Coach	AC&F	1944	1960	1968	26
45	Coach	AC&F	1944	1964	1968	27
46	Coach	AC&F	1944	1965	1968	28
50	Coach	B&S	1911	1911	1950	29
51	Coach	B&S	1911	1911	1949	30
52	Coach	B&S	1911	1911	1950	31
51	Dining-bar-lounge	AC&F	1944	1947	1959	32
52	Dining-bar-lounge	AC&F	1944	1947	1959	33
53	Dining-bar-lounge	AC&F	1944	1948	1959	34
58	Dining-parlor-observation	AC&F	1944	1948	1959	34A
59	Dining-parlor-observation	AC&F	1944	1948	1959	34B
60	Business	CI&L	1926	1926	1948	35
61	Coach	Pullman	1923	1923	1954	
62	Coach	Pullman	1923	1923	1954	
63	Coach	Pullman	1923	1923	1954	
64	Coach	Pullman	1923	1923	1954	
65	Grill-coach	AC&F	1944	1947	Rblt.	36

Carbuilder and other codes

AC&F = American Car & Foundry
StLC = St. Louis Car Company
B&S = Barney & Smith Car Company
OFCC = Ohio Falls Car Company
TC = Tennessee Central Railway
CI&L = Lafayette Shops
M/W = Maintenance-of-way
P-S = Pullman Standard
Rblt. = Rebuilt
R/N = Road Number
Renum. = Renumbered

Notes

1. Ex-Tennessee Central 100. Sold to Green Bay Railway Museum.
2. *Lynne* rebuilt from Pullman *Great Spirit* sold to Brown Inc.
3. Purchased from B&O. Resold to L&N.
4. Ex-USA 89397. Trucks removed, used at Lafayette Shops.
5. Ex-USA 89395. Trucks removed, used at Lafayette Shops.
6. Rebuilt from 430-series cars.
7. Renumbered from 508 in 2/48.
8. 609 renumbered to 512 in 5/46, renumbered again in 3/48 to 18.
9. Ex-USA 89377. Rebuilt 2/60 to coach 43.
10. Ex-USA 89371.
11. Ex-USA 89394. Rebuilt 12/60 to coach 44.
12. Ex-USA 89372.
13. Ex-USA 89390.
14. Ex-USA 89396. Rebuilt 8/64 to coach 45.
15. Ex-USA 89386.
16. Ex-USA 89381.
17. Ex-USA 89382. Rebuilt 5/59 to coach 42.
18. Ex-USA 89393.
19. Ex-USA 89367.
20. Ex-USA 89366.
21. Ex-USA 89349.
22. Ex-USA 89380. Rebuilt 9/65 to coach 46.
23. Rebuilt from grill-coach 65.
24. Rebuilt from Deluxe coach 29.
25. Rebuilt from coach 21.

R/N	Type	Original Builder	Year Built	Monon Acqu'd	Monon Retired	Notes
66	Grill-coach	AC&F	1944	1948	1959	37
67	Grill-coach	AC&F	1944	1948	1959	38
68	Grill-coach	AC&F	1944	Rblt.		39
69	Grill-coach	AC&F	1944	Rblt.		40
71	Parlor-observation	AC&F	1944	1959		41
72	Parlor-observation	AC&F	1944	1959		42
75	Parlor	Pullman	1927	1946	1959	43
81	Dinette-coach	AC&F	1944	1949	1959	44
82	Dinette-coach	AC&F	1944	1949	1959	45
85	Coach	AC&F	1906	1906	1949	46
90	Business	CI&L	1916	1916	1948	47
101	Baggage	Pullman	1929	1947	1968	49
102	Baggage	Pullman	1923	1947	1968	49
103	Baggage	Pullman	1924	1947	1968	49
104	Baggage	Pullman	1917	1949	1968	49
106	Baggage	StLC	1942	1942	1968	50
107	Baggage	StLC	1942	1942	1968	50
108	Baggage	StLC	1942	1942	1968	50
109	Baggage	StLC	1942	1942	1968	50
110	Parlor	AC&F	1909	1909	1950	48
115	Dining-lounge	B&S	1912	1912	1949	51
116	Dining-lounge	B&S	1912	1912	1949	52
201	Head-end	AC&F	1944	1947	Renum.	53
202	Head-end	AC&F	1944	1948	Renum.	54
203	Head-end	AC&F	1944	1955	Renum.	55
204	Head-end	AC&F	1944	1955	Renum.	55
205	Head-end	AC&F	1944	1955	Renum.	55
206	Head-end	AC&F	1944	1955	Renum.	55
250	Head-end	Pullman	1952	1952	—	56
251	Head-end	Pullman	1952	1952	—	73
317	Baggage-coach	B&S	1912	1951		57
406	Baggage	OFCC	1893	1893	1950	58
430	Baggage	StLC	1942	1942	1968	59
431	Baggage	StLC	1942	1942	1968	60
432	Baggage	StLC	1942	1942	1968	61
433	Baggage	StLC	1942	1942	1968	59
434	Baggage	StLC	1942	1942	1968	59
435	Baggage	StLC	1942	1968		62
436	Baggage	StLC	1942	1942	1968	59
508	Baggage	B&S	1913	1913	Renum.	60
512	Baggage	B&S	1913	1913	Renum.	61
609	Baggage	B&S	1913	1913	Renum.	62
610	Mail car	B&S	1913	1913	1951	
611	Mail car	B&S	1913	1913	1951	63
641	Head-end	Pullman	1952	1952	—	64
775	Head-end	Pullman	1952	1952	—	64
784	Head-end	Pullman	1952	1952	—	64
820	Head-end	Pullman	1952	1952	—	64
2200	Power car	AC&F	1944	1948	1964	65
2203	Head-end	AC&F	1944	1948	1959	66
2204	Head-end	AC&F	1944	1948	1959	66
2205	Head-end	AC&F	1944	1948	1968	66
2206	Head-end	AC&F	1944	1948	1968	66
2207	Head-end	AC&F	1944	1948	1968	67
2208	Head-end	AC&F	1944	1948	1968	67
2209	Head-end	AC&F	1944	1948	1968	67
2210	Head-end	AC&F	1944	1948	1968	67
X-5	Power car	AC&F	1944	1948	Renum.	68
	Sleeper	Pullman	—	1949	1953	69
	Sleeper	Pullman	—	1949	1960	70
	Sleeper	Pullman	—	1949	1960	71
	Sleeper	Pullman	—	1949	1953	72

26. Rebuilt from coach 23.
27. Rebuilt from coach 26.
28. Rebuilt from Deluxe coach 34.
29. Retired, converted to crew quarters at McDoel in 1950.
30. Retired, converted to crew quarters at South Hammond.
31. Retired, converted to crew quarters at Lafayette in 1950.
32. Ex-USA 89389.
33. Ex-USA 89379.
34. Ex-USA 89388.
34A. Ex-USA 89346.
34B. Ex-USA 89373.
35. Retired, carbody sold to CI&L director Lyons 11/10/48.
36. Ex-USA 89392. Rebuilt 5/56 to coach 41.
37. Ex-USA 89370.
38. Ex-USA 89355. Used as temporary station at Lafayette 1959-60.
39. Ex-USA 89374. Rebuilt in 1949 to dinette 81.
40. Ex-USA 89375. Rebuilt in 1949 to dinette 82.
41. Ex-USA 89364.
42. Ex-USA 89384.
43. Purchased from Pullman 1/1/46.
44. Rebuilt from grill-coach 68.
45. Rebuilt from grill-coach 69.
46. Retired, converted to crew quarters at South Hammond.
47. Retired. Leased to St. Louis Museum of Transportation.
48. Rebuilt from coach 48 in 1946. Retired and converted to crew quarters at Belt Junction in Indianapolis in 1950.
49. Pullman tourist car conversion at Lafayette Shops.
50. Renumbering of CI&L 430, 433, 434 and 436.
51. Rebuilt from 96. Converted to M/W X-156.
52. Rebuilt from 97. Converted to M/W X-157.
53. Ex-USA kitchen car. Converted to rider car 220 in 3/53.
54. Ex-USA kitchen car. Converted to rider car 221 in 3/53.
55. Renumbered to 2200 series in 1956.
56. P-S boxcar renumbered from 635. Express service 1955-1959.
57. Retired for use at station at Monon.
58. Converted to M/W service.
59. To 106-109 series.
60. Converted to mail-baggage 13.
61. Converted to mail-baggage 14.
62. Converted to mail-baggage 19.
63. Rebuilt from mail-baggage 507 in 1928.
64. Renumbered from 601-851 boxcar series. In express service 1955-1959.
65. Renumbered from X-5 in 1957.
66. Renumbering of 203-206.
67. Ex-USA kitchen cars. Converted to express service 1955-56.
68. Ex-USA kitchen car. Renumbered 2200 in 1957.
69. *Camp Dix.*
70. *Camp Meigs.*
71. *Fort Canby.*
72. *Sir Henry W. Thorton.*
73. P-S Boxcar 837. In express service 1955-1959.

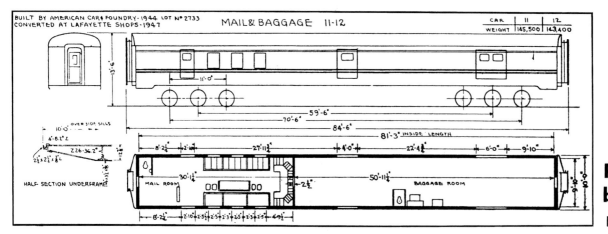

RPO-baggage

Nos. 11-12

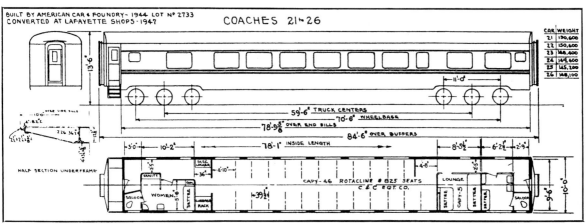

Coach

Nos. 21-26

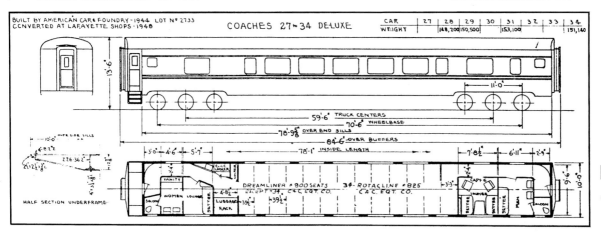

Deluxe coach

Nos. 27-34

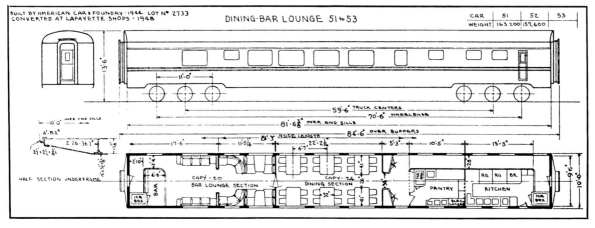

Dining-bar lounge

Nos. 51-53

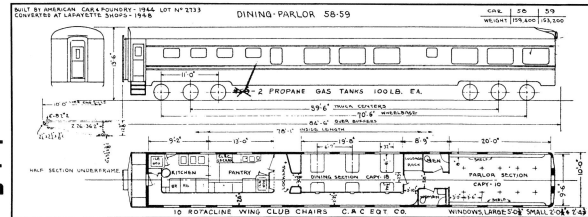

Dining-parlor-observation
Nos. 58-59

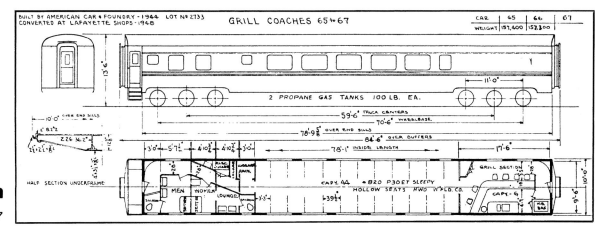

Grill coach
Nos. 65-67

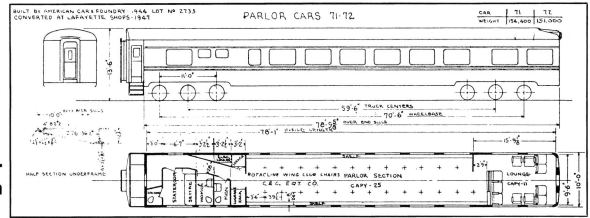

Parlor-observation
Nos. 71-72

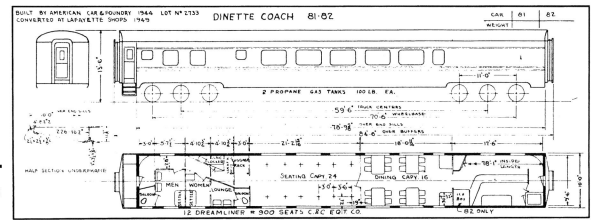

Dinette-coach
Nos. 81-82

INDEX

(Italicized page numbers indicate illustrations.)

A pair of Monon's familiar semaphores frame the Hoosier Line's longest-lived postwar passenger train, the *Thoroughbred,* south of the railroad's namesake town. Farewell, Monon. *(DAVE FERGUSON'S PHOTO ART)*

GARY W. DOLZALL

has no difficulty explaining his fascination with the Monon. Living first in Bedford and then in Bloomington, Indiana, he spent his first two decades near Hoosier Line rails. A lifelong student of the railroad industry, Gary has written numerous magazine articles and three books in addition to this one:

• *Diesels from Eddystone: The Story of Baldwin Diesel Locomotives* (with Stephen Dolzall),

• *Steel Rails across America* (with Mike Danneman),

• *The Spirit of Railroading* (with Mike Danneman).

Other interests include model railroading, auto racing, and the American Civil War; on the latter subject he has also published a number of magazine articles. An Indiana University graduate, Gary lives with his wife and three children in Connecticut.

STEPHEN F. DOLZALL

received a Lionel train set at age two which served to establish a lifelong interest in railroading. A family move to Bedford, Indiana, in 1948 afforded Steve first a glimpse at Monon steam and later a ringside seat for the final chapter of the Monon story. Steve has co-authored:

• *Diesels from Eddystone: The Story of Baldwin Diesel Locomotives*

and several magazine articles with Gary. Although the Monon remains a favorite, other specialties are the products of all the locomotive builders and the history of railroads in Southern Indiana. His other interests include model railroading, the Indianapolis 500, automobile restoration, and automotive history. Steve is a graduate of Indiana University. He and his wife, Lana, live in Amhurst, Virginia, and have two married children.

THE MONON IN COLOR

Left: In a red-and-gray tribute to the Barriger-era Monon, the new *Hoosier*—fresh from Lafayette Shops—stands for its portrait in the summer of 1947. On the point, Electro-Motive F-3 No. 81, the first of the original eight-unit set of passenger F's delivered in May 1947. **Above:** In the dark environs of Chicago's Dearborn Station on August 17, 1947, John Barriger and famed cartoonist John T. McCutcheon prepare to splash parlor-observation No. 71 with champagne before the *Hoosier's* first scheduled run. *(BOTH PHOTOS, DAVE FERGUSON'S PHOTO ART)*

Raymond Loewy's styling of Monon's post-war passenger cars resulted in memorable interior fittings, including a grand bar and Kentucky Derby theming (**above**, in dining-bar-lounge No. 51) and plush parlor seats (**right**, in parlor-observation No. 71). (BOTH PHOTOS, DAVE FERGUSON'S PHOTO ART)

Above: Steam meets diesel, Southern meets Monon, at the Kentucky & Indiana Terminal's Youngtown Yard, Louisville, in 1948. Monon F-3A 65B is northbound with a mainline freight while Southern Railway 2-8-0 No. 838 powers a short local. *(JACK B. FRAVERT)* **Right:** Crewmen chat and baggage is loaded on head-end cars at Louisville Union Station (also known as 10th Street Station) in preparation of a 1954 departure of train 6, the northbound *Thoroughbred*. Eight years into its career, Monon F-3A has lost little of its appeal. *(CHARLES B. CASTNER)*

Right: Dressed in the black-and-gold livery that symbolized Monon's postwar freight operations, Hoosier Line F-3A 65B draws tonnage into New Albany's streets in September 1956. (*JACK B. FRAVERT*) **Below:** Ducking through the truss bridge over Fall Creek, Monon F-3A 82B with the southbound *Tippecanoe* rolls off the final miles toward Indianapolis Union Station in April 1959. (*RICHARD BALDWIN*)

The trainshed of Indianapolis Union Station frames Monon F-3A 83A as it arrives in the Hoosier capital with train 11, the *Tippecanoe*, in April 1959. Only days remained in the train's life. *(RICHARD BALDWIN)*

White flags fly from Alco RS-2's 24 and 26 as the veterans draw a local through Vernia, north of New Albany, on December 3, 1960. Right behind the duo was the ubiquitous (to Monon local freights) "head-end caboose." *(TOM SMART, DOLZALL COLLECTION)*

Red-and-gray F-3A 83A off the morning *Tippecanoe* run from Chicago takes a spin on the turntable at Monon's Belt Junction roundhouse in Indianapolis in 1959. The unit will probably return to the Windy City with the "5 o'clock Monon," a.k.a. *Hoosier.* (RICHARD BALDWIN)

Left: First of Monon's Alco C-628's, No. 400, leads two sisters out of McDoel Yard, Bloomington, with southbound train 73 in May 1967. A meet is occurring, with northbound 72 holding the main and No. 73 easing out of McDoel's passing track. *(FRED CLINE)* **Below:** A traffic glut on the Hoosier Line in 1966 required Monon to borrow motive power from another road which favored Alcos—Spokane, Portland & Seattle. SP&S RS-2 No. 63 idles away the evening at South Hammond with Century 628 No. 403 in August 1966. *(MIKE SCHAFER/JIM BOYD)*

New Alco C-420's 516, 517 and 518 stand at Lafayette Shops in September 1967. "Shops" would apply the lower headlight (taken off a trade-in C-628). Monon 518 was destined to be the last of a long line of Alco's that Monon purchased. *(J. ANTHONY KOESTER)*

Honorary EMD's: On the outside they look different from the Electro-Motive power they're coupled to, but inside Fairbanks-Morse H-15-44's 45 and 46 have the same power plants—EMD's 567-series V-16's. Repowering of the FM's took place at Lafayette Shops in 1960; scene is at McDoel Yard on March 1, 1964. *(TOM SMART, DOLZALL COLLECTION)*

An aluminum FM noseplate, brass builder's plate and a red horn punctuate a classy-looking, glistening new H-10-44 for Monon standing at the Fairbanks-Morse plant in Beloit, Wis., in late autumn of 1946. The 18—Monon's only FM switcher (H-15-44's 45 and 46 were road-switchers)—sported the short-lived black-and-yellow paint scheme that adorned a few early Monon diesels. *(FAIRBANKS-MORSE, COLLECTION OF JIM WALTER)*

The date is October 24, 1964, and the *Thoroughbred* has been fully transformed from red-and-gray to black-and-gold livery. F-3A 207 (ex-84A) is doing the honors at Salem with train 6, just pulling away from the depot. *(TOM SMART, DOLZALL COLLECTION)*

The final version of the *Thoroughbred*—with a high-nose C-420 (No. 501) on the point—eases north on 5th Street past Monon's old Lafayette station. It is September 1967, and the *Thoroughbred* is in its final month of operation. The limestone station, built in 1902, still stands, and Amtrak passenger trains still glided by it in 1987. *(J. ANTHONY KOESTER)*

Monon had but one train into Dearborn station by the 1960's, but the arrival of the last *Thoroughbred* on Sept. 30, 1967, was an event duly recognized by Chicago media. The conductor of last No. 6 is interviewed by television personalities as C-420 510 (running backwards) chants alongside. The freight unit was swapped at Shops for high-nose 501, which was called to duty for a football special which met final 6 in Lafayette. *(MIKE SCHAFER)*

Right: The *Thoroughbred's* F-3's share locomotive facilities with the F's of future merger partner Louisville & Nashville at the K&IT in Louisville in the wee hours of a July 1966 morning. *(GEORGE STROMBECK)* **Below:** Southbound train 73 is strung across the Ohio River on Kentucky & Indiana Terminal's mammoth bridge as a 6250-h.p. C-420/U23B/C-420 team headed by Century 513 heads into Louisville on June 24, 1971. *(TOM SMART, DOLZALL COLLECTION)*

A Century 420 duo rides high above the Tippecanoe River near Monticello, Ind., with Indianapolis-bound tonnage in June 1971. Monon's Chicago-Indianapolis route may have been the shortest between those two points, but now it's the quietest—most of it has been abandoned south of Delphi, Ind. (MIKE SCHAFER)

Train 73 breaks the Saturday morning humdrum of downtown Lafayette as it begins its journey out of Shops to Louisville in June 1971. U23B 605 leads two C-420's and two RS-2's. (MIKE SCHAFER)

An Indianapolis-bound Penn Central freight has been halted at the Monon crossing to wait as the latter's train 73 roars south along the White River through Gosport behind one of the new U23B's. The famous run-through depot here both pre- and post-dated the Chicago, Indianapolis & Louisville/ Monon Railroad—the structure was built in the mid-1800's and was torn down by L&N in the mid-1970's. This blend of ancient and contemporary at Gosport, Ind., illustrates the paradox of the Monon—a progressive railroad with a storybook charisma. *(MIKE SCHAFER)*

Above: Monon caboose 81531 was one of eight uncommon "bay window cupola" cabooses assembled at Lafayette Shops in 1956-1957. A combination of red, black, silver and white paints lent these waycars even more personality. Number 81531 trailed train 72 at McDoel Yard in May 1967. *(FRED CLINE)* **Right:** Handsome even in old age, F-3A 204 (ex-82B) noses out of Lafayette Shops in March 1967. The cab unit would survive until the Monon merged into the L&N. *(J. ANTHONY KOESTER)*